专业 让保险更保险

中国再保险行业发展报告

(2022)

中国再保险(集团)股份有限公司 ◎ 编著

中国金融出版社

责任编辑：张智慧　　王雪珂
责任校对：潘　洁
责任印制：陈晓川

图书在版编目(CIP)数据

中国再保险行业发展报告. 2022 / 中国再保险（集团）股份有限公司编著. —北京：中国金融出版社，2022.12

ISBN 978-7-5220-1851-5

Ⅰ.①中… Ⅱ.①中… Ⅲ.①再保险—保险业—经济发展—研究报告—中国—2022　Ⅳ.①F842.69

中国版本图书馆CIP数据核字 (2022) 第228298号

中国再保险行业发展报告（2022）

ZHONGGUO ZAIBAOXIAN HANGYE FAZHAN BAOGAO (2022)

出版发行	中国金融出版社
社址	北京市丰台区益泽路2号
市场开发部	(010) 66024766，63805472，63439533 (传真)
网上书店	www.cfph.cn
	(010) 66024766，63372837 (传真)
读者服务部	(010) 66070833，62568380
邮编	100071
经销	新华书店
印刷	北京侨友印刷有限公司
尺寸	169毫米×239毫米
印张	20.5
字数	280千
版次	2022年12月第1版
印次	2022年12月第1次印刷
定价	168.00元

ISBN 978-7-5220-1851-5

如出现印装错误本社负责调换　　联系电话 (010) 63263947

编委会名单

主　　　编： 和春雷

执行副主编： 庄乾志

副　主　编： 朱海林　肖　笠　朱晓云
　　　　　　　雷建明

编委会成员： 张仁江　田美攀　钭旭杰
　　　　　　　曹顺明　朱日峰

序 一

党的十八大以来，以习近平同志为核心的党中央统揽全局、把握大势，深刻把握中国社会发展规律，擘画了立足新发展阶段、贯彻新发展理念、构建新发展格局、实现高质量发展的新时代宏伟蓝图，推动党和国家事业取得历史性成就、发生历史性变革。

当前，百年变局加速演进，世界地缘政治局势震荡、经济低迷，全球疫情反复，气候变化导致极端天气、气象地质灾害时有发生，中国经济发展的外部环境更趋复杂严峻，风险和不确定性进一步增加。保险，作为降低风险、减少不确定性的主要手段，在提供风险保障、服务实体经济、护航人民美好生活中将发挥更加重要的作用。

在中国银行保险监督管理委员会（以下简称中国银保监会）正确领导下，伴随着中国经济的持续增长和行业的共同努力，中国已成为全球第二大保险市场和最重要的新兴保险市场，保险业支持国民经济稳定运行、服务实体经济、护航人民美好生活的能力不断提升。站在"两个一百年"的历史关口，中国保险业正在加快转型升级，围绕安全、数字、绿色、养老、普惠等关键词，从被动的风险承担转向主动的风险减量管理，从单一的经济补偿转向综合的服务保障，全面融入社会风险管理大生态系统，充分发挥保险保障功能，有力服务国家战略、参与社会治理、保障人民群众的生命财产安全，将行业的涓涓细流汇入国家和人民事业的大江大河，与民族复兴的时代脉搏同频，与人民对美好生活的追求向往共振。

从国际保险业发展历程中可以看到，任何一个发达保险市场背后，都有一个强大和完善的再保险体系的支持。再保险，作为"保险的保险"，在中国金融业中率先全面开放，现已形成500多家中外资、在岸离岸机构争相竞争的市场格局，充分发挥了风险分散、技术引导和资金融通作用，成为中国保险市场的"稳定器"和"调控器"。作为中国再保险行业的奠基人和主力军，中国再保险（集团）股份有限公司（以下简称中再集团）始终坚定不移落实党中央、国务院决策部署，坚守再保险主责主业，坚持再保直保化，加快数字化转型，持续完善行业基础设施，推进产品和服务创新，携手合作伙伴打造一站式、定制化的风险管理综合解决方案，全力服务国家战略、分散经济风险、护航美好生活。

在中国银保监会和中国保险行业协会悉心指导下，在国内保险、再保险同业大力支持下，中再集团中国再保险研究院组织编写的行业首部年度发展报告——《中国再保险行业发展报告（2022）》（以下简称《报告》）正式发布。《报告》系统总结了党的十八大以来中国再保险行业发展成就，展示了再保险市场发展全景图。相信《报告》的出版，会为广大读者全面了解和深入研究中国再保险行业发展状况提供有益参考，对扩大国内外行业交流、提升再保险行业社会影响力起到积极的促进作用。

中再集团董事长　和春雷

2022年12月

序 二

党的十八大以来、特别是第五次全国金融工作会议以来，保险业深入贯彻落实党中央、国务院决策部署，强化保障功能，深化改革开放，服务实体经济，守住风险底线，高质量发展取得重大成就，实现了跨越式发展。保险业总资产从2012年底的7.4万亿元增加到2021年底的24.9万亿元；保费规模从2012年底的1.5万亿元增加到2021年底的4.5万亿元，复合年均增长率超过12%，稳居全球第二大保险市场；保险深度从2.98%上升至3.93%，保险密度从1 144元/人上升至3 179元/人，与发达国家的差距进一步缩小。

再保险是"保险的保险"。近年来中国保险业高质量发展，再保险发挥了不可或缺的重要作用。再保险是行业健康发展的安全阀和稳定器。在防范化解行业系统性风险、降低直保公司的经营活动风险，特别是在巨灾赔付、风险管理、技术支持等方面，再保险发挥了至关重要的作用。再保险依托其承保能力、模型定价和专业人才等优势，对重大、巨额、特殊风险提供高层级、高限额保障，承担了国内财产与工程险超过50%的巨灾损失和农业保险近40%的巨灾损失。再保险也是行业改革创新的重要助推器，利用平台和技术优势，汇聚起保险行业及所承保领域的数据，通过数据分析研发，形成新的保险产品，推动直保行业产品组合升级，是保险行业产品服务创新升级的主要推动力。在为中国实体企业拓展"一带一路"业务保驾护航征程中，再保险牵头推出首张中文政治风险保单；在面对国内疫情防控和复工复产需求时，再保险牵头开发出多款保险产品；在应对气候变化挑战、助力"双碳"战略的过程中，再保险牵头开拓清洁能源保险、储能保险、碳保险、天气保险、生物多样性保护保险等新型绿色保险产品。

在中国保险行业协会统计研究专委会指导下，专委会主任委员单位中再集团牵头，首次出版发行《中国再保险行业发展报告（2022）》，全面梳理中国再保险近十年来的发展历程，充分展示中国再保险在服务保险业转型发展、推动实体经济发展、维护国家金融安全等方面发挥的重要作用，是近年来中国再保险行业高质量发展成果的高度浓缩，也是中再集团强化央企责任担当、以实际行动庆祝党的二十大胜利召开的重要载体。

期待《中国再保险行业发展报告（2022）》为中国再保险行业发展提供更多更有用的理论成果，更好地服务保险业高质量发展。

中国保险行业协会会长　于华

2022年12月

前　言[①]

当前,世界百年未有之大变局加速演进,新冠肺炎疫情影响广泛深远。全球范围的不稳定性因素日益增多,自然灾害、极端天气、公共卫生事件等成为全球重要的议题。中国进入新发展阶段,面对人民对美好生活的向往,必须统筹好发展和安全、处理好稳增长和防风险的关系,增强经济体系的韧性和活力,确保行稳致远。

保险是现代风险管理的基本手段,再保险是分散风险、提升保险业风险保障能力、维护保险市场平稳运行的有效机制。编写《中国再保险行业发展报告（2022）》,回顾历史、展望未来、对标全球,全面展现行业发展全景,有利于社会各界深入了解再保险的功能作用和独特价值,可以加快推动中国保险和再保险业高质量发展,更好维护国家安全和社会稳定。

一、再保险的功能作用

再保险又称分保,是保险人通过签订合同,将自己所承保的风险责任的一部分或全部转移给其他保险人的保险。再保险由保险派生发展而来,保险是再保险的基础和前提,没有保险,再保险无从做起。再保险是保险的后盾和保障,没有再保险支撑,保险的发展会受较大

[①] 本报告中"中国再保险行业"或"中国保险业"是指中国大陆保险再保险行业及市场,不含港澳台地区。本报告中主要数据来自历年《中国保险年鉴》、中国银保监会官方、再保险公司年报等公开披露数据信息,以及撰写期间再保险行业调研数据信息。

影响。再保险与保险密切相关、相辅相成、相互促进。

作为"保险的保险",再保险在宏观、中观和微观层面均发挥着不可替代的作用。从宏观层面社会经济体系角度看,再保险是缓释"黑天鹅""灰犀牛"对经济体系冲击的市场化、商业化"安全垫",能够发挥减轻国家财政负担、降低公共管理成本的社会作用,同时也是开展国际经济合作的有效手段。从中观层面保险行业角度看,再保险是保险业发展的"安全阀"和"稳定器",对于保障保险市场安全、辅助保险市场调控以及强化行业风险管理发挥了重要的作用。从微观层面保险公司角度看,再保险在为直接保险公司分散赔付风险、扩大承保能力、提供巨灾保障功能等方面作出了重要贡献。

二、再保险的发展历程

再保险萌芽于14世纪海上保险,至19世纪中叶开始公司化经营。现代再保险业开端于1347年意大利热那亚商人签发第一张海上保险保单。1370年,意大利商人承保了从热那亚出发经西班牙加的斯至荷兰斯卢丝的海上保险,并将加的斯至斯卢丝的海上运输风险进行转移,成为再保险的起源。1846年科隆再保险公司[①]作为世界上第一家专业再保险公司在德国成立,其后,瑞士再保险公司和慕尼黑再保险公司先后于1863年和1880年成立。从此再保险深入人心,成为各国保险公司普遍运用的风险控制手段。

中国再保险业与全球再保险业相比,发展历史较短。中国再保险业萌芽于解放前,随着新中国发展而发展。1949—1979年为行业初步发展阶段。1949年,中国人民保险公司成立,专设海外业务室经营

---

① 1994年,科隆再保险公司被通用再保险集团收购。

国际保险和再保险业务；国民经济恢复时期，再保险通过分保在国际范围内分散风险，有效减轻国家外汇补充负担；在时任国家领导人高度关注的海后轮被劫持与跃进轮触礁沉没事件中，再保险分别从国际再保市场摊回98%、83%的赔款，为国家挽回了重大经济损失；特殊时期，国内保险业务全面停办，国际再保险业务虽然也受到冲击，但通过存续业务的管理，保障了对外交流的重要渠道。1980—1995年为业务恢复阶段。1980年，中国人民保险公司开始恢复停办20余年之久的国内保险业务，并在原有基础上大力发展国外保险业务；1995年，第一部《中华人民共和国保险法》（以下简称《保险法》）颁布，规定国内保险公司应当将其承保的每笔保险业务按照规定办理再保险，再保险第一次通过法律条文得到了界定和规范。1996—2001年为机构专业发展阶段。1996年，再保险业务经营从原中国人民保险公司独立出来，成立中保再保险有限公司进行专业化经营，这是国内第一家经营再保险业务的专业公司；1999年，在中保再保险公司的基础上，中国再保险公司成立，具有完全独立的法人资格，法定分保业务快速增长，商业分保也逐步展开。2002—2005年为有序对外开放阶段。2001年中国正式加入世界贸易组织（WTO），金融领域首先实现开放的便是再保险市场，从2002—2005年底逐步取消再保险和再保险经纪业务跨境交易限制，法定分保市场完全被商业性再保险市场取代，同时允许国外再保险人在国内设立机构开展经营活动，慕尼黑再保险、瑞士再保险、科隆再保险等国际知名的专业再保险公司陆续在中国开设了分支机构；为有效应对商业分保市场的到来和全球市场竞争的需要，中国再保险公司于2003年完成股份制改造，成立中国再保险（集团）公司，下设中国财产再保险股份有限公司、中国人寿再保险股份有限公司、中国大地财产保险股份有限公司、中再资产管理股份有限公司、华泰保险经纪股份有限公司等子公司。2006年至今为全面开放阶段。自2006年完全取消法定分保尤其是2009年《保险法》第二次修订以来，中国再保险业开启了全面开放历程；全球主要再保险机构在中国布局设点不断提速，离岸再保险公司参与中国市场力度逐步加大；为有效应对市场竞争，中资机构加快改革步伐，2007年4月11日，中央汇金投资有限责任公司向中再注资40亿美元，标志着中国再保险（集团）公司由有限责任公司转变成股份有限公司；2007年10月30日，中国再保险（集团）股份有限公司挂牌，率先在国有保险集团公司中完成整体改制；2015年，中再集团成功登陆香港资本市场，成为赴港上市的第一家再保险公司；同年，太平再保险（中国）有限公司成立，是中国境内第二家具有再保险独立法人牌照的中资再保险公司；此后，前海再保险股份有限公司、人保再保险股份有限公司相继成立；中国再保险市场体系愈趋成熟，全球影响力逐步提升。

三、中国再保险行业主要成就

党的十八大以来，中国持续深化金融供给侧结构性改革，稳步扩大金融开放，有力推动了经济高质量发展，中国保险和再保险业也完成了从高速增长向高质量发展新阶段的迈进。

十年来，中国国内生产总值（GDP）从2012年的53.9万亿元增长到2021年的114.4万亿元，经济总量占世界经济的比重达18.5%，提高7.2个百分点，稳居世界第二位；人均GDP从39 800元增加到81 000元。

十年来，中国保险业总资产从2012年的7.4万亿元增加到2021年的24.9万亿元，增长2.4倍；保费规模从1.5万亿元增加到4.5万亿元，年均增速超过12%，从2017年起连续五年稳居全球第二大保险市场；

保险深度从2.98%上升至3.93%，保险密度从1 144元/人上升至3 179元/人，与发达国家的差距进一步缩小。从2017年到2021年，为实体经济发展和人民生产生活提供保险保障从4 154万亿元增加到12 146万亿元、增长192.4%，提供保险赔付从11 181亿元增加到15 609亿元、增长39.6%，服务实体经济发展、保障人民生产生活的水平不断提升。

十年来，伴随着中国经济的快速增长和中国保险行业的发展壮大，中国再保险行业呈现六大发展特征。一是专业主体逐渐丰富。截至2021年底，国内专业再保险公司数量自2000年的1家增加到15家，2012年后新增6家再保险主体。二是市场规模稳步扩大。分出保费由2012年的862.9亿元增长至2021年的2 456.8亿元，年均增长率约为12.3%；分保费收入由2012年的691.2亿元增长至2021年的2 090.2亿元，年均增长率约为13.1%，占全球再保险市场份额约9.3%。三是功能作用持续发挥。再保险充分发挥损失补偿和风险分散功能，降低重大灾害事故冲击，有力维护社会经济与行业稳健发展。2021年再保险赔付金额852.6亿元，较2012年增长2.8倍。2013年无锡海力士半导体厂火灾事故、2015年天津港爆炸事故，保险公司分别从再保险人摊回赔款53亿元和81亿元，分别占保险赔付责任的97%和83%。再保险提供充足承保能力和风险管理技术，为农业、交通、能源、核电等大型风险、特殊风险提供保险保障，如中国核保险共同体2021年为境内所有17座运行核电厂的53台运行核电机组提供全方位保险保障，涉核财产近万亿元、涉核企业一线人员2.4万人，有力支持中国核电事业发展。再保险在服务国家战略方面发挥了重要作用，在服务社会治理、助力科技创新、保障国计民生、服务"一带一路"、推进乡村振兴及推广绿色保险等领域作出积极贡献。四是开放程度不断扩大。2021年，外资专业再保险公司分保费收入占国内专业再保险公司分保费收入的31.9%，超过500家境外再保险人通过跨境交易的形式参与中国保险市场，再保险成为中国金融业中开放程度最深、国际化程度最高的领域之一。五是国际竞争力不断增强。行业龙头企业中再集团在香港整体上市、全资收购英国百年老店桥社保险公司，2020年首次跻身《财富》世界500强、成为亚洲最大、全球第六的再保险公司，境外机构已拓展到英国、中国香港、爱尔兰、丹麦、挪威、阿联酋、新加坡、马来西亚、澳大利亚、百慕大等11个国家/地区，覆盖财产再保险、人身再保险、资产管理三大业务板块。中国建设国际再保险中心不断加速，向着立足中国、面向亚洲、辐射全球的亚洲区域性再保险中心目标持续迈进。六是创新能力持续提升。中再集团迭代开发了具有自主知识产权的地震、台风、洪水等巨灾模型，持续打造生命表、重疾表等行业设施，为保险业风险定价和产品创新奠定了重要基础；先后在百慕大和中国香港地区首次发行巨灾债券，为利用资本市场构建多渠道的巨灾风险分散机制做出了有益探索。慕再支持中国首单草原碳汇遥感指数保险，瑞再助力中国首个湿地碳汇生态价值保险方案落地。总体而言，再保险在引领保险行业产品创新、模式创新、服务创新上发挥了重要作用。

四、2021年中国再保险市场概况

2021年，面对新冠肺炎疫情与全球经济复杂形势，中国再保险市场稳健运行，业务规模持续增长、经营效益稳步提升、国际影响力不断增强、风险防控有力有效，实现"十四五"良好开局。

一是市场规模。2021年，分出保费合计2 456.8亿元，较上年增长1.2%；其中：财产险市场分出保费1 460.5亿元，较上年增长5.6%，

占总分出保费的59.4%；人身险市场分出保费996.3亿元，较上年下降4.5%，占总分出保费的40.6%；分出率约为5.2%，其中，财产再保险分出率约为10.6%，人身再保险分出率约为3.0%。分保费收入2 090.2亿元，较上年增长15.5%；其中：6家中资公司（不含中再集团）分保费收入1 422.9亿元，较上年增长20.6%，占比约68.1%；8家外资公司分保费收入667.3亿元，较上年增长6.1%，占比约31.9%。全球前50大再保险公司2021年分保费收入约3 537.5亿美元[①]，中国再保险市场分保费收入占全球再保险市场规模约9.3%。赔付支出852.6亿元，较上年增长14.2%。其中：6家中资公司赔付支出491.0亿元，较上年增长13.5%；8家外资公司赔付支出361.6亿元，较上年增加15.2%。总资产规模6 057.5亿元，较年初增长22.2%；再保险行业总资产占保险业总资产规模约2.4%。

二是市场格局。专业再保险公司共有15家，其中，7家中资再保险公司（含1家集团公司，即中再集团），8家外资再保险公司。百余家财产险、人身险公司不同程度参与再保险市场竞争；超过500家境外再保险主体虽未在国内设立分支机构、但通过离岸交易的形式接受国内分出业务。财产再保险领域，市场份额超过20%的公司1家，市场份额10%～15%的公司1家，市场份额5%～10%的公司3家，市场份额低于5%的公司7家；人身再保险领域，市场份额超过50%的公司1家，市场份额10%～15%的公司1家，市场份额5%～10%的公司5家，市场份额低于5%的公司3家。目前国内专业再保险公司机构布局主要集中在北京、上海、深圳等中国经济最为发达的核心城市。截至2021年底，9家再保险公司在北京设有机构，8家在上海设有机构，3家在深圳设有

---

① 数据来源：A.M.Best数据。

机构。其中,将北京作为总部或区域中心的再保险公司有9家,占比最高,其次为上海。

三是业务结构。按照业务类型划分,2021年合约业务分保费收入2 070.7亿元,较上年增长16.7%,占比约为97.7%;临分业务分保费收入49.5亿元,较上年增长8.1%,占比约为2.3%。按照险种划分,财产险分保费收入1 075.6亿元,较上年增长28.0%,占比约为51.5%;寿险分保费收入445.0亿元,较上年增长0.79%,占比约为21.3%;健康险分保费收入496.5亿元,较上年增长9.2%,占比约为23.8%;意外险分保费收入73.1亿元,与上年持平,占比约为3.5%。

四是风险管理。再保险公司偿付能力情况和国际评级指标整体表现较好,为业务拓展、风险管理、声誉形象等提供了有效支撑。

五、中国再保险市场趋势展望

展望未来,面对中国经济与保险业高质量发展新阶段,再保险市场具有更加广阔的发展空间。

一是中国再保险市场未来一段时期仍将保持稳中有进发展态势,但不确定性带来的经营风险与波动性显著增强。中国经济发展"稳中向好"基本面没有改变,保险业发展空间依然巨大、市场需求更为多元,再保险市场发展与国民经济和保险业发展密切相关,将继续保持稳中有进的发展态势,保险公司分出保费及再保险分保费收入都将保持良好增长趋势。与此同时,气候变化带来的全球自然灾害事件频发,新冠肺炎疫情持续反复,国际局势复杂多变,保险业转型进入深水区,多重因素叠加影响下再保险经营波动性将显著上升,对再保险行业经营稳健性与风险管控能力都提出了更高要求。

二是中国再保险市场将以服务实体经济作为中长期发展的关键着力点。当前中国经济已由高速增长阶段转向高质量发展阶段，再保险作为重要的"安全阀"和"稳定器"，将在保障实体经济发展中创新拓展业务机遇。在碳中和、乡村振兴、科技强国、健康中国、应对人口老龄化等重大国家战略加快推进过程中，在中等收入群体不断扩大、公众保险意识持续增强的过程中，再保险能够利用其在专业技术、资源、人才等方面的独特优势，在服务国家战略、参与国家治理和社会服务方面拓展新的战略机遇与业务增量。

三是中国再保险市场将以创新引领为重点，在保险产业链中发挥更大价值。再保险将逐步适应在承担巨灾风险方面的功能扩展，适应全球化激烈竞争的新形势，加快技术创新和商业模式创新步伐，在提升技术和资本实力的基础上，从简单提供承保能力支持向一揽子的新型风险管理产品的批发商转变、向资本和技术的综合提供商转变、向资本市场中介功能延伸，推动再保险价值链向供应链、渠道和客户价值链的移动，占据价值链的高端。与政府机构、保险公司、科技平台等各方的合作将更为深化，构建再保险特色生态圈，大力推动产业链和合作网络建设，升级经营模式与服务模式。强化再保险的风险管理和技术传导功能，提高再保险对直接保险市场的覆盖面与渗透力，在促进保险市场健康发展方面发挥更大价值。再保险将进一步发挥在数据、技术及人才等方面的专业优势，加强业务模式研发，以产品创新为突破口，为财产损失和人身健康，特别是一系列新兴风险提供更加全面的保险保障，如专利、数据、算法等无形资产保险，恐怖主义、政治暴乱等"一带一路"保险，以及巨灾保险、网络安全保险、特殊风险保险等多类型创新产品。

习近平总书记强调，金融要为实体经济服务，满足经济社会发展和人民群众需要。立足新发展阶段、贯彻新发展理念，再保险业必将在服务保险业供给侧结构性改革大局、服务实体经济、维护社会稳定、支持重大战略实施、服务民生风险保障等方面发挥更加重要的作用。希望《中国再保险行业发展报告（2022）》在理论与实践方面的探索，能够启迪智慧、促进交流，为行业高质量发展贡献绵薄之力！

目 录

第一章 再保险市场2021年总体发展情况及发展展望　1

一、再保险市场发展概况　3

二、再保险服务保险行业制度体系与基础设施建设情况　23

三、再保险数字化发展情况　27

四、再保险发展趋势展望　31

第二章 财产再保险市场2021年发展情况及发展展望　37

一、财产再保险市场规模　39

二、财产再保险需求侧分析　41

三、财产再保险供给侧分析　43

四、财产再保险主要业务　43

五、财产再保险发展展望　45

第三章 人身再保险市场2021年发展情况及发展展望　49

一、人身再保险市场规模　51

二、人身再保险需求侧分析　53

三、人身再保险供给侧分析　54

四、人身再保险主要业务　54

五、人身再保险发展展望　56

第四章 外资再保险公司2021年发展情况及发展展望　59

　一、外资再保险公司在中国发展基本情况　61
　二、外资再保险公司在中国发展历程　62
　三、外资再保险公司在中国经营情况　65
　四、外资再保险公司在中国人力资源情况　71
　五、外资再保险公司在中国发展展望　75

第五章 再保险行业2021年监管政策及趋势展望　79

　一、再保险行业现行监管架构　81
　二、再保险行业特别监管政策　86
　三、再保险行业2021年重要监管政策　89
　四、再保险行业监管趋势展望　94

专题报告　97

　专题一　再保险助力巨灾风险管理与巨灾保险发展专题报告　99
　专题二　再保险支持农业保险发展专题报告　117
　专题三　再保险服务"一带一路"建设专题报告　129
　专题四　再保险推动绿色保险发展、助力实现碳中和目标专题报告　140

附录 中国再保险行业发展大事记（1949—2021年）　153

后记　161

第一章 再保险市场2021年总体发展情况及发展展望

一、再保险市场发展概况

二、再保险服务保险行业制度体系与基础设施建设情况

三、再保险数字化发展情况

四、再保险发展趋势展望

2021年是"十四五"开局之年，面对新冠肺炎疫情与复杂的内外部形势，中国再保险市场保持稳健运行，业务规模持续增长，经营效益稳步提升，国际影响力不断增强，风险防控有力有效，行业发展实现良好开局。

一、再保险市场发展概况

（一）市场规模

1．原保险分出保费

2021年，国内保险市场分出保费2 456.8亿元，较上年增长1.2%。其中：财产保险市场分出保费合计1 460.5亿元，较上年增长5.6%，占总分出保费的59.4%；人身保险市场分出保费合计996.3亿元，较上年下降4.5%，占总分出保费的40.6%。同期，国内原保险保费合计47 452.1亿元，较上年增长4.9%。

总体来看，一是分出保费小幅增长，增长率低于原保险约3.7个百分点，主要源于保险市场政策变化及结构调整，特别是车险综合改革（以下简称车险综改）、中国第二代偿付能力监管制度体系建设（以下简称偿二代）等对再保险分出需求的显著影响；二是从历年分出保费看再保险市场总体结构，财产保险与人身保险分出保费占比约为6∶4，再保险以财产保险分出为主。

图 1　2012—2021 年财产险与人身险分出保费占比情况

（数据来源：中国保险年鉴、中国银保监会）

总结2012年以来发展成效，2012—2021年，伴随中国保险市场不断发展，再保险需求持续提升，分出保费规模从862.9亿元增长至2 456.8亿元，年均增长率约为12.3%。同期，原保险保费由15 487.9亿元增长至47 452.1亿元，年均增长率约为13.2%。总体来看，分出保费与原保险保费平均增速基本一致，但各年增速差异较大，分出保费波动性明显高于原保险保费，这也是再保险经营模式的显著特征，体现出再保险对原保险经营周期发挥风险分散和平滑波动作用。

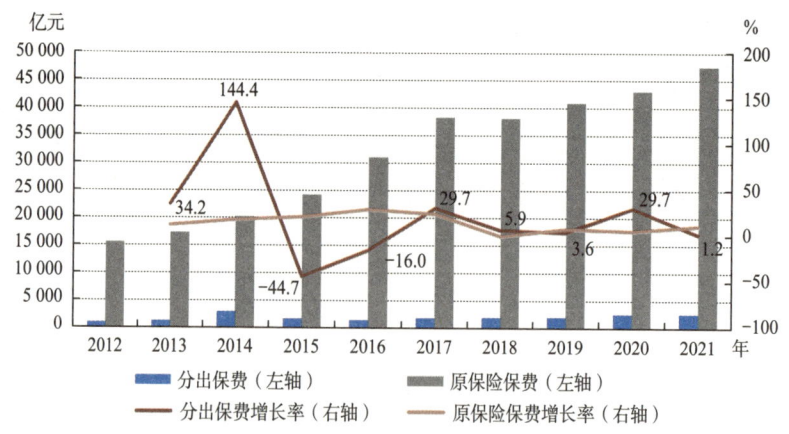

图 2　2012—2021 年原保险保费、分出保费及增长率情况

（数据来源：中国保险年鉴、中国银保监会）

表 1　2012—2021 年分出保费、原保险保费及再保险分出率情况

单位：亿元、%

年份	分出保费	增长率	原保险保费	增长率	再保险分出率
2012	862.9	—	15 487.9	—	5.6
2013	1 157.8	34.2	17 222.2	11.2	6.7
2014	2 829.8	144.4	20 133.2	16.9	14.1
2015	1 564.8	-44.7	24 167.6	20.0	6.5
2016	1 314.5	-16.0	30 957.6	28.1	4.2
2017	1 705.0	29.7	38 188.2	23.4	4.5
2018	1 806.2	5.9	38 032.8	-0.4	4.7
2019	1 871.0	3.6	40 857.7	7.4	4.6
2020	2 427.1	29.7	42 952.4	5.1	5.7
2021	2 456.8	1.2	47 452.1	10.5	5.2

数据来源：中国保险年鉴、中国银保监会。

从分出保费规模看，再保险需求在2014—2016年经历较大波动，主要源于"偿二代"影响。"偿二代"建设于2012年启动，于2015年2月正式发布并进入实施过渡期，2016年第一季度起正式实施。相比于以规模为导向的"偿一代"，"偿二代"强调以风险为导向，使得保险业不同风险的业务对资本的需求出现显著变化，从而显著影响保险公司对再保险的分出需求及分保策略。2014—2016年，保险公司分出保费由2 829.8亿元大幅下降至1 314.5亿元，降幅超过50%。自2016年起，保险公司分出保费规模趋于平稳，呈逐年上升趋势。

2021年，国内再保险市场分出率约为5.2%，其中，财产再保险分出率约为10.6%，人身再保险分出率约为3.0%。由于财产保险市场风险更多样且巨灾风险较为突出，相比于人身保险市场，财产保险市场对再保险需求更大，分出率也明显更高。

2012—2021年，国内再保险市场分出率平均约为6.2%，其中

2014—2016年"偿二代"监管政策过渡期间，分出率大幅波动，2014年分出需求猛增、分出率高达14.1%，随后逐步回落。不考虑2014—2016年波动影响，分出率平均约为5.3%。自2016年至今，再保险分出率总体呈上升趋势，体现出保险市场对再保险的风险分散需求正在逐步增强。

图3　2012—2021年再保险分出率情况

（数据来源：中国保险年鉴、中国银保监会）

2．再保险分保费收入

2021年，国内再保险市场分保费收入2 090.2亿元，较上年增长15.5%。其中，6家中资公司分保费收入1 422.9亿元，较上年增长20.6%，占比约为68.1%；8家外资公司分保费收入667.3亿元，较上年增长6.1%，占比约为31.9%。

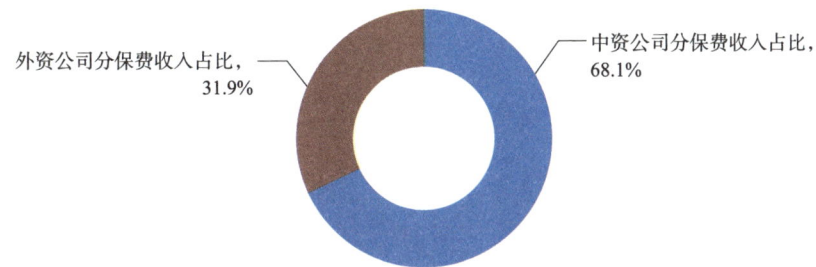

图 4　2021 年中资及外资再保险公司分保费收入占比情况

（数据来源：中国保险年鉴、中国银保监会）

总体来看，再保险分保费收入保持两位数增长速度，高于原保险保费增速，行业整体呈现良好发展态势；中资与外资公司市场占比保持相对稳定。

总结2012年以来发展成效，2012—2021年，国内再保险市场分保费收入从691.2亿元增长至2 090.2亿元，年均增长率约为13.1%。其中，中资公司分保费收入由400.3亿元增长至1 422.9亿元，年均增长率约为15.1%；外资公司分保费收入由290.9亿元增长至667.3亿元，年均增长率约为9.7%。总体来看，再保险分保费收入与原保险保费平均增速一致，但再保险分保费收入各年增速差异较大、波动性较高。特别是2014—2016年，受"偿二代"监管政策过渡期影响，再保险公司分保费收入显著波动。自2016年"偿二代"正式实施后，分保费收入呈逐年稳步增长趋势。其中，中资再保险公司分保费收入在2012—2021年保持正增长；外资再保险公司分保费收入波动性较大，2014年分保费收入增长率超过100%，2015年降幅近47%，体现出中资与外资公司经营策略的差异性。

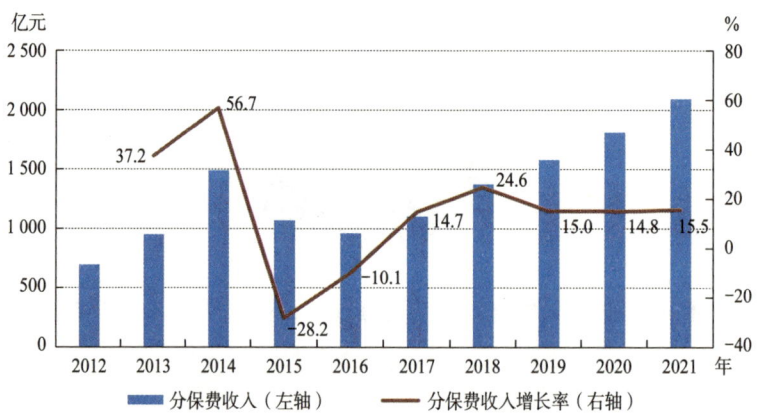

图 5　2012—2021 年再保险公司分保费收入及增长率情况

（数据来源：中国保险年鉴、中国银保监会）

表 2　2012—2021 年中资与外资再保险公司分保费收入及增长率情况

单位：亿元、%

年份	分保费收入	中资公司分保费收入	增长率	占比	外资公司分保费收入	增长率	占比
2012	691.2	400.3	—	57.9	290.9	—	42.1
2013	948.6	466.8	16.6	49.2	481.8	65.6	50.8
2014	1 486.0	502.5	7.6	33.8	983.5	104.1	66.2
2015	1 066.3	543.4	8.1	51.0	522.9	-46.8	49.0
2016	958.6	552.0	1.6	57.6	406.6	-22.2	42.4
2017	1 099.6	778.7	41.1	70.8	320.9	-21.1	29.2
2018	1 370.1	949.8	22.0	69.3	420.2	31.0	30.7
2019	1 576.1	1 044.9	10.0	66.2	533.0	26.8	33.8
2020	1 809.2	1 180.1	13.1	65.2	629.1	18.0	34.8
2021	2 090.2	1 422.9	20.6	68.1	667.3	6.1	31.9

数据来源：中国保险年鉴、中国银保监会。

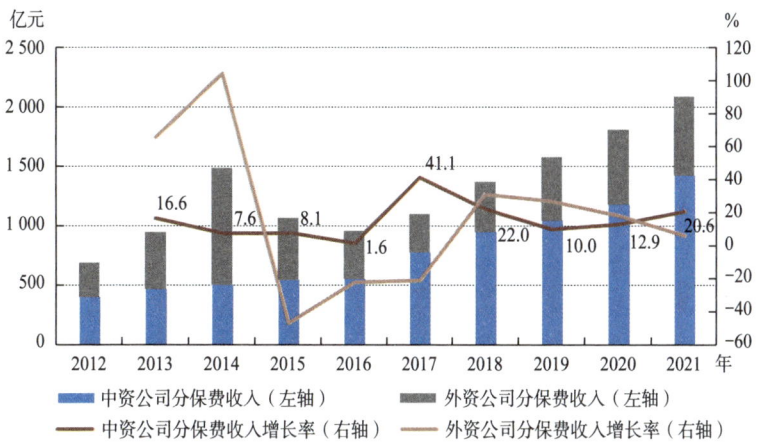

图 6 2012—2021 年中资与外资再保险公司分保费收入及增长率情况

（数据来源：中国保险年鉴、中国银保监会）

2021年，全球前50大再保险公司分保费收入约为3 537.5亿美元[①]，约合22 554.0亿元[②]；中国再保险市场分保费收入2 090.2亿元，占全球再保险市场规模约9.3%。

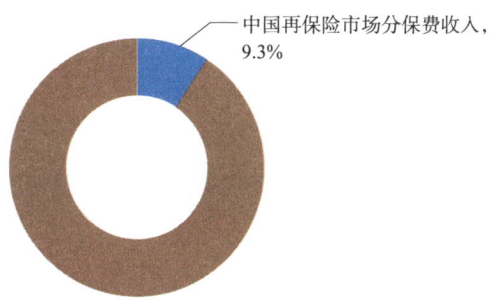

图 7 2021 年中国再保险市场分保费收入占全球份额

（数据来源：中国保险年鉴、中国银保监会、A.M.Best 数据）

---

① 数据来源：A.M.Best数据。
② 2021年12月31日银行间外汇市场人民币汇率：1美元=6.3757元人民币。

3．赔付支出

2021年，国内再保险行业赔付支出852.6亿元，较上年增长14.2%，占当年分保费收入比重为40.8%。其中，6家中资公司赔付支出491.0亿元，较上年增长13.5%；8家外资公司赔付支出361.6亿元，较上年增长15.2%。

图8　2012—2021年再保险业赔付支出情况

（数据来源：中国保险年鉴、中国银保监会）

表3　　2012—2021年再保险赔付支出情况

单位：亿元、%

年份	赔付支出	增长率	占分保费收入
2012	303.8	—	44.0
2013	383.7	26.3	40.5
2014	433.2	12.9	29.2
2015	668.5	54.3	62.7
2016	1 119.3	67.4	116.8
2017	489.0	-56.3	44.5
2018	541.2	10.7	39.5
2019	677.6	25.2	42.5
2020	746.5	10.2	41.3
2021	852.6	14.2	40.8

数据来源：中国保险年鉴、中国银保监会。

总结2012年以来发展成效，2012—2021年，国内再保险行业赔付支出从303.8亿元增长至852.6亿元，年均增长率为12.2%。总体来看，再保险赔付支出在2016年"偿二代"实施初期大幅增长，其中人身再保险赔付支出大幅增加，2017年明显回落，政策变化期的波动性较大。

4．资产规模

2021年，国内再保险行业总资产规模6 057.5亿元，较年初增长22.2%，高于分保费收入增速6.7个百分点。

总结2012年以来发展成效，2012—2021年，国内再保险行业总资产规模从1 437.2亿元增长至6 057.5亿元，年均增长率约为17.3%，高于再保险分保费收入年均增长率。总资产规模同样受到"偿二代"影响，在2014—2016年呈现较大波动性。自2016年开始，再保险行业总资产规模呈稳步增长趋势，与分保费收入变化趋势保持一致。

2012—2021年，再保险行业总资产占保险业总资产规模比重相对稳定，2021年底约为2.4%，体现了再保险行业伴随保险市场发展而逐步发展壮大，在监管政策与市场环境变化下保持整体稳步增长。同时，保险业总资产占金融业总资产规模比重稳步上升，从2018年的5.6%上升至2021年的6.5%，保险业在金融行业中的作用和地位正在不断增强。

图 9　2012—2021 年再保险行业总资产规模及增长率情况

（数据来源：中国保险年鉴、中国银保监会）

表 4　2012—2021 年再保险业、保险业、金融业总资产规模及占比情况

单位：亿元、%

年份	再保险业总资产	保险业总资产	再保险业总资产占保险业比重	金融业总资产	保险业总资产占金融业比重
2012	1 437.2	68 425.6	2.1	—	—
2013	1 765.4	77 576.7	2.3	—	—
2014	3 183.2	96 177.8	3.3	—	—
2015	4 722.0	119 295.7	4.0	—	—
2016	2 343.9	142 659.0	1.6	—	—
2017	2 699.3	146 816.7	1.8	—	—
2018	3 358.3	163 641.0	2.1	2 940 000	5.6
2019	4 261.3	187 495.6	2.3	3 186 900	5.9
2020	4 956.3	216 156.5	2.3	3 531 900	6.1
2021	6 057.5	248 874.0	2.4	3 819 500	6.5

数据来源：中国保险年鉴、中国银保监会、中国人民银行网站。

（二）市场格局

1．市场主体

截至2021年底，国内再保险市场专业再保险公司共有15家，其中

7家中资再保险公司（含1家集团公司，即中再集团），8家外资再保险公司。此外，百余家财产险和人身险直保公司不同程度参与再保险市场竞争；超过500家境外再保险主体虽未在国内设立分支机构，但通过离岸交易的形式接受国内分出业务。

表5　　　　　　　　　国内专业再保险公司情况概览[①]

公司名称	成立时间	注册地	注册性质	企业性质
中国再保险（集团）股份有限公司	1996年	北京	集团公司	中资
中国财产再保险有限责任公司	2003年	北京	公司	中资
中国人寿再保险有限责任公司	2003年	北京	公司	中资
慕尼黑再保险公司北京分公司	2003年	北京	分公司	外资
瑞士再保险股份有限公司北京分公司	2003年	北京	分公司	外资
德国通用再保险股份公司上海分公司	2004年	上海	分公司	外资
法国再保险公司北京分公司	2008年	北京	分公司	外资
汉诺威再保险股份公司上海分公司	2008年	上海	分公司	外资
信利再保险（中国）有限公司[②]	2011年	上海	公司	外资
RGA美国再保险公司上海分公司	2014年	上海	分公司	外资
太平再保险（中国）有限公司	2015年	北京	公司	中资
前海再保险股份有限公司	2016年	深圳	公司	中资
人保再保险股份有限公司	2017年	北京	公司	中资
大韩再保险公司上海分公司	2020年	上海	分公司	外资
中国农业再保险股份有限公司	2020年	北京	公司	中资

资料来源：中国保险年鉴、各再保险公司年报。

总结2012年以来发展成效，2012—2021年，国内再保险市场的主体数量不断增长，从9家增加至15家，其中中资公司新增4家，外资公司新增2家。2014—2017年，年均有一家新设再保险公司，2020年增加

[①] 各再保险主体在文中使用以下简称：中再集团或中再、中再产险或中再、中再寿险或中再、慕再或慕再北分、瑞再或瑞再北分、通用再或通用再上分、法再或法再北分、汉再或汉再上分、信利再、RGA美再或RGA美再上分、太平再（中国）、前海再、人保再、大韩再或大韩再上分、中国农再。

[②] 信利保险（中国）有限公司成立于2011年，2020年变更为信利再保险（中国）有限公司。

2家再保险公司。

2．机构布局

与保险公司以机构拓展拉动业务增长的特点不同，再保险公司机构精简、人员资源集中，目前国内专业再保险公司机构布局主要集中在北京、上海、深圳等中国经济发达的核心城市。

截至2021年底，15家再保险公司中有9家在北京设有机构、8家在上海设有机构、3家在深圳设有机构。其中，将北京作为总部或区域中心的再保险公司有9家，占比最高，其次为上海。

表6　　　　　专业再保险公司国内机构布局情况

公司名称	机构布局情况
中国再保险（集团）股份有限公司	总部位于北京
中国财产再保险有限责任公司	总部位于北京；在上海、深圳设有分公司
中国人寿再保险有限责任公司	总部位于北京；在上海、深圳设有分公司
慕尼黑再保险公司北京分公司	分公司位于北京
瑞士再保险股份有限公司北京分公司	分公司位于北京
德国通用再保险股份有限公司上海分公司	分公司位于上海
法国再保险公司北京分公司	分公司位于北京
汉诺威再保险股份公司上海分公司	分公司位于上海
信利再保险（中国）有限公司	公司位于上海
RGA美国再保险公司上海分公司	分公司位于上海
太平再保险（中国）有限公司	总部位于北京；在上海设有分公司
前海再保险股份有限公司	公司位于深圳
人保再保险股份有限公司	公司位于北京
大韩再保险公司上海分公司	分公司位于上海
中国农业再保险股份有限公司	公司位于北京

资料来源：中国保险年鉴、各再保险公司年报。

（三）业务结构

1．分业务类型分保费收入

2021年，国内再保险市场分保费收入2 090.2亿元，其中合约业务分保费收入2 070.7亿元，较上年增长16.7%，占比约为97.7%[①]；临分业务分保费收入49.5亿元，较上年增长8.1%，占比约为2.3%。合约业务保持稳健增长，临分业务增长速度有所放缓。

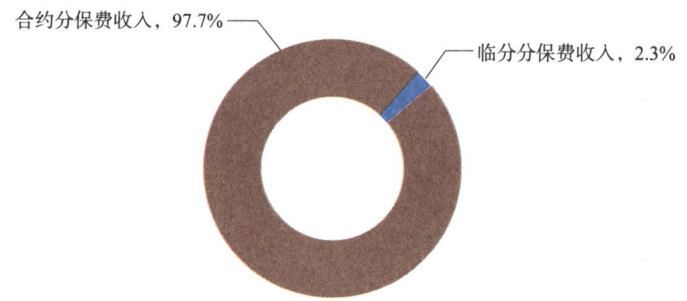

图10　2021年再保险合约与临分业务分保费收入占比情况

（数据来源：中国银保监会）

总结2012年以来发展成效，2012—2021年，合约业务分保费收入从681.9亿元增长至2 070.7亿元，年均增长率约为13.1%；临分业务分保费收入从9.3亿元增长至49.5亿元，年均增长率约为20.4%。总体来看，合约业务是再保险主要业务类型，占比保持在95%以上，发展速度较为平稳；临分业务占比较小，发展速度较快，但历年增长速度有较大波动，与业务性质密切相关。

---

① 分保费收入已考虑公司间关联交易影响，分业务类型分保费收入未考虑关联交易影响。

表7 2012—2021年再保险合约与临分分保费收入、增长率及占比情况

单位：亿元、%

年份	合约业务分保费收入	增长率	占比	临分业务分保费收入	增长率	占比
2012	681.9	—	98.7	9.3	—	1.3
2013	940.3	37.9	99.1	8.3	-10.7	0.9
2014	1 476.7	57.1	99.4	9.23	11.6	0.6
2015	1 055.2	-28.5	99.0	11.0	19.2	1.0
2016	917.9	-13.0	95.8	37.9	243.7	4.0
2017	1 080.2	17.7	98.2	19.4	-48.9	1.8
2018	1 339.4	24.0	97.8	30.7	58.5	2.2
2019	1 539.8	15.0	97.7	36.3	18.1	2.3
2020	1 774.3	15.2	97.5	45.8	26.2	2.5
2021	2 070.7	16.7	97.7	49.5	8.1	2.3

数据来源：中国保险年鉴、中国银保监会。

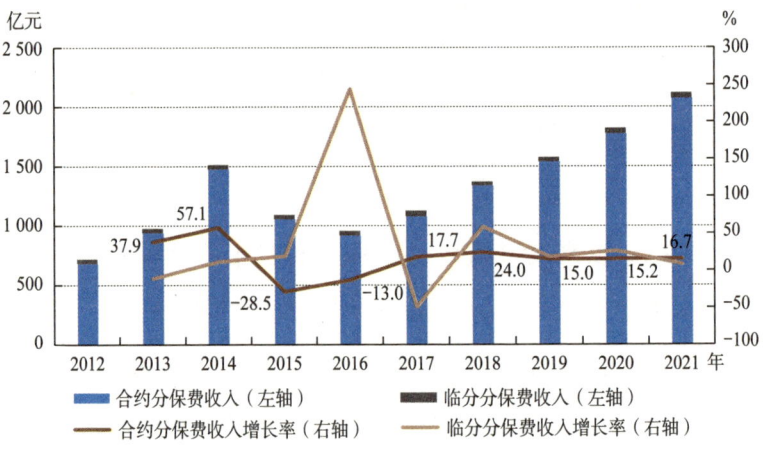

图11 2012—2021年再保险合约、临分分保费收入及增长率情况

（数据来源：中国保险年鉴、中国银保监会）

2．分险种分保费收入

2021年，国内再保险市场财产险分保费收入1 075.6亿元，较上年增长28.0%，占比约为51.5%；寿险分保费收入445.0亿元，较上年增长0.79%，占比约为21.3%；健康险分保费收入496.5亿元，较上年增长

9.2%，占比约为23.8%；意外险分保费收入73.1亿元，与上年持平，占比约为3.5%。总体来看，一是各险种分保费收入增长率有所分化，财产险增长较快，其次为健康险，寿险和意外险规模与上年基本持平；二是健康险分保费收入增速较往年明显放缓，与保险市场健康险发展态势一致，健康险分保需求在2021年减速明显；三是与2020年比较，财产险分保费收入占比小幅上升，寿险、健康险和意外险的分保费收入占比小幅下降，体现了保险市场业务结构调整对再保险的影响。

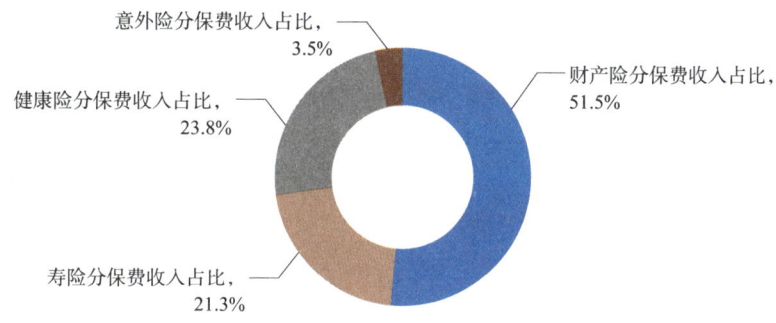

图 12　2021 年分险种分保费收入占比

（数据来源：中国银保监会）

总结2012年以来发展成效，2012—2021年，国内再保险市场财产险分保费收入由462.6亿元增长至1 075.6亿元，年均增长率约为9.8%；寿险业务由153.0亿元增长至445.0亿元，年均增长率约为12.6%；健康险业务由50.6亿元增长至496.5亿元，年均增长率约为28.9%；意外险业务由25.0亿元增长至73.1亿元，年均增长率约为12.7%。其中，健康险是增长最快的险种，分保费收入占比逐年上升，2019年首次超过20%，2020年分保费规模超过400亿元，是发展潜力最大的险种，但近年来健康险增长速度正在放缓。随着财产险公司健康险业务比重的不断上升，对健康险的再保险分出需求也在持续增加，特别是对短期健康险需求的增加带来了较高的分保费收入。

表8　　　　2012—2021年各险种分保费收入及增长率

单位：亿元、%

年份	财产险	增长率	寿险	增长率	健康险	增长率	意外险	增长率
2012	462.6	—	153.0	—	50.6	—	25.0	—
2013	562.8	21.7	297.3	94.3	63.5	25.6	24.8	-0.6
2014	588.0	4.5	799.6	168.9	65.7	3.4	32.7	31.7
2015	598.1	1.7	320.9	-59.9	112.1	70.7	35.1	7.4
2016	480.7	-19.6	285.9	-10.9	100.1	-10.8	43.5	23.9
2017	484.9	0.9	430.2	50.5	136.1	36.0	48.4	11.3
2018	600.4	23.8	484.4	12.6	218.2	60.4	67.1	38.5
2019	729.9	21.6	421.3	-13.0	353.0	61.8	73.6	9.7
2020	840.1	15.1	441.6	4.8	454.5	28.7	73.1	-0.7
2021	1 075.6	28.0	445.0	0.8	496.5	9.2	73.1	0.0

数据来源：中国保险年鉴、中国银保监会。

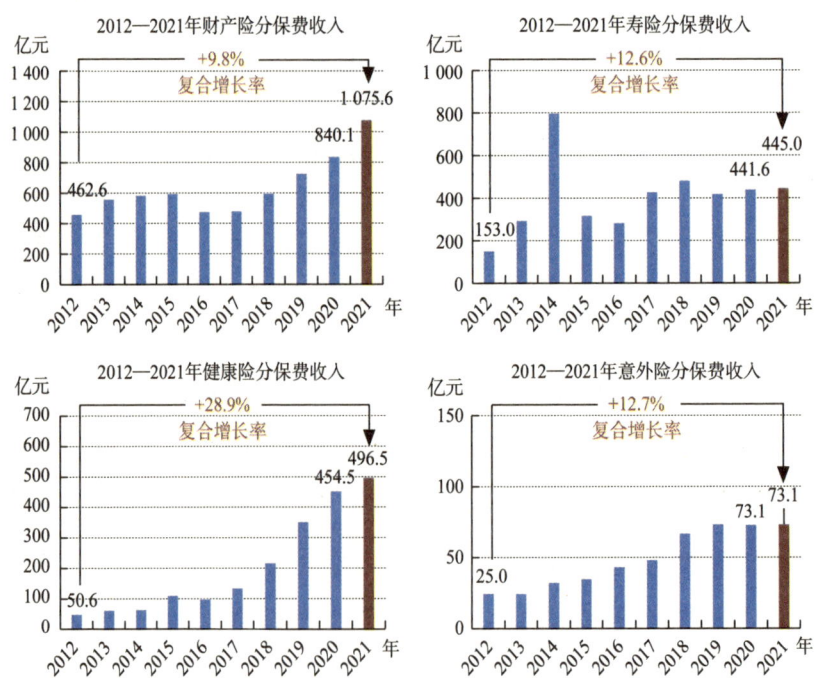

图13　2012—2021年各险种分保费收入

（数据来源：中国保险年鉴、中国银保监会）

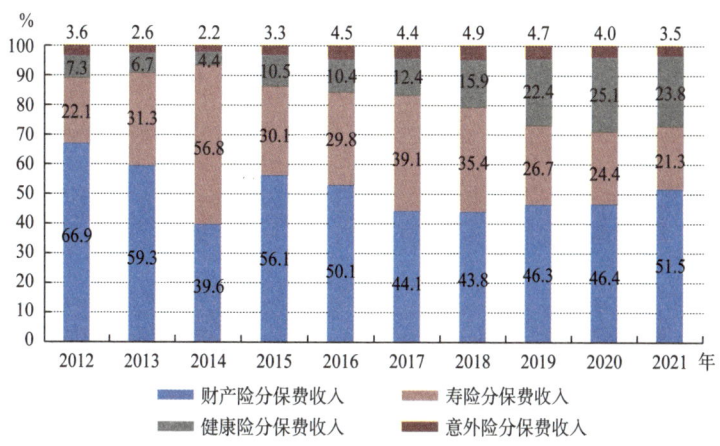

图14　2012—2021年分险种分保费收入占比情况

（数据来源：中国保险年鉴、中国银保监会）

（四）风险管理情况

再保险承担着为保险业进一步转移、分散风险的职能，特别是针对巨灾风险、重大风险以及特殊风险，再保险的高风险分散作用更加突出，能够使保险公司跨越危险单位限制、突破区域限制，在全球更为广泛的时间和空间中承接业务、分散风险。因此，再保险业相较保险业，对风险管理的要求更高、系统重要性更为突出，特别是更加注重对巨灾等重大风险累积责任的管理。风险管理已成为再保险业的核心竞争力之一，获得再保险公司高度关注。

近年来，再保险行业整体风险管理体系建设不断完善，风险管控手段更为丰富，在风险指标监测方面，主要关注偿付能力与国际评级指标。2021年，各家再保险公司偿付能力和评级指标整体表现较好，为其业务拓展、风险管理、声誉形象等提供了有效支撑。

1. 偿付能力情况[①]

（1）核心偿付能力充足率、综合偿付能力充足率情况

核心偿付能力充足率是保险公司核心资本与最低资本的比值，衡量公司高质量资本的充足状况，监管达标值为50%；综合偿付能力充足率是实际资本与最低资本的比值，衡量公司资本的总体充足状况，监管达标值为100%。

2021年第一至第四季度，再保险公司的平均核心偿付能力充足率分别为313.7%、286.9%、284.2%和288.9%，均高于监管达标值50%和当季财产险公司、人身险公司的充足率水平。

2021年第一至第四季度，再保险公司的平均综合偿付能力充足率分别为336.2%、307.4%、307.3%和311.2%，均高于监管达标值100%和当季财产险公司、人身险公司的充足率水平。

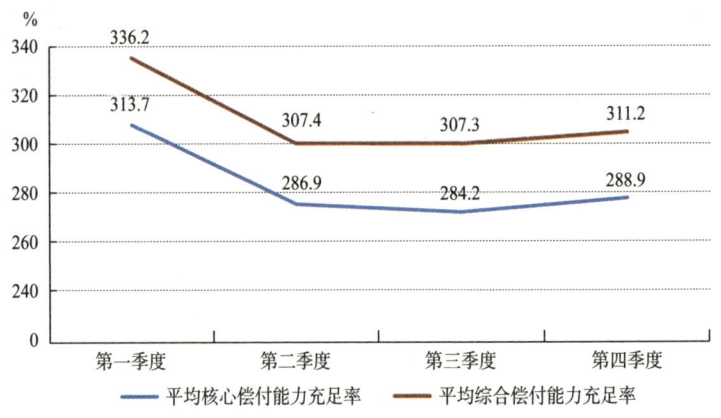

图 15　2021年再保险公司偿付能力情况

（数据来源：中国银保监会网站）

[①] 下文中偿付能力相关数据为"偿二代"一期规则下的统计数据。

（2）风险综合评级（IRR）情况

风险综合评级是对保险公司偿付能力综合风险的评价，衡量保险公司总体偿付能力风险的大小，分为A、B、C、D四类，监管达标值为B类。

2021年，共有14家再保险公司获得并披露了季度风险综合评级情况，评级结果均在B类及以上，其中7家再保险公司在四个季度的评级结果为A类。

（3）风险管理能力（SARMRA）情况

风险管理能力通过制度健全性和遵循有效性反映保险公司的风险管理水平。中国银保监会对保险公司的风险管理能力开展监管评估，评估分值高于80分可提高偿付能力充足率。

截至2021年底，共有13家再保险公司接受了风险管理能力监管评估。各公司最近一次监管评估的平均得分为79.24分，并有6家再保险公司得分在80分以上。

（4）流动性情况

保险公司主要通过净现金流、综合流动比率和流动性覆盖率等指标反映其流动性风险。

净现金流方面，根据14家再保险公司的公开披露信息，2021年各季度内，各家再保险公司净现金流之和为第一季度流出27.30亿元、第二季度流入19.83亿元、第三季度流入27.92亿元、第四季度流出47.96亿元。8家再保险公司各季度净现金流之和为正向流入，6家再保险公司各季度净现金流之和为负向流出。

综合流动比率方面，该指标为现有资产的预期现金流入合计与现有负债的预期现金流出合计的比值，反映保险公司各项资产和负债在未来期间现金流分布情况以及现金流入和现金流出的匹配情况。根据

15家再保险公司的公开披露信息，2021年第四季度末，各家再保险公司三个月内的综合流动比率均值为246.37%，一年以内综合流动比率均值为207.21%，一年以上综合流动比率均值为208.75%。

流动性覆盖率方面，该指标为优质流动资产的期末账面价值与未来一个季度的净现金流的比值，反映保险公司在压力情景下未来一个季度的流动性水平。根据15家再保险公司的公开披露信息，2021年第四季度末，假设发生巨灾事件，导致预测期内分保赔付的现金流出较基本情景增长50%的压力情景下，各家再保险公司的流动性覆盖率均值为2 265.50%；假设预测期内到期的固定收益类资产20%无法收回本息的压力情景下，各家再保险公司的流动性覆盖率均值为2 423.45%。

2．国际评级情况

2021年，共有14家再保险公司获得信用评级机构给予的评级，且多家公司采取多评级策略，其中12家公司获得标准普尔评级，评级结果均在A-级及以上；12家公司获得贝氏评级，评级结果均在A-级及以上；6家公司获得穆迪评级，评级结果均在A1级及以上；3家公司获得惠誉评级，评级结果均在AA-级及以上。

（五）再保险中介发展情况

再保险中介主要以再保险经纪公司为主。再保险经纪公司是促成再保险分出公司与接受公司建立再保险关系的中介机构。再保险经纪公司凭借其对市场信息全面及时的把握、丰富的专业知识和实务经验，为再保险交易双方提供高质量的服务，设计再保险方案、落实再保险安排、提供专业培训。

中国再保险经纪市场是最为开放的金融领域之一。与境内经纪公司类似，境外经纪公司只要在中国再保险登记系统注册并通过审核，就可以同等地发起再保险业务。中国再保险登记系统信息显示，2021年，再保险经纪人共232家，其中境外机构120家，占比51.7%；境内机构112家，占比48.3%。

从全球市场格局来看，怡安（Aon）、佳达（Guy Carpenter）和韦莱（Willis Re）[①]为国际排名前三的再保险经纪公司。其中，排名第一的怡安和第二的佳达市场规模接近。从中国市场格局来看，呈现由外资机构主导、中资机构快速成长的基本格局。上述三家公司也是国内再保险经纪市场的主要参与者。佳达和怡安再保险经纪营业收入稳居中国市场前两名。除市场规模外，这三家再保险经纪公司在国际市场排分、精算服务、风险咨询等方面也发挥着市场主导作用。

目前上述三家国际再保险经纪公司均已在中国境内注册机构，其中佳达和韦莱为外资独资企业，怡安与中粮集团成立了合资公司。除以上境内注册机构外，这三家公司在中国香港、新加坡等地的机构也积极参与中国保险市场再保险业务排分。

二、再保险服务保险行业制度体系与基础设施建设情况

再保险公司经营更具宏观系统性、数据更有广泛枢纽性，在保险行业监管制度建设、重大行业性基础设施建设等方面具有一定比较优势，持续贡献专业价值。

---

① 2021年，Arthur J. Gallagher & Co.宣布以35亿美元收购Willis Re，目前并购在大部分地区已完成。

(一)参与保险行业监管制度体系建设

偿付能力监管是保险行业监管的核心,相关制度体系建设直接关系到保险业的发展方向及轨道。2014—2021年期间,相关再保险公司协助监管机构论证、制定、修订了中国第二代偿付能力监管制度。此外,相关再保险公司还协助制定、修订了《再保险业务管理规定》、车险综改费率相关制度、《核保险巨灾责任准备金管理办法》等重要规章制度。在《企业会计准则第25号——保险合同》《保险业监管数据标准化规范(再保险公司版)》相关编制工作当中,再保险业也发挥了积极作用。

(二)聚合数据资源,开发风险模型

数据与分析工具是保险业风险管理的基石。再保险公司凭借数据和技术优势,汇总整合多领域、多维度、长时间数据,搭建分析数据库,开发专业风险模型。

一是聚合连接多方数据资源。在巨灾风险管理领域,再保险积极构建多维度、立体化的自然灾害数据库,加强在应急管理、生态环境、气象水利等自然灾害管理重要领域的数据积累与跨部门数据协同共享,推动巨灾风险的多方共治。

二是自主开发巨灾风险模型。作为保险业风险管理与定价的重要工具,模型必不可少。中再集团在2018年8月成立中再巨灾风险管理股份有限公司,专注巨灾风险管理和巨灾模型研发,于2018年成功研发中国首个基于国内数据、具有完全自主知识产权的地震巨灾模型;2019年研发中国第一个集成强风、暴雨、风暴潮、洪涝四大致灾因子的台风巨灾模型,正在加快推进洪水巨灾模型开发,将从根本上解决

中国长期以来使用国外模型的"卡脖子"问题。目前巨灾模型已应用于保险行业，在实践中不断迭代升级，可以让巨灾风险"看得清、算得明、管得好"。

（三）助力行业技术标准升级，丰富定价工具箱

一是助力行业生命表、重疾表、意外险发生率表编制。再保险牵头参与行业第三套生命表编制和重大疾病经验表修订。在重大疾病经验表修订中，再保险牵头数据标准和数据清洗职能小组，完成从重疾产品问世以来共约4亿条承保数据、587万条理赔数据的收集、清洗和验收工作，进一步夯实了行业数据基础，同时固化形成了数据收集、校验、理赔病理等重疾数据信息标准以及可直接对行业外输出的技术和应用工具。在意外险发生率表编制过程中，再保险提供丰富的承保与理赔数据，协助编制团队建立保险行业意外险数据库，为发生率的测算提供了重要参考。

二是发布国内首组水险风险曲线，推出健康险承保定价系统平台，扩充丰富行业风险定价工具、提升定价能力。水险风险曲线包含国内货运险风险曲线、进出口货运险风险曲线、沿海内河船舶险风险曲线、远洋船舶险风险曲线共4条，同时形成了水险曲线定价工具的功能化、软件化、平台化，可简便运用于直保与再保的承保定价。健康险承保定价系统平台首次将国内产险业与寿险业健康险数据融合，有助于避免产险公司或寿险公司单纯采用本行业数据为健康险业务进行定价的片面性，有利于保险公司全面认识和理解健康险业务风险。基于再保险公司收集到的商业医疗保险数据和社保医疗保险数据，对当前中端健康险市场的覆盖率超过60%。

（四）开展前瞻性、理论性研究

一是搭建行业智库平台、强化机制保障。再保险发挥连接多方的平台优势和技术领先的专业优势，从技术孵化角度，于2017年成立国内首个再保险巨灾研究中心；于2018年进一步孵化升级为中国首家专注巨灾风险管理的保险科技公司，平台优势持续扩大并向专业产品和服务转化落地。从智库资源平台角度，2021年先后成立中国再保险研究院与中国亚太再保险研究中心，不断提升再保险理论和政策研究水平，搭建互联互通、共商共享的跨学科、跨行业研究平台，持续深化再保险中心建设各领域重点问题研究，为保险行业高质量发展贡献智慧力量。

二是加强对新兴风险的前瞻性研究。新能源汽车风险领域，再保险公司持续加强新能源车险、自动驾驶风险、UBI等前沿风险研究，积极参与新能源车险费率测算等行业技术性工作，同时以研究为切入点、加大外部合作力度，打造保险生态圈，例如中再与中国汽车工程研究院于2021年成立汽车保险联合实验室，开展前沿性、探索性研究。气候变化风险领域，以推动绿色保险发展为核心，再保险公司加入中国人民银行研究局牵头的中国金融标准化技术委员会绿色金融标准工作组；承担《保险公司环境压力测试》行业标准的研究工作，积极参与《ESG评价规范》《上市公司ESG评价标准》《企业环境信息披露标准》等绿色金融标准的研究制定工作。网络风险领域，再保险公司持续推动网络安全保险的前瞻性研究，2021年推出《我国网络安全保险发展蓝皮书（2021）》，同时协助国家工业信息安全发展研究中心编写《我国网络安全保险产业发展白皮书（2021年）》，再保险专业能力获得国家部委与市场高度认可。

三是为行业性平台设立提供重要技术支撑。在中国城乡居民住宅地震巨灾保险共同体设立中，再保险公司深度参与地震巨灾保险的顶层制度设计、产品开发与费率测算等工作，牵头参与开发住宅地震巨灾保险产品，形成了《城乡居民住宅地震巨灾保险示范条款》，在地震巨灾保险产品设计中发挥了关键作用。在中国"一带一路"再保险共同体设立中，再保险公司不但是倡议者更是实践引领者，对业务规则、核保指引、承保能力、成员发展等工作做了扎实系统的研究论证，为共同体成功设立和稳健运行发挥了重要作用。在中国集成电路共保体设立中，再保险公司凭借长期在集成电路产业风险管理方面积累的经验，积极参与调研国际保险市场、测算承保能力并设计共保体顶层机制，为国家集成电路保险保障的发展提供了全球视角和具体解决方案。

三、再保险数字化发展情况

再保险业加快数字化发展步伐，持续加大科技投入，推进科技领域布局，加强多领域场景共建，打造数字保险服务新生态，通过保险科技不断优化客户体验、升级服务体系，满足客户多样化、差异化和品质化的保险需求，实现降本提效增收。再保险与科技深入融合，进一步适应数字经济发展新形势，从模式创新、产品创新、技术创新、服务创新等角度助力行业突破发展困境和瓶颈，不断提升服务实体经济能力。

（一）战略层面高度重视数字化转型

一是数字化转型成为中长期核心战略。国内再保险公司的数字化转型与国际同业比较起步较晚，但发展步伐正在提速。特别是近年来在行业政策的大力推动下，在市场激烈竞争的要求下，国内再保险公司纷纷将数字化转型作为中长期战略发展重心和打造自身核心竞争力的重要驱动力，从顶层设计上进一步明确愿景目标、发展思路和具体举措。例如，中再集团将"科技赋能"作为"十四五"四大战略支点之一，制定了"数字中再2.0"专项规划，从传统轨、创新轨、组织变革三条主线描绘公司"十四五"数字化发展总体框架，加快推动再保险业务与科技融合发展，更好助力业务创新、提升运营效率、赋能行业发展。数字化也是国际再保险公司总体发展战略的重要组成部分，如瑞再明确提出数字化转型中长期目标和年度重点工作，慕再将"数字要素"嵌入其整体发展战略并设立具体数字目标。国际再保险公司在中国市场也在积极践行其数字化发展的总体战略要求。

二是投入大量资源和人力，支持数字化转型发展落地。例如，中再近年来在支持数字化发展方面持续加大资金投入，2021年科技投入近8.5亿元，组建了近400人的科技人才队伍，培养造就保险业务与科技复合型人才和创新团队，打通技术人才成长通道，加大专业技术序列机制建设，保障各项科技化建设举措具备充足的人力基础和技术积淀。

（二）持续拓展战略布局，加强战略合作

一是积极探索设立金融科技子公司、科技创新中心等，在战略布局上不断取得新突破。慕再在中国设立思韬咨询（北京）有限公司，

专注于智能保险解决方案；法再在中国设立保险科技子公司一蜂科技，为直保公司提供科技服务，打通营销、产品、风控、理赔全流程；RGA美再在中国设立科技子公司RGAX专注于推进全球人寿和健康保险业转型，每年度主办Big Ideas保险科技创新大赛，深入挖掘保险科技创新应用，解决人寿和健康保险行业发展痛点；中再于2018年成立国内第一家巨灾科技公司中再巨灾风险管理股份有限公司，并在总部设立了创新孵化中心。

二是加强多渠道战略合作，一方面通过孵化、投资等方式加速与科技公司的合作共赢，另一方面探索多元合作方式。例如，瑞再在中国市场投资了平安好医生、水滴保险等保险科技新平台，并与复旦大学等高校联合，加强对中国保险科技发展的深度研究，与分子实验室等科技平台合作，举办中国保险科技创新大赛和乌镇保险科技大会。中再与国家部委、地方政府、金融机构、科技企业、科研院所等均有广泛合作，在巨灾模型、建筑工程质量潜在缺陷保险信息平台等方面成效显著。中再还与光大科技成立联合创新实验室，打造基于数据安全融合的联邦学习平台，利用数据融合技术构建创新平台，打造对数据"可用不可见"的使用模式，在充分保护数据和隐私安全的前提下，实现数据价值的转化和释放，构建客户智能营销的生态体系。

（三）创新服务手段，提高运营管控质效

一是科技赋能提升服务能力。通过数字化、科技化手段，打造服务保险行业的新平台、新工具。例如，中再积极推动平台生态化，巨灾领域推出"再商""再瞰""再型"等平台，建筑业领域推出工程质量潜在缺陷保险、安责险和建筑业质量手册平台，"一带一路"领域推出"再医"、"再通"平台，大健康领域推出健康服务和"天玑"平台，农业领域推出白灾、农业服务平台等,是再保险通过科技手段打造行业服务平台的突出代表。

二是将新技术融入业务场景,降低运营成本,提升经营效率和客户满意度,推动商业模式转型。在营销方面,通过银保跨界数据融合分析用户资信和消费偏好、大数据分析确定代理人客户分配,实现精准营销。在产品和定价方面,通过物联网、第三方数据,优化产品设计和再保定价。在风控方面,通过人工智能和大数据建立反欺诈模型,防范理赔风险。在理赔方面,利用深度学习和图像识别技术,开发人工智能定损,完成实时结算和赔付,提升理赔效率。在再保交易方面,通过区块链技术,将再保、直保、渠道打通,实现从低频再保交易向高频实时交易转变。

(四)开展前瞻性研究,为创新发展蓄力蓄能

一是开拓新业务领域。以推动网络保险发展为典型,再保险依托数据积累、资源整合优势,在网络风险安全保障方面发挥突出作用,一方面可通过与专业的学术机构、政府部门和保险科技公司合作,结合最前沿的专业知识和最先进的技术,加强网络安全风险相关的创新性研究与产品开发;另一方面,因网络风险具有动态性、来源多样性和传导性等特点,导致其影响因素复杂、数据收集困难且难以预测潜在经济损失,再保险借助量化风险评估模型和平台,全方位衡量投保企业的网络安全风险状况,结合大数据综合分析,为保险业承保网络安全相关风险提供重要技术支撑。例如,中再发布《我国网络安全保险发展蓝皮书(2021)》,将保险商业运营与社会责任相结合,这也是再保险公司首次从行业和技术角度全面阐述中国网络安全保险整体情况。瑞再积极为市场提供网络安全风险相关的创新性研究与产品开

发，推出全面可定制的网络安全保险产品开发工具包。

二是聚焦新技术服务。例如，2018年，由原上海保监局牵头，中再联合众安科技等合作伙伴打造了国内首个区块链再保险实验平台，利用去中心化、开放性、独立性、安全性和匿名性等特征，大幅提高交易处理的准确性和效率，有效化解行业痛点。同年，中再、汉再、通用再联合众安保险、众安科技、英特尔等共同发布中国首个经过实验验证的再保险区块链指导性纲要《再保险区块链（RIC）白皮书》，进一步推动再保险区块链应用落地。中再还开发上线了全球核保险共同体体系中首个应用区块链技术的运营服务平台"核·星"平台，与轻松筹等机构联合发布首款区块链保险产品。

四、再保险发展趋势展望

（一）机遇与挑战

发展机遇方面：一是中国经济具有坚强韧性和强大动能，2021年中国GDP达到114.4万亿元，同比增长8.1%，在全球主要经济体中名列前茅。根据《中共中央关于制定国民经济和社会发展第十四个五年规划和二〇三五年远景目标的建议》（以下简称《国家"十四五"规划》）测算，未来15年GDP年均增速约为4.74%，"十四五"期间保持较好增长态势。"双循环"新发展格局将重新定位中国在全球经济中的驱动作用，经济稳中向好、长期向好的基本面不会改变，为保险业高质量发展打下坚实基础。二是中国保险业发展空间依然广阔，2021年国内保费收入4.5万亿元，在全球占比约为10%，远低于GDP和人口的全球占比，未来10~15年中国仍是全球保险业最重要的增长区域。《国家"十四五"规划》35次提到"保险",乡村振兴、制造强国、科技强国、社会治理现代化、应对人口老龄化、健康中国等国家战略加快推进,中等收入群体扩大、公众保险意识增强,保险特别是再保险服务国家战略、参与国家治理和社会服务的空间巨大。三是中国保险市场业务结构加速变化。强监管成为主基调,为行业高质量发展创造良好环境。伴随国家深入推进制造强国、乡村振兴、社会治理现代化等战略部署,农业保险、责任保险等非车险有望加快增长。实现碳达峰、碳中和将为经济社会带来一场系统性变革,绿色发展将成为提升经济发展效益和群众生活质量的重要力量,为以绿色保险为代表的创新产品带来发展机遇。随着中国医疗体制改革持续深化,健康保险已经超越车险成为中国保险行业第二大险种,2025年保费收入有望达到2万亿元。伴随着应对人口老龄化上升为国家战略和居民财富积累,商业养老保险有望迎来快速发展。受益于保险保障需求、财富管理需求和养老金管理需求增长,保险资产管理仍有长足发展空间,第三方资产管理业务有望成为重要利润增长点。四是保险科技带来新变革,数字经济成为国际竞争主战场并引领产业变革。保险市场发展要求保险业通过建平台、造生态深度融入产业发展,以BASIC[①]为代表的新技术加速应用,保险业风险管理将从事后赔付向事前风险预测和预防延伸,保险科技将成为保险业数字化转型、商业模式变革和高质量发展的助推器,再保险有望通过平台生态赋能重塑保险价值链。五是国际市场面临发展机遇,受巨灾损失以及新冠疫情影响,全球保险费率明显上涨,国际财产再保险市场呈现明显走硬趋势,为国际业务高质量发展创造较好条件。人民币国际化进程持续推进,国际人身再保险市场储

---

① BASIC指以区块链(Blockchain)、人工智能(AI)、安全(Security)、物联网(IoT)、算力(Computing)为代表的新技术。

蓄型业务需求持续存在。

发展挑战方面：一是中国宏观环境更为复杂多变，新冠疫情影响持续，全球经济不确定性因素显著增加，金融市场波动未知性趋强，气候变化导致巨灾事件频发，低利率环境对保险资产负债管理和资产配置提出较大挑战，经济社会复杂性提高导致风险管理难度加大，保险公司经营面临的外部风险因素大幅增加。二是政策准则大幅变化，国际会计准则IFRS17、车险综改、"偿二代"二期工程[①]等政策陆续落地实施，极大影响保险公司经营行为，对再保险公司的产品形态、服务模式、服务领域和技术水平提出较大挑战，改革发展面临的约束条件和规则要求显著增多。三是保险市场竞争越发激烈，中国金融保险业加快双向开放，直保市场增速放缓，龙头企业强者恒强、马太效应越发明显；外资再保险公司、保险头部企业和互联网科技平台令再保险市场主体层次更加丰富，市场竞争手段更为多样化；保险科技加速推进数字化转型和产业融合，对传统保险和再保险公司的产品创新速度、客户服务效率和平台运营能力提出更高要求。四是国际再保险市场面临不确定性，当前国际力量对比深刻调整，贸易保护主义盛行，地缘政治风险逐步加大，全球主要再保险市场持续提高对离岸经营再保险业务的市场准入标准。

（二）发展展望

从保险业整体来看：

一是"偿二代"二期实施，监管规则将全面优化升级。"偿二

[①] "偿二代"二期工程建设工作于2017年9月启动，结合金融工作新要求和保险监管新形势，中国银保监会对"偿二代"监管规则进行了全面修订升级，以提升偿付能力监管制度的科学性、有效性和全面性。2021年12月30日，中国银保监会发布《保险公司偿付能力监管规则（Ⅱ）》，标志着"偿二代"二期工程建设顺利完成。

代"二期风险因子调高，保险行业风控体系迎来新的变化。一方面，由于"偿二代"二期新增保单未来盈余分组且限额计入核心资本，同时普遍调高了风险因子，预计短期内行业偿付能力充足率或将普遍下降，未来增资或发行债券等资本补充需求将有所增加。另一方面，"偿二代"二期解决了资本不实、数据不实、底层资产不清等问题，能更科学评估资本占用需求，更准确反映保险公司的风险暴露情况，有利于促进保险公司优化资产负债匹配、关注长期价值投资，也有利于促进保险行业回归保险保障本源。

二是车险综改将进一步深化，财产险发展逐步回归平稳。车险综改以来，保险公司在激烈竞争中主动调整策略，提升发展能力，车险单月保费从2021年第四季度以来逐步实现正增长。在国家对汽车消费的激励政策影响下，预计行业车险保费将实现修复性增长。龙头险企在车险领域的竞争优势将更为凸显，业务集中度进一步提升。

三是人身险转型调整仍在持续。受行业经营环境变化影响，人身险核心指标新业务价值增长率自2018年进入负增长区间，并在疫情持续的两年中加速下滑。2021年，人身险见证了历史上最大规模的代理人流失，标志着代理人升级转型进入深水区。个险渠道同时面临代理人队伍减员和展业难度加大的问题。行业销售端的低迷之势仍将持续，但最剧烈的调整期已经过去，代理人产能将持续提升，产品利润率基本稳定。人身险公司在达成短期业务目标的基础上，更加注重推动中长期的转型与改革。健康险、养老险市场将是未来发展的重点。

四是加快推进数字化转型。保险业正处于向数字化、信息化转型的重要时期，下一步在建立数据联通与共享机制、打破险企的数据茧房效应、推动行业全域数据采集方面，监管机构与行业组织将提供更有力的支撑。保险业将聚焦"数据+新场景"，营造线上新生态，为精细管理、精准服务和优化传统金融保险业务提供数字化方案。

从再保险行业来看：

一是未来一段时期仍将保持稳中有进发展态势，但不确定性带来的经营风险与波动性显著增强。中国经济发展"稳中向好"基本面没有改变，保险业发展空间依然巨大、市场需求更为多元，再保险市场发展与国民经济和保险业发展密切相关，将继续保持稳中有进的发展态势，保险公司分出保费及再保险分保费收入都将保持良好增长趋势。与此同时，气候变化带来的全球自然灾害事件频发，新冠肺炎疫情持续反复，国际局势复杂多变，保险业转型进入深水区，多重因素叠加影响下再保险经营波动性将显著上升，对再保险行业经营稳健性与风险管控能力都提出了更高要求。

二是服务实体经济将成为行业中长期发展的关键着力点。当前中国经济已由高速增长阶段转向高质量发展阶段，再保险作为重要的"安全阀"和"稳定器"，将在保障实体经济发展中创新拓展业务机遇。在碳中和、乡村振兴、科技强国、健康中国、应对人口老龄化等重大国家战略加快推进过程中，在中等收入群体不断扩大、公众保险意识持续增强的过程中，再保险能够利用其在专业技术、资源、人才方面的独特优势，在服务国家战略、参与国家治理和社会服务方面拓展新的战略机遇与业务增量。

三是以引领创新为重点，在保险产业链中将发挥更大价值。再保险将逐步适应在承担巨灾风险方面的功能扩展，适应全球化激烈竞争的新形势，加快技术创新和商业模式创新步伐，在提升技术和资本实力的基础上，从简单提供承保能力支持向一揽子的新型风险管理产品的批发商转变、向资本和技术的综合提供商转变、向资本市场中介功能延伸，推动再保险价值链向供应链、渠道和客户价值链的移动，占据价值链的高端。与政府机构、保险公司、科技平台等各方的合作将更为深化，构建再保险特色生态圈，大力推动产业链和合作网络建设，升级经营模式与服务模式。强化再保险的风险管理和技术传导功能，提高再保险对直接保险市场的覆盖面与渗透力，在促进保险市场健康发展方面发挥更大价值。再保险将进一步发挥在数据、技术及人才等方面的专业优势，加强业务模式研发，以产品创新为突破口，为财产损失和人身健康，特别是一系列新兴风险提供更加全面的保险保障，如专利、数据、算法等无形资产保险，恐怖主义、政治暴乱等"一带一路"保险，以及巨灾保险、网络安全保险、特殊风险保险等多类型创新产品。财产再保险方面，将加强新能源、绿色建筑、减碳技术的风险研究，开展新能源汽车、天气风险、森林碳汇等绿色保险产品创新；将加快商业农险产品创新，积极推进指数保险、价格保险、涉农保险等创新型农险产品发展；将围绕集成电路、软件质量、知识产权等新兴领域，开展科技保险产品创新与服务；将围绕新的社会治理需求，研发推广新型责任保险产品和解决方案。人身再保险方面，将重点服务健康中国战略和应对人口老龄化，围绕健康医疗、护理、医疗器械等领域开展产品创新，积极服务第三支柱养老建设，整合优质健康管理服务资源，以产品创新助力保险业转型升级。

第二章 财产再保险市场2021年发展情况及发展展望

一、财产再保险市场规模

二、财产再保险需求侧分析

三、财产再保险供给侧分析

四、财产再保险主要业务

五、财产再保险发展展望

一、财产再保险市场规模

(一)分出保费规模

2021年,国内财产保险公司再保险分出保费合计1 460.5亿元,较上年增长5.6%;同期,财产保险公司原保险保费合计13 816.2亿元,较上年增长1.8%;再保险分出保费增速高于同期原保险保费增速约3.8个百分点。

2012—2021年,国内财产保险公司再保险分出保费从739亿元增长至1 460.5亿元,年均增长率约8.1%;同期,财产保险公司原保险保费由5 529.9亿元增长至13 816.2亿元,年均增长率约10.7%,再保险分出保费年均增速低于同期原保险保费增速2.6个百分点。自2016年以来,分出保费增长速度加快,2016—2021年五年数据显示,财产保险公司再保险分出保费的年均增长率约10.4%;同期,财产保险公司原保险保费年均增长率约8.3%,再保险分出保费年均增速已高于同期原保险保费年均增速约2个百分点。

图1 2012—2021年财产险公司原保险保费、分出保费及增长率情况

(数据来源:中国保险年鉴、中国银保监会)

表1 2012—2021年财产保险公司分出保费、原保险保费及再保险分出率情况

单位：亿元、%

年份	分出保费	增长率	原保险保费	增长率	分出率
2012	739.0	—	5 529.9	—	13.4
2013	865.2	17.1	6 480.9	17.2	13.3
2014	929.8	7.5	7 544.4	16.4	12.3
2015	946.0	1.7	8 423.3	11.6	11.2
2016	887.9	-6.1	9 266.2	10.0	9.6
2017	938.8	5.7	10 541.4	13.8	8.9
2018	1 072.3	14.2	11 755.7	11.5	9.1
2019	1 207.7	12.6	13 016.3	10.7	9.3
2020	1 383.4	14.5	13 583.7	4.4	10.2
2021	1 460.5	5.6	13 816.2	1.8	10.6

数据来源：中国保险年鉴、中国银保监会。

（二）再保险分出率

2021年，财产保险公司的再保险分出率约10.6%，连续第二年超过10%，较上年提升0.4个百分点。

2012—2015年，再保险分出率逐年下降，但均高于10%。2016—2021年，再保险分出率呈现先降后升的变化趋势。2016年主要受"偿二代"实施的影响，再保险分出率大幅下降至不足10%；2017年，"偿二代"影响延续，再保险分出继续降低至不足9%；2018年以来，受非车险业务增长的拉动，再保险分出率逐年提升；2020年，再保险分出率提升至10%以上；2021年，再保险分出率进一步提升，较2016年高出近1个百分点。

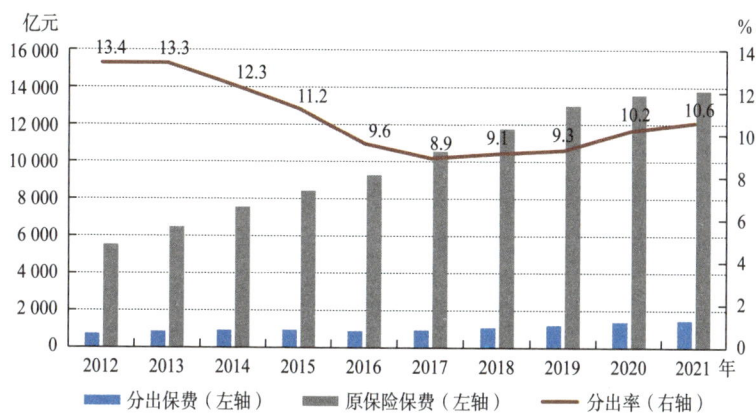

图 2　2012—2021 年财产保险公司再保险分出率情况

（数据来源：中国保险年鉴、中国银保监会）

二、财产再保险需求侧分析

（一）财产保险公司分出保费分布情况

2021年，财产再保险分出保费规模超过100亿元的财产保险公司共4家，合计分出保费929.2亿元，占全行业分出保费规模的63.6%；再保险分出保费规模在10亿~100亿元的财产保险公司共14家，合计分出保费335.7亿元，占全行业分出保费规模的23.0%；再保险分出保费规模在1亿~10亿元的财产保险公司共51家，合计分出保费189.3亿元，占全行业分出保费规模的13.0%；再保险分出保费规模不足1亿元的财产保险公司共19家，合计分出保费6.3亿元，占全行业分出保费规模的0.4%。

（二）财产保险公司分出保费变化

2021年，财产再保险分出保费较上年增长的财产保险公司数量61家，占比69.3%，其中：较上年增长10%以内的公司数量16家，占比18.2%；较上年增长10%~20%的公司数量10家，占比11.4%；较上年增长超过20%的公司数量35家，占比39.8%。2021年，财产再保险分出保费较上年减少的财产保险公司数量27家，占比30.7%，其中：较上年减少10%以内的公司数量8家，占比9.1%；较上年减少10%~20%的公司数量7家，占比8.0%；较上年减少超过20%的公司数量12家，占比13.6%。

（三）财产保险公司分出率分布情况

2021年，财产再保险分出率超过20%的财产保险公司数量39家，占比44.3%，较上年增加7家；再保险分出率15%~20%的公司数量5家，占比5.7%，较上年减少5家；再保险分出率10%~15%的公司数量8家，占比9.1%，较上年增加1家；再保险分出率5%~10%的公司数量18家，占比20.5%，较上年增加6家；再保险分出率低于5%的公司数量18家，占比20.5%，较上年减少9家。

表2　2016—2021年财产保险公司再保险分出率分布情况

单位：家

分出率区间	2016	2017	2018	2019	2020	2021
>20%	26	26	28	34	32	39
15%~20%	4	5	8	2	10	5
10%~15%	12	12	11	15	7	8
5%~10%	14	17	15	11	12	18
<5%	24	24	25	25	27	18
合计	80	84	87	87	88	88

三、财产再保险供给侧分析

从供给侧结构来看，中再产险充分发挥国内再保险主渠道作用，市场份额排名第1位。与此同时，财产再保险市场近年来新增多家本土再保险主体，包括中国农再、人保再、太平再（中国）、前海再等；外资再保险人也高度重视中国再保险市场，瑞再、汉再等外资再保人于2021年纷纷增资、加紧国内市场布局。

2021年，在境内注册、经营财产再保险业务的专业再保险公司共12家（含劳合社中国）。其中，市场份额超过20%的公司1家，市场份额10%~15%的公司1家，市场份额5%~10%的公司3家，市场份额低于5%的公司7家。

四、财产再保险主要业务

（一）财产再保险安排方式

财产再保险公司通过合约分保和临时分保，以比例再保险[①]、非比例再保险[②]方式等再保险安排为直保客户转移和分散风险。

（二）财产再保险主要业务类型

1．合约分保

（1）非水险业务

国内财产保险公司对以企业财产险、工程险为主的非水险业务，

---

① 比例再保险，是指以保险金额为基础确定再保险分出人自留额和再保险接受人分保额的再保险方式。

② 非比例再保险，是指以赔款金额为基础确定再保险分出人自负责任和再保险接受人分保责任的再保险方式。

通常采取比例再保险与非比例再保险并重的再保险安排方式。比例再保险安排，通常以组建溢额合约或成数溢额①合约为主要的再保险安排方式，其中成数溢额的分保方式占主流。非比例再保险安排，通常以组建险位损失超赔②合约、事故损失超赔③合约（巨灾损失超赔合约）、险位损失/事故损失混合超赔合约为主要的再保险方式，其中：大型财产保险公司分别组建险位损失超赔合约和事故损失超赔合约，中小型财产保险公司组建险位损失/事故损失混合超赔合约。

（2）农险业务

国内财产保险公司对农险业务的再保险安排主要包括与中国农再的约定分保和商业市场分保。在约定分保方面，2021年，中国农再与国内农业保险承保机构签署再保险标准协议，约定承担行业20%的农业风险分保保障。在商业市场分保方面，比例再保险安排通常体现为组建成数分保合约，非比例再保险安排通常体现为组建赔付率超赔合约。

（3）其他险种

国内财产保险公司对其他险种的再保险安排主要结合险种自身情况选择再保险方式。以船舶险、船建险、货运险为主的水险业务通常选择组建成数溢额合约，并对净自留损失安排超赔合约保障；责任险

---

① 成数再保险，是指原保险人将保险标的的保险金额，按照约定的分保比率分给再保险人的保险方式。
  溢额再保险，是指原保险人将每一危险单位的保险金额超过约定自留额的部分（即溢额部分）分给再保险人的保险方式。
② 险位损失超赔再保险，是指以每一危险单位所发生的赔款为基础来确定分出公司自负责任和分入公司分保责任的再保险方式。
③ 事故损失超赔再保险，是指以一次事故所发生的总赔款为基础来确定分出公司自负责任和分入公司分保责任的再保险方式。

业务通常选取某项或某几项细分险种组建成数合约，并对各类责任险业务的净自留损失安排超赔合约保障；信用保证险业务通常选择组建成数合约；特殊风险业务通常选择组建成数合约，并对净自留损失安排超赔合约保障；意外险业务通常选择组建超赔合约保障；短期健康险业务通常结合具体产品的情况组建成数合约。

2．临时分保

国内财产保险公司的临时分保安排主要涉及以下情况：一是未安排再保险合约保障或通常再保险市场不提供合约再保险支持的险种或业务，如航天险等；二是属于再保险合约除外责任的险种或业务，如恐怖主义风险、涉水工程险等；三是超出再保险合约保障限额的业务，如超高保额项目等。

五、财产再保险发展展望

（一）财产再保险市场的机遇与挑战

发展机遇方面：一是车险综改重塑行业经营模式。市场逐步消化保费规模下降的不利冲击后，承保效益的压力接踵而至；细分领域，新能源车专属保险率先破冰，但"高增长、高赔付"的特点加剧挑战，再保险将更加积极地协同直保公司开展风险研究和风险减量管理，管控风险、改善承保业绩。二是非车险仍处于增量市场阶段。大型险企全面转型为客群经营模式，有望加速创新产品的探索和落地，在新兴险种及创新产品领域的再保险需求保持强劲。三是政策性险种及政务场景业务、个人险业务强劲增长。控风险、持续改善承保业绩已成共识，再保险保障是必不可少的环节。

发展挑战方面：一是异常天气为代表的灾害损失加重，再保险人的累计责任风险突出，灾害损失面临较大幅度波动的风险。二是新兴风险及创新领域的再保险需求激增，再保险人的承保定价面临较大不确定性风险。三是受直保市场价格竞争影响，原保险业务定价不足的情况较为普遍，再保险人的承保业绩进一步承压。

（二）对财产保险公司再保险分出需求变化的展望

在传统险种领域，财产保险公司的再保险需求整体平稳。分散巨灾风险、平滑经营波动为再保险安排的主要诉求。一是传统险种的整体再保险分出率保持在合理区间。二是在一定程度内，财产保险公司能够接受市场对再保险合约条件的合理调整。三是在超赔合约保障的再保险安排中，财产保险公司在一定程度上能够提高成本预算，以保证其在再保险市场硬周期下能够获得足额的风险保障。

在新兴险种及创新产品领域，财产保险公司的再保险需求保持强劲。一是战略性新兴产业快速发展，拉动风险保障需求增加。近年来，以集成电路、海上风电等为代表的新兴产业快速发展，风险保障需求及相应的再保险保障需求强劲。二是政策支持类的保险业务快速发展，推高再保险需求。以促进建筑质量提升的建筑工程质量潜在缺陷保险、促进保险替代保证金降低企业成本的工程履约保证保险、服务健康中国战略的中端健康保险及城市普惠型健康保险等为代表，均保持较高的再保险分出率。三是再保险公司更主动地输出数据和技术经验，与直保公司合作开发创新型保险产品和风险解决方案。在新能源汽车及产业链的相关保险、网络安全保险等领域，再保险公司对新兴领域的风险研究和产品研发参与度提高，也从供给端进一步助推了风险分散需求向再保险业务合作的转化。

（三）对专业再保险公司业务承保策略变化的展望

再保险市场的承保能力供给整体偏紧、再保险市场的报价条件局部趋严。财产再保险市场将延续"稳中趋严"的市场态势，再保险人更加关注风险对价，严控自然灾害的累计责任、严控部分特定领域的风险敞口、严控已过剩承保能力的进一步投放仍将是主流再保险市场的普遍诉求。

离岸再保险人继续将承保能力向价格涨幅大的国家和地区转移，中国市场吸引力有所下降。一是近年来巨灾损失呈现高频高损态势，叠加美国冬季风暴、欧洲洪水以及美国飓风"艾达"等巨灾影响，国际再保市场承保利润不断受到侵蚀。二是再保险资本供给增长有限，持续亏损使再保险人不得不寻求价格上涨，收缩承保能力并择优投放。三是由于非模型灾害频发，通货膨胀严重，国际再保险公司总部普遍要求减少巨灾类业务承保能力的投放。

再保险人关注直保端价格竞争对风险定价充足度的影响，局部收紧承保条件以控制风险敞口。一是受车险综改、"偿二代"二期实施等多重因素叠加影响，市场形势趋于复杂。二是灾害损失偏重，市场遭受了河南暴雨洪水灾害及多个大赔案损失。三是受直保市场的价格竞争影响，原保险业务定价不足的情况较为普遍，再保险人的承保效益进一步承压。

第三章

人身再保险市场2021年发展情况及发展展望

一、人身再保险市场规模

二、人身再保险需求侧分析

三、人身再保险供给侧分析

四、人身再保险主要业务

五、人身再保险发展展望

一、人身再保险市场规模

（一）分出保费规模

2021年，国内人身险公司再保险分出保费996.3亿元，较上年下降4.5%。同期，人身险公司原保险保费收入33 635.9亿元，较上年增长6.2%。总体来说，人身再保险分出保费规模不同年份之间呈波动趋势。当前，在宏观经济面临"需求收缩、供给冲击、预期转弱"三重压力、"偿二代"等监管政策切换以及直保市场转型和增速放缓的背景下，再保险市场增长面临一定冲击和挑战。

2012—2021年，国内人身险公司再保险分出保费从140.4亿元增长至996.3亿元，年均增长率约24.3%，整体呈现稳中有升趋势。其中，2012—2014年，分出保费迅速提升；2015—2016年大幅回落；2017—2020年波动上涨；2021年，分出保费较上年又稍有下降。

图1 2012—2021年人身险公司原保险保费、分出保费及增长率情况

（数据来源：中国保险年鉴、中国银保监会）

表1　2012—2021年人身险公司原保险保费、分出保费及再保险分出率情况

单位：亿元、%

年份	分出保费	增长率	原保险保费	增长率	分出率
2012	140.4	—	9 957.9	—	1.4
2013	298.8	112.8	11 010.0	10.6	2.7
2014	1 937.4	548.4	12 592.3	14.4	15.4
2015	555.6	−71.3	15 724.0	24.9	3.5
2016	435.9	−21.5	21 662.8	37.8	2.0
2017	722.4	65.7	25 972.7	19.9	2.8
2018	736.2	1.9	26 232.5	1.0	2.8
2019	673.9	−8.5	27 792.6	5.9	2.4
2020	1 043.7	54.9	29 500.7	6.1	3.5
2021	996.3	−4.5	33 636.0	14.0	3.0

数据来源：中国保险年鉴、中国银保监会。

（二）再保险分出率

2021年，国内人身险公司再保险分出率约为3%，连续第二年超过3%，较上年下降0.5个百分点。当前，国内人身再保险分出率与全球趋同，基本稳定在3%左右，主要受业务结构以及人身险直保市场变化影响，以风险保障为目的的传统再保险业务分出比例较大，储蓄型为主的人身险则分出较低；境外存量市场格局稳定，增长有限，业务变动主要受国际并购、年金业务等大宗交易业务影响。

2012—2021年，人身险公司再保险分出率整体呈现稳中有升趋势。其中，2012—2014年，人身再保险分出率逐年提升并达到高峰；2015年大幅回落；2016—2020年，分出率稳步提升；2021年，分出率较2020年稍有降低。整体来说，与2012年相比，10年来再保险分出率翻倍，高出2012年1.6个百分点。这一变化很大程度源于中国医疗险市场的高速发展，相较重疾溢额分保方式，医疗险多采用成数分保，人身险公司分出需求有较大程度提升。

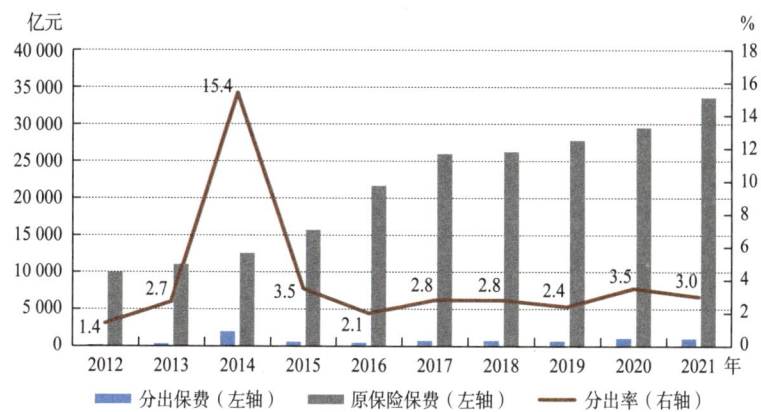

图 2　2012—2021 年人身保险公司再保险分出率情况

（数据来源：中国保险年鉴、中国银保监会）

二、人身再保险需求侧分析

2021年，中国人身险原保险保费收入3.36万亿元，同比上升6.2%。展望未来，疫情下经济下行压力凸显，人均收入增幅减慢，行业监管持续加强，代理人持续脱离等影响，作为一项非刚性消费支出，人身险增长也会面临压力，增速预计将放缓。

从再保险需求来看，虽然行业发展面临压力，但是出于产品创新、风险分散等目的，2021年分出保费较上年增长的人身险公司数量仍然达到了56家，占比达63%，再保险需求依然在增长。其中，较上年增长超过50%的公司数量24家，较上年增长20%~50%的公司数量15家，较上年增长0~20%的公司数量17家。

2021年[①]，人身再保险分出保费规模超过50亿元的人身险公司共9家，合计分出保费688.2亿元，占全行业分出保费规模的69.1%；分出

---

① 2021年数据显示，部分人身险公司分出保费为负数。人身险公司分出保费整体净值为996.3亿元。以此为基础计算分出保费占比，合计占比超过100%。

保费规模在10亿~50亿元的人身险公司共18家，合计分出保费439.5亿元，占全行业分出保费规模的44.1%；分出保费规模在1亿~10亿元的人身险公司共29家，合计分出保费108.5亿元，占全行业分出保费规模的10.9%；分出保费规模不足1亿元的人身险公司共27家，合计分出保费7.2亿元，占全行业分出保费规模的0.7%。

三、人身再保险供给侧分析

从供给侧结构来看，中再寿险充分发挥国内再保险主渠道作用，市场份额排名第一。其他主要参与者包括国际大型再保险公司，以及前海再、太平再（中国）、人保再等本土再保险公司。

2021年，在境内注册、经营人身再保险业务的专业再保险公司共10家。其中，市场份额超过50%的公司1家，市场份额10%~15%的公司1家，市场份额5%~10%的公司5家，市场份额低于5%的公司3家。

四、人身再保险主要业务

（一）人身再保险安排方式

人身再保险公司通过提供合同分保和临时分保，以风险保费方式、共保方式/修正共保方式[①]等再保险安排为直保公司转移和化解风险。

[①] 风险保费方式又称年度可续保方式，年度可续保的再保险是指分出公司将长期险业务或短期险业务的风险保额以一定比例分出，分出公司付给分入公司一定金额的再保险费，由分入公司承担分出业务的保险责任。共保方式是指分出公司将某一长期寿险的全部风险转移给再保险公司的分保方式，分出公司将被保险人的原始保费按比例支付给再保险公司，同时也将发生率风险和投资风险转移给再保险公司。修正共保方式是上述两种方式的综合，分出公司将原始保费按比例支付给再保险公司，但保费中准备金部分则留存在分出公司。

（二）人身再保险主要业务类型

1. 传统再保险业务

（1）寿险再保险业务

国内寿险再保险业务主要以长期人寿再保险和短期人寿再保险为主，主要承担发生率风险。长期人寿险的再保险一般分为YRT[①]、共保和修正共保三种方式。短期人寿再保险期限较短且标的风险分散性较好，很少采用成数方式，主要以溢额方式进行分保。

（2）健康险再保险业务

近年来，国内健康险业务主要以重疾险和医疗险为主，前者主要承担发生率风险，以溢额分保为主；后者主要承担医疗费用风险，以成数分保为主。在健康险开发中，人身再保险公司通常依托强大的数据库，汇集住院率、发病率、医疗费用分布、发病人群特征等丰富的数据信息，对数据的时间横截面及随时间的纵向趋势进行深度挖掘研究，为人身险公司健康险新产品开发提供技术支持。

（3）意外险再保险业务

人身再保险公司以丰富的承保经验，为人身险公司和部分健康险公司提供各类意外伤害保险的再保险服务。无论是个人意外险产品或是团体意外险产品，人身再保险公司均可以提供分保方式多样的、涵盖各种意外保障责任的再保险安排。

人身再保险公司为多种职业类别的高风险业务提供再保险保障，包括政府企业的职员和社会知名人士的保险、赴境外高风险国家人士

---

① YRT是指分出公司将长期险业务的发生率风险按照年度续保的方式转移给再保险公司。

的保险、煤矿从业人员的保险、各种地质考察人员的保险、从事各种高风险运动人员的保险、高保额人员的保险等。同时，可以为直接保险公司提供人身险类的巨灾保障，如事故超赔和巨灾超赔再保险安排，为各家保险公司的业务风险管理提供支持。

2．其他再保险业务

除传统再保险业务外，人身再保险公司积极开展业务创新，如在监管合规的前提下，为人身险公司缓解偿付能力压力；根据经济周期及市场判断帮助人身险公司转移投资端风险，承接寿险、两全险、年金险等业务。

五、人身再保险发展展望

（一）人身再保险市场的机遇与挑战

发展机遇方面：一是健康中国、乡村振兴、"一带一路"等落地带来对"惠民保"[①]、罕见病保险、防返贫保险等保险创新产品的需求，再保险能够在产品创新和风险管理方面提供重要支撑、发挥引领作用。二是在行业渠道升级、产品服务供给侧结构性改革的背景下，保险公司对再保险公司在数据、产品、服务、销售支持等方面的综合需求进一步提升，再保险在新风险定义、产品开发、风险定价和管理方面的价值输出越发重要。三是在保险行业与健康产业融合实践中，市场迫切需要再保险公司凭借专业中立的站位，贯通各环节服务链条并进行产品化运营支持。四是保险行业基础设施建设如重疾表、意外表、

---

① "惠民保"又称城市定制型商业医疗保险，其具有低价格、低门槛、高保障等特点，有效弥补了多层次医疗保障体系缺口。

生命表的制定工作，需要再保险发挥数据技术方面的优势，为行业整体发展贡献力量。五是在"偿二代"二期工程下，保险公司偿付能力普遍下降，再保险需求呈上升趋势，蕴含一定业务机会。

发展挑战方面：一是宏观经济面临三重压力，金融环境更为复杂。利率方面，2021年长端利率呈现下行趋势；投资方面，股市和债市波动加大。二是直保行业转型压力加大，受新冠肺炎疫情持续影响，保险线下经营活动受到限制，业务拓展与队伍建设面临困难，2021年中国境内代理人数量为641.9万人，与上年末的842.8万人相比，减少252.1万人，同比下降近30%，对再保险经营带来压力。三是新检测技术大幅提升疾病的检出率，使得基于既往经验定价的重疾险业务面临挑战。医疗险长期化也使经营面临更大不确定性。

（二）对再保险分出需求变化的展望

从需求端看，在传统型业务方面，健康险是重要的人身险增长来源，短期也面临挑战。健康险自2013年起步至今，保费规模超过8 400亿元，年均增长率达到32.8%。商业健康险在人身险业务中的占比呈现逐年提升趋势，2021年达到25.4%，成为人身险市场增长主要驱动力。此外，健康险产品在保险公司产品线中扮演着不可替代的角色。重疾险是代理人渠道传统的"打底产品"，是稳定代理人队伍的重要工具。百万医疗险成为代理人渠道的主要获客产品，也是互联网流量平台的主要变现产品。"惠民保"是医保商保融合的成功模式。在其他再保险业务方面，需要充分考量IFRS17、"偿二代"二期的影响，不断创新综合解决方案，提升资本使用效率，丰富服务客户手段。与此同时，需要进一步提升资产负债匹配能力和逆周期管理能力。未来，人身险短期挑战或将向再保险市场传递，人身险公司再保险分出需求预计将随着传统和非传统业务的快速发展而有所波动。

（三）对专业再保险公司业务承保策略变化的展望

从供给端看，人身再保险公司将积极落实"健康中国"战略，围绕民生需求坚定不移推进健康险创新发展。一是发挥产品优势，推动供给侧结构性改革。发挥人身再保险在人身险产品设计创新领域发动机的作用，从"健康中国"战略提出的"立足全人群和全生命周期两个着力点"出发，在满足人民对美好生活的向往、填补国内医疗保障体系缺口方面持续发力。二是适应数字化时代需要，推动构建数据优势。推动内部数据标准化建设，提升数据安全性和流转效率；精选医药、医疗服务等细分场景，丰富大健康数据储备；积极开展数据融合及共创项目，加快跨界数据集中和脱敏共享。三是夯实技术优势。提升风险模型、精算定价、风险评估等核心技术，结合技术研究和数据分析提升精准核保与定价能力；深刻认知医疗技术进步的影响，精准界定责任、疾病定义和分类，洞察理赔趋势，强化业务追踪和质量检测。未来，人身再保险公司将更加注重发挥产品创新和数据优势，提升专业技术和服务能力，以推动健康险发展作为重要着力点，带动业务增长，拓展战略布局，培育核心竞争力。

第四章　外资再保险公司2021年发展情况及发展展望

一、外资再保险公司在中国发展基本情况

二、外资再保险公司在中国发展历程

三、外资再保险公司在中国经营情况

四、外资再保险公司在中国人力资源情况

五、外资再保险公司在中国发展展望

一、外资再保险公司在中国发展基本情况

近年来全球再保险市场增速放缓，但以中国为代表的新兴再保险市场一枝独秀。全球主要再保险公司将中国市场视为战略目标市场，依托其强大的专业能力和资本优势，加大对中国市场投入。

市场主体方面，截至2021年底，国内再保险市场专业再保险公司共15家，其中，中资7家（含1家集团公司，即中再集团），外资8家。在8家外资公司中，有7家位列A.M.Best数据世界再保险公司排行榜。此外，百余家财产险、人身险公司不同程度参与再保险市场竞争；超过500家境外再保险主体虽未在国内设立分支机构、但通过离岸交易的形式接受国内分出业务。

表1　　　　国内外资专业再保险公司情况概览

公司名称	成立时间	注册地	注册性质	企业性质
慕尼黑再保险公司北京分公司	2003年	北京	分公司	外资
瑞士再保险股份有限公司北京分公司	2003年	北京	分公司	外资
德国通用再保险股份公司上海分公司	2004年	上海	分公司	外资
汉诺威再保险股份公司上海分公司	2008年	上海	分公司	外资
法国再保险公司北京分公司	2008年	北京	分公司	外资
信利再保险（中国）有限公司	2011年	上海	公司	外资
RGA美国再保险公司上海分公司	2014年	上海	分公司	外资
大韩再保险公司上海分公司	2020年	上海	分公司	外资

资料来源：中国保险年鉴、各再保险公司年报。

受益于宏观经济和保险市场的快速发展，中国再保险市场也呈现出快速增长态势，分保费收入增长速度显著高于成熟市场平均增速，国内市场也呈现出充分竞争的格局。目前，财产再保险市场从分保费收入规模和偿付能力来看，已形成多梯队、共参与的局面。在宏观经

济面临三重压力、"偿二代"等监管政策切换以及直保市场转型和增速放缓的背景下，人身再保险市场则呈波动趋势。随着外资再保险公司的不断投入，中国再保险市场充分竞争的局面不断深化且日趋激烈。

二、外资再保险公司在中国发展历程

自2001年中国加入世界贸易组织（WTO）后，中国再保险市场率先向外资全面开放，中国再保险市场从无到有、从小到大，已成为全球最为开放、最具成长性的再保险市场之一。

（一）在中国开设分支机构情况

瑞再与慕再先后于1996年和1997年在上海设立代表处，是最早进入中国的全球头部再保险公司。2003年，两家公司分别获得在北京开设分公司的执业牌照。中国再保险市场对外开放的大门向外资再保险公司打开。瑞再、慕再等头部再保险公司率先布局，其他再保险公司陆续发力。从实施路径来看，都是从设立代表处开始，逐步过渡为经营性公司。目前除信利再外，其余7家外资在中国再保机构均以分公司的形式开展业务。

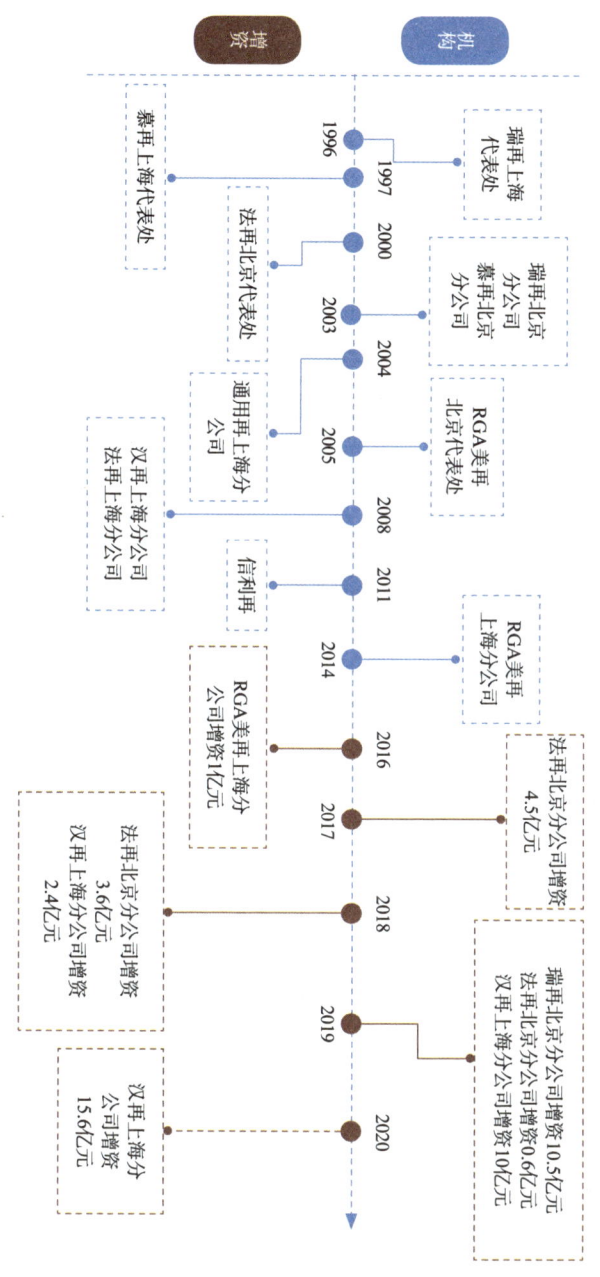

图 1　外资再保险公司在中国发展时间表

（资料来源：各再保险公司年报）

（二）经营资本持续增加

继2015年慕再北京分公司增加13亿元营运资金、成为第一家增资的外资再保险公司后，2017—2021年，外资再保险公司持续增资其在中国的经营机构，5年合计增资金额为49.6亿元。其中，汉再上海分公司增资额合计达28亿元，瑞再北京分公司增资额达10.5亿元。特别是在2019—2021年，外资再保险公司对中国机构的增资力度明显加大，合计增资36.7亿元，明显高于中资再保险公司合计增资14亿元的水平。

表2　　　　2017—2021年再保险主体资本变动一览表

单位：亿元

公司	2017	2018	2019	2020	2021	累计增资	期末注册资本
人保再	20.0		10.0			30.0	40.0
太平再（中国）	5.0		4.0			9.0	19.0
前海再						—	30.0
小计						39.0	89.0
瑞再北京分公司			10.5			10.5	13.1
慕再北京分公司						—	16.5
汉再上海分公司		2.4	10.0	15.6		28.0	41.0
法再北京分公司	4.5	3.6	0.6			8.7	20.7
通用再上海分公司		1.4				1.4	4.4
RGA美再上海分公司						—	3.0
小计						49.6	115.4
合计	29.5	7.4	35.1	15.6	0	88.6	204.4

数据来源：中国银保监会官网。

（三）服从集团总体战略，全球化发展一盘棋

外资再保险公司在中国发展拥有明确的、与集团整体发展战略保持一致的经营目标。一是外资再保险公司有明确的收益回报要求；二

是外资再保险公司有较高的偿付能力约束要求,确保公司的实际偿付能力水平维持在目标区间;三是外资再保险公司注重前瞻性资本规划;四是外资再保险公司拓展替代资本,充分利用巨灾债券、次级债等多种资本补充工具;五是以风险资本管理为导向,借助内部统一的财务标准评估并分配资本。

（四）员工人数稳步增长

从员工规模看,外资再保险公司由最初代表处层级的2~10人,发展到经营层级的百人以上规模。外资再保险公司从业务规模到员工人数、年龄结构和教育背景等发展变化进一步表明其核心竞争力不断增强。

（五）风险管理治理架构与风险管理文化相适应

外资再保险公司在总部层级均设有强大的风险管理部门,对公司面临的固有风险和非固有风险等进行统一管理,为每个风险类别设定最佳风险容忍水平。同时,外资再保险公司风险管理治理架构与风险管理文化相适应,注重资源的整合与共享。一是通过集团统一的资本模型实现对不同区域和市场的资本管理与风险管理;二是建立健全风险偏好和传导机制,偏好的设置最终与经济资本回报、评级资本和监管资本要求相适应;三是强调信息系统集中、统一建设。

三、外资再保险公司在中国经营情况

近年来,外资再保险公司已经成为中国再保险市场的重要组成部分,其业务规模整体呈稳健增长态势,盈利能力不断提升,竞争力进一步增强。

（一）业务规模情况

2017—2021年，外资再保险公司业务规模整体稳健增长。其中，瑞再北京分公司业务规模排名外资再保险公司首位，2021年分保费收入达192.19亿元；慕再、汉再和法再紧随其后。

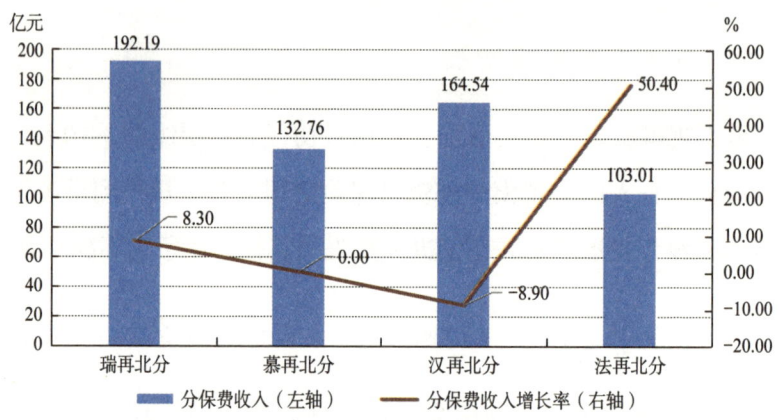

图2　2021年外资再保险公司分保费收入及增长率情况

（数据来源：各再保险公司年报）

1．瑞再北分

从分保费收入看，瑞再北分2021年总保费收入达192.19亿元，同比增长8.3%。近年来瑞再集团的财产险业务增幅明显，瑞再北分的财产险业务贡献了其总保费收入的七成以上，远高于寿险和健康险。

从业务结构看，2021年瑞再北分财产险分保费收入占比高达72.21%，其中占比较高的财产责任险和车险分别为41%和22.3%。人身险分保费收入占比为27.79%。近两年，由于中国市场寿险及健康险发展前景广阔，且相关业务受疫情影响较小，人身险分保费收入呈现上升趋势。

表3　　　　　　　　　　瑞再北分业务结构情况

单位：亿元、%

业务条线	2021年分保费收入	2021年分保费占比
人身险	53.41	27.79
寿险	4.85	2.52
健康险	48.56	25.27
财产险	138.78	72.21
车险	42.87	22.30
财产责任险	78.80	41.00
水险	12.85	6.69
其他	4.26	2.22
合计	192.19	100.00

数据来源：公司年报。

2．法再北分

从分保费收入看，2021年法再北分分保费收入达103.01亿元，同比增长50.4%。其中寿险分保费收入高达40.05亿元，占全部分保费收入的39%，同比增长397.5%，其增长主要来自财务再保险业务。

从业务结构看，法再北分人身险业务占比逐年上升，并超过财产险业务成为公司第一大业务险种，占总分保费收入的64.41%。财产险业务分保费收入36.67亿元，同比上升23.2%，占总分保费收入的35.59%。财产险业务的主要增长点集中在农险、货运险、特险，2021年分保费增长率分别达到140.42%、96.84%、86.66%。

表4　　　　　　　　　　法再北分业务结构情况

单位：亿元、%

业务条线	2021年分保费收入	2021年分保费占比
短期健康险	15.30	14.85
车险	4.32	4.19
信用保证险	7.02	6.81
寿险	40.05	38.88
长期健康险	11.00	10.68

续表

业务条线	2021年分保费收入	2021年分保费占比
责任险	7.14	6.93
企财险	5.49	5.33
工程险	2.03	1.97
意外险	2.64	2.56
农险	4.80	4.66
船舶险	0.88	0.85
货运险	1.41	1.37
特险	0.95	0.92
合计	103.01	100.00

数据来源：公司年报。

3．汉再上分

从分保费收入看，汉再上分2021年保险业务收入164.54亿元，同比下降8.9%，自2021年开始业务有所收缩。尽管如此，汉再上分2021年的分保费收入仅次于瑞再北分，位居外资再保险公司中的第2位。

从业务结构看，汉再上分人身险与财产险业务各占一半左右。人身险业务中占比最高的为健康险，占比35.51%；财产险业务占比较高的有责任险，占比9.81%；财产险，占比9.70%；信用险，占比9.42%；车险，占比8.85%等。

业务增速方面，2021年信用险保费增幅明显，达21.41%；责任险、车险、财产险、工程险、货运险等保费均小幅增长；农险大幅下滑，降幅达65.98%。

表 5　　　　　　　　　汉再上分业务结构情况

单位：亿元、%

业务条线	2021年分保费收入	2021年分保费占比
寿险	81.58	49.58
健康险	58.43	35.51
人寿险	16.37	9.95
意外险	6.78	4.12
非寿险	82.96	50.42
责任险	16.15	9.81
车险	14.56	8.85
农险	7.83	4.76
信用险	15.50	9.42
财产险	15.96	9.70
工程险	6.96	4.23
货运险	2.55	1.55
船舶险	1.00	0.61
健康险	1.23	0.75
意外险	0.54	0.33
其他	0.68	0.42
合计	164.54	100.00

数据来源：公司年报。

4．慕再北分

从分保费收入看，慕再北分2021年总保费收入达132.76亿元，与上年基本持平。寿险及健康险保费收入呈现出下降趋势，在总分保费收入中占比大幅减少，非寿险成为主要业务。

从业务结构看，慕再北分财产险业务占六成左右，寿险及健康险占四成左右。2021年，其财产险分保费收入77.54亿元，同比上升14.75%，在总保费收入中占58.41%；寿险及健康险保费收入55.22亿元，同比下降15.27%，在总保费收入中占41.59%。

表6　　　　　　　　　慕再北分业务结构情况

单位：亿元、%

业务条线	2021年分保费收入	2021年分保费占比
财产险	77.54	58.41
寿险及健康险	55.22	41.59
合计	132.76	100.00

数据来源：公司年报。

（二）盈利情况

2021年，外资再保险公司在中国机构的整体盈利情况较好。部分外资再保险公司业务线均衡，互联网和中端医疗保险布局较早，重疾险业务占比较少，盈利性较好。还有部分外资再保险公司重疾业务减损压力较大，导致利润有所下滑。由于外资再保险机构的转分率较高，盈利水平会受到一定程度影响，因此净利润指标不能完全反映其经营状况。

表7　　　　　　　外资再保险公司在中国机构净利润情况

单位：万元、%

	2021年净利润	2021年ROE
瑞再北分	8 069	1
慕再北分	37 700	9
汉再上分	-2 940	-1
法再北分	18 113	8

数据来源：各再保险公司年报。

（三）偿付能力情况

偿付能力方面，上述四家外资再保险公司2021年偿付能力充足率均显著高于中资机构，其中瑞再北分偿付能力充足率最高，达到392%。外资再保险公司整体资本实力强劲，有较大潜力承保高质量业务，为其深耕中国再保险市场提供了坚实基础。

表8　　　　　　外资再保险公司在中国机构偿付能力情况

单位：%

保险集团	2021年偿付能力充足率	在中国分公司	2021年偿付能力充足率
慕再集团	227	慕再北分	305
瑞再集团	223	瑞再北分	392
汉再集团	243	汉再上海分公司	285
法再集团	226	法再北分	276

数据来源：各再保险公司年报。

四、外资再保险公司在中国人力资源情况

外资再保险公司高度重视中国市场管理人员安排和人才培养，前期通过在中国选用熟悉本地市场的经理人增进对中国市场的了解，进而逐步派遣具备丰富管理经验、公司长期培养的核心人员，确保集团总部的重要战略可以在区域市场顺利实施。与此同时，外资再保险公司也高度重视本地人才培养。

（一）外资再保险公司在中国人力发展主要举措

1．加强条线垂直化管理

一是通过加强条线垂直化管理，进一步获取其在中国机构信息，提高对中国机构管理的全面性及可视度。二是通过外资公司与在中国机构相互学习，形成优势互补或者强强联合，为拓展未来业务提供能力基础。

2．加强人员派驻

一是对在中国重要岗位及职能派驻高管，以实现对在中国机构的

有效控制和决策效力，常见重要派驻岗位如CEO、CFO。在考虑到当地监管要求的前提下，母公司负责对派驻高管进行选拔、考核、聘用。二是派驻经营中层，获取在中国机构实际运营信息并锻炼中层骨干，同时可以把控关键的职能及部门。常见派驻部门如业务部门、财务部门、法律合规部门、审计部门、风险管理部门等，总部负责对派驻经营层进行选拔、考核、聘用。三是建立集团总部优秀员工到海外机构派驻、轮岗制度，有效培养优秀员工的国际视野及忠诚度，储备未来管理人才。常见的交换部门包括业务部门、财务部门、人力部门等，总部负责对交换员工进行选拔、考核、聘用。

3．注重文化交流

一是展开短期（1个月以内）的交流互访，通过参观、培训、讲座、论坛等形式促进总部与在中国机构的沟通理解。二是联合举办文化交流互动活动，设立文化工作坊，讨论文化差异，增进对不同国家文化的理解，促进文化融合。

4．建立协同机制

一是设立高管层对话委员会，中国机构就工作要点与集团总部高管层直接对话，以高效达成共识并推动落地。二是在中国机构内部设置联系小组，横向负责收集各职能部门信息，与相关职能部门就日常运营问题进行沟通，同时负责纵向与集团总部相应部门沟通联系。三是设置临时协同工作组，通过搭建项目机制，推动协同项目逐步落地。

（二）外资再保险公司在中国人力发展情况

1. 人员数量增长情况

近年来，外资再保险公司着力建设中国市场团队，以人才驱动业务发展，在中国员工数量增幅明显。当前，部分外资再保险公司为在中国长期发展建立了较为完备的人才队伍，员工人数已接近中资再保险公司。

2. 年龄结构与性别结构

年龄结构方面，近年来外资再保险公司员工年龄趋向年轻化，员工队伍整体较为年轻。其中，主要外资再保险公司35岁以下员工占比约47%，45岁以上员工占比约12%。

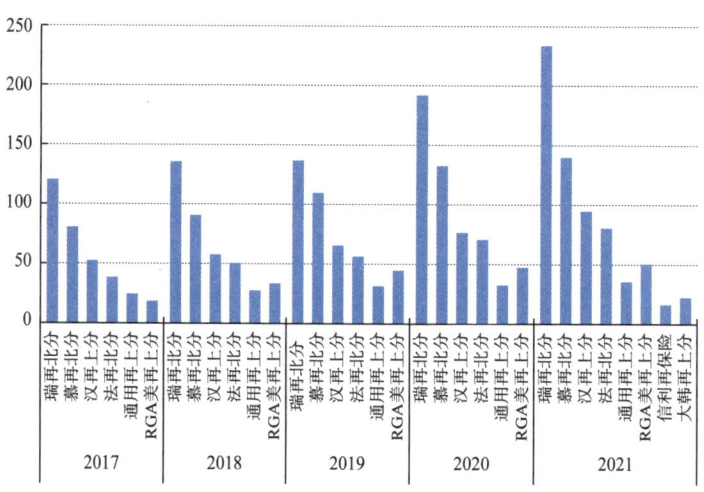

图3 外资再保险公司人力增长情况

（数据来源：2017—2021年中国保险年鉴）

性别结构方面，外资再保险公司女性员工占比较高，慕再北分、瑞再北分、法再北分、汉再上分女性员工比例均超过60%。

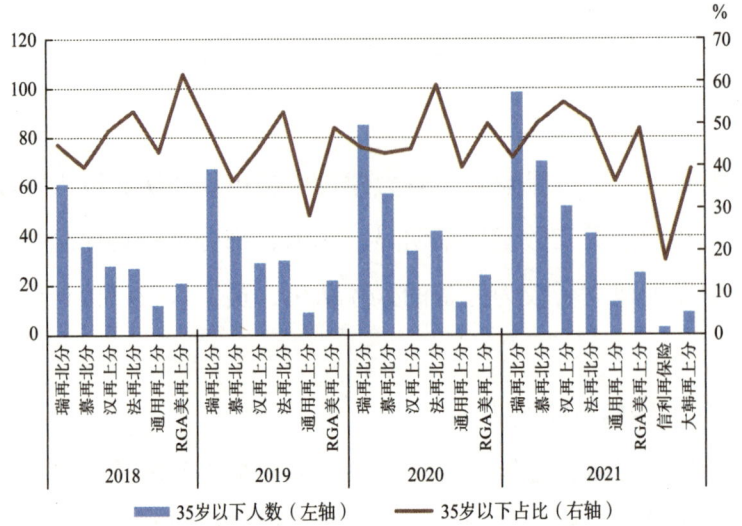

图 4　外资再保险公司 35 岁以下员工情况

（数据来源：2018—2021 年中国保险年鉴）

3．人员学历结构

从人员学历结构来看，大部分外资再保险公司硕士及以上学历员工占比在50%~70%之间。部分外资再保险公司重视市场研究和产品创新与开发，博士学历的员工较多。

表9　　　　　　主要外资再保险公司人力结构

公司	总人数			受教育程度				年龄结构		
	合计	男性	女性	博士	硕士	学士	大专以下	35岁以下	36~45岁	46岁以上
慕再北分	140	56	84	3	83	53	1	70	50	20
瑞再北分	234	84	150	17	140	73	4	98	107	29
法再北分	81	31	50	0	60	21	0	41	30	10
汉再上分	95	36	59	3	52	38	2	52	38	5
大韩再上分	23	11	12	0	4	19	0	9	13	1

数据来源：2021年中国保险年鉴。

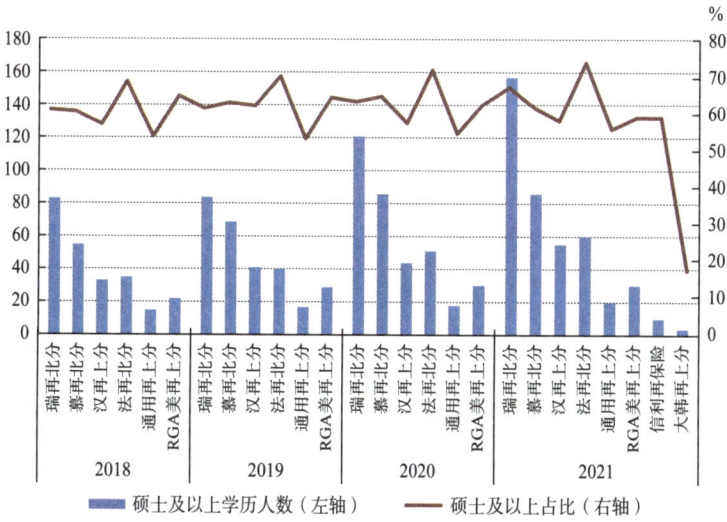

图 5　外资再保险公司硕士以上学历员工情况

（数据来源：2018—2021 年中国保险年鉴）

五、外资再保险公司在中国发展展望

随着外资再保险公司对中国市场的认知逐步加深，中国市场的战略地位也在快速提升，外资再保险公司对中国市场未来发展较为乐观。

（一）外资再保险公司在中国发展的机遇与挑战

发展机遇方面：一是中国保险市场规模巨大且具备持续发展潜力。经过多年高速发展，中国保险市场仍然保持着较快增长速度，且未来20~30年仍具备维持较高增速的预期。二是中国保险市场持续对外开放、监管环境友好。近年来中国持续扩大对外开放，2018—2019年期间，中国银保监会先后对外出台了涉及保险业对外开放的措施14

条，包括放宽和取消外资持股比例的限制，放宽外资机构在总资产、经营年限、股东资质等方面的限制等，鼓励有特色、专业的外资公司进入中国市场，以共同推动行业整体高质量发展。同时，中国市场对于保险行业、外资保险公司的支持力度较大，能够给外资保险公司提供国民待遇和稳定的政策预期，这也是其他新兴市场难以比拟的。

发展挑战方面：一是由于费率不足、商业财产险承保质量欠佳、加上越发频繁的极端天气，外资再保险公司在中国财产险合约业务普遍表现不佳，而一揽子成数合同的利润边际也因车险综改、过度竞争、中国农再成立、离岸再保人参与等因素而有所稀释，部分外资再保险公司近年来出现承保亏损的现象。二是在人口老龄化背景下，受通货膨胀和人口结构变化影响，虽然部分寿险产品需求增长，但传统模型对死亡率、发病率、被保险人生活方式等假设也存在不适用的可能性，中国人身再保险业务长期面临挑战。

（二）发展展望

从外资再保险公司在中国总体战略来看，外资再保险公司在中国市场的中长期发展战略具有一定相似性。一是坚持在中国市场进行长期投入。外资再保险公司普遍看好中国市场中长期巨大发展潜力，基于"长期主义"理念进行长期持续投入。二是普遍提高在中国市场资本投入力度。2019—2021年，外资再保险公司对中国机构合计增资36.7亿元，远超同期中资再保险公司资本补充额。增资后，外资再保险公司均维持了较高的偿付能力充足性水平，为其开拓市场、拓展业务、扩招人员等都预留了更多空间。三是继续充分利用内部转分，平衡业务发展和资本使用效率，加大自身竞争优势。

从外资再保险公司在中国业务策略来看，一是外资再保险公司持续关注中国市场发展潜力,在"双碳"战略、绿色金融、乡村振兴、健康中国、应对人口老龄化等重大国家战略加快推进过程中,积极探索相关条线的业务机会。二是外资再保险公司在国际市场经营多年,拥有较为成熟的产品线和产品创新开发经验,可以为国内客户提供多元化、定制化的风险解决方案,进一步加强对中国市场的客户服务力度。三是外资再保险公司的数字化转型领先于同业机构,已基本实现业务线上化和智能化。未来面向行业客户,将继续把数字化全方位融入业务场景,进一步提升客户体验。四是外资再保险公司重视与政府、专业机构的合作,对于中国政府重点关注的医疗、"三农"、环境污染及食品安全等领域,在相应的健康险、农险、责任险等业务条线均重点投入,提供专业化服务。

第五章 再保险行业2021年监管政策及趋势展望

一、再保险行业现行监管架构

二、再保险行业特别监管政策

三、再保险行业2021年重要监管政策

四、再保险行业监管趋势展望

2021年，中国银保监会积极推动保险行业高质量发展，发布多项对行业有较大影响的监管政策。一是优化偿付能力监管机制。中国银保监会修订发布《保险公司偿付能力监管规则（Ⅱ）》（以下简称《规则Ⅱ》）和《保险公司偿付能力管理规定》，进一步完善了保险机构偿付能力监管机制。二是加强公司治理监管。中国银保监会发布《银行保险机构公司治理准则》等多项公司治理监管政策，全方位强化对保险机构的公司治理要求。三是完善再保险业务管理规范。中国银保监会修订发布《再保险业务管理规定》，进一步规范再保险业务开展，着重强调再保险作为"保险的保险"的核心定位，并允许境内保险公司通过特殊目的保险公司在香港市场发行巨灾债券分散巨灾风险。四是推进保险资金市场化运用。中国银保监会进一步放开保险资金运用范围，并修改保险资金运用领域部分规范性文件，减少对保险资金投资的限制，引导保险资金更好支持经济社会发展。

一、再保险行业现行监管架构

国内再保险行业与直保行业在法律层面均由《保险法》进行规范，行业监管机构为中国银保监会。中国银保监会对再保险行业的监管政策主要分为两类：一是适用于保险行业整体的监管政策，如对偿付能力、公司治理以及保险资金运用等的监管政策。此类监管政策基于再保险行业和直保行业的共同特点制定，通常同时适用于再保险公司和直保公司，或者适用于直保公司，参照适用于再保险公司。二是适用于再保险行业的特别监管政策，主要体现在再保险市场行为监管领域，以及针对再保险行业国际化特征所做的特别监管。

为保障各项监管政策有效施行，中国银保监会将现场监管与非现场监管相结合，对保险机构采取制定管理标准、开展能力评估以及对违法违规行为实施行政处罚等监管方式，促使保险机构保持合理偿付能力，提升公司治理水平，规范市场经营行为。

此外，在反洗钱、反恐怖融资以及国有金融资产管理等方面，再保险行业也同时受到中国人民银行、财政部等机构的监管。

（一）保险行业"三支柱"监管架构

自国内保险行业全面恢复发展以来，行业监管从初期以市场行为监管为主，逐步过渡到以市场行为监管和偿付能力监管并重，目前形成以偿付能力监管为核心、公司治理监管为基础、市场行为监管为抓手的"三支柱"监管架构。

1. 偿付能力监管

偿付能力监管是现代保险业监管的核心，重在对保险公司偿付能力充足率状况、综合风险、风险管理能力等进行全面评价和监督检查，确保保险公司偿付能力满足风险保障需求。2001年3月，原中国保监会[①]发布《保险公司最低偿付能力及监管指标管理规定（试行）》，细化规定财产保险公司、人身险公司和再保险公司的最低偿付能力要求以及相应监管指标计算方式；后经三轮优化，中国银保监会于2021年1月修订发布《保险公司偿付能力管理规定》，将偿付能力监管指标由单一的偿付能力充足率扩展为核心偿付能力充足率、综合偿付能力充足率以及风险综合评级三个有机联系的指标。2012年4月，原中国保监会启动以风险为导向的"偿二代"建设，确立定量资本要求、

[①] 即成立于1998年的中国保险监督管理委员会，是统一监督管理全国保险市场，维护保险业合法、稳健运行的中华人民共和国国务院原直属正部级事业单位。2018年3月，根据《第十三届全国人民代表大会第一次会议关于国务院机构改革方案的决定》，撤销中国保险监督管理委员会，职能划归中国银保监会。

定性监管要求、市场约束机制的偿付能力"三支柱"监管体系。2017年9月,中国保监会启动"偿二代"二期工程建设,对偿付能力监管体系进行全面优化升级,中国银保监会于2021年12月正式发布《规则Ⅱ》,宣告"偿二代"二期工程建设的顺利完成。

2. 公司治理监管

公司治理是现代企业制度的基石,旨在通过建立包括股东(大)会、董事会、监事会、高级管理层(以下简称"三会一层")等治理主体在内的公司治理架构,明确各治理主体的职责边界、履职要求,完善风险管控、制衡管制及激励约束机制,不断提升公司治理水平。良好的公司治理能对保险机构健康稳定运营起到至关重要的作用。2006年1月,随着国内保险公司改制上市并逐步建立现代企业制度,原中国保监会发布《关于规范保险公司治理结构的指导意见(试行)》,要求保险机构强化主要股东义务、加强董事会建设、发挥监事会作用、规范管理层运作以及加强关联交易和信息披露管理,从而在国内保险行业监管领域正式引入公司治理监管。2021年6月,中国银保监会修订发布《银行保险机构公司治理准则》,将党的领导融入保险机构公司治理各个环节,进一步明确"三会一层"组成、职责及运作机制,全面系统地强化了对保险机构公司治理的规范性要求。此外,监管机构针对保险机构股东行为规范、董监事履职评价以及董监高任职资格管理等公司治理监管细分领域发布系列监管政策,不断优化完善公司治理监管体系。

3. 市场行为监管

市场行为监管是保险市场有序运行的重要保障,主要包括对保险条款与费率、保险销售行为、保险中介行为、保险服务行为以及保险欺诈行为等方面的监管,强调通过规范保险机构市场行为维护保险消费者权益和保险市场正常秩序。市场行为监管具体方式与被监管主体的市场行为特点紧密联系，因财产保险、人身保险以及再保险在交易主体、业务性质以及风险特征等方面存在一定差异，监管机构采取分类监管方式，通常针对不同类型的保险机构和保险业务制定不同的监管政策。如对于保险条款和保险费率监管，监管机构分别针对人身保险、财产保险发布《人身保险公司保险条款和保险费率管理办法（2015年最新修订）》、《财产保险公司保险条款和保险费率管理办法（2021年最新修订）》。

总体而言，再保险行业和直保行业的经营主体及其业务开展均受到国家严格监管。在偿付能力监管、公司治理监管以及市场行为监管的保险行业"三支柱"监管架构下，对再保险行业与直保行业的监管存在诸多共同之处，但同时也因二者行业特性方面的差异存在一定区别。

（二）其他重要监管

除中国银保监会的专业监管以外，中国人民银行、财政部等机构同时从反洗钱、反恐怖融资以及国有资产管理等方面对包括再保险公司在内的金融机构实施监管。

中国人民银行履行对金融机构反洗钱和反恐怖融资工作的监管职责，其发布的《金融机构反洗钱和反恐怖融资监督管理办法》等规章制度明确规定金融机构应建立符合要求的反洗钱和反恐怖融资内部控制和风险管理机制，履行客户尽职调查、客户身份资料和交易记录保存以及大额交易和可疑交易报告等义务。同时因再保险业务中，分入人和分出人均为受到严格监管的保险机构，不涉及自然人和现金交易，发生洗钱和恐怖融资的风险较小，因此部分反洗钱和反恐怖融资监管政策适用于再保险行业时具有一定灵活性，如中国人民银行于2022年1月发布的《金融机构客户尽职调查和客户身份资料及交易记录保存管理办法》特别说明"保险公司在办理再保险业务时，履行客户尽职调查义务不适用本办法"。

财政部根据国务院授权，履行国有金融资本出资人职责，其发布的《金融企业国有资产转让管理办法》等规章制度对持有国有资产的金融企业的相应资产管理和处置工作提出了详细要求。同时财政部制定并组织实施国家统一的会计制度，其发布的《企业会计准则第25号——保险合同》全面规范包括再保险合同在内的保险合同确认、计量和相关信息的列报，从而影响再保险业务的保险收入和经营策略。

同时，党中央、国务院以及相关监管机构关于国家经济金融工作的指导意见和发展规划对再保险行业及其监管政策也会产生深远影响。如中国为履行加入世界贸易组织承诺，于2006年1月彻底取消法定分保，并于当年6月发布《国务院关于保险业改革发展的若干意见》，明确此后一段时期保险业改革发展的指导思想、目标任务和政策措施，要求加强偿付能力监管、深入推进保险公司治理结构监管并强化市场行为监管。2007年6月，为贯彻落实《国务院关于保险业改革发展的若干意见》，并适应加入世界贸易组织后快速发展、高度竞争的再保险市场发展需求，原中国保监会发布《中国再保险市场发展规划》，进一步明确国内再保险市场发展的总体思路、目标和政策措施。在上述指导意见和发展规划的框架下，原中国保监会于此后5年内陆续发布《关于再保险业务安全性有关问题的通知》、《保险公司偿付能力报告编报规则第15号——再保险业务》以及《财产保险公司再保险管理规范》等规章制度，并对2005年10月发布的《再保险业务管理规定》进行第一次修订，逐步完善再保险市场监管，保障再保险行业健康稳定发展。

二、再保险行业特别监管政策

监管机构关于再保险行业的监管政策，除上述适用于保险行业整体的监管政策外，还包括针对再保险行业特点，特别是其国际化特征制定的特别监管政策。

（一）规范再保险公司的设立

2001年12月，中国正式加入世界贸易组织（WTO）。2002年3月，原中国保监会发布《关于印发我国加入世界贸易组织（WTO）法律文件有关保险业内容的通知》，公布国内有关保险业对外承诺的内容，其中对于再保险的承诺内容包括：中国在加入WTO时，即允许外国保险公司跨境从事再保险业务，允许外国保险公司以分公司、合资公司或独资子公司的形式提供寿险和非寿险的再保险业务，没有地域限制或发放营业许可的数量限制。相比直保行业，国内再保险行业更早、更快地向外资开放。2002年9月，为明确中国入世开放新格局下再保险公司的设立条件，原中国保监会发布《再保险公司设立规定》，对国内再保险公司的设立审批、业务经营范围、资本金以及人员配置等提出了具体要求。

（二）明确再保险业务管理规范

2005年10月，原中国保监会发布国内第一部全面系统地规范再保险市场的法规——《再保险业务管理规定》，初步明确保险公司、保险联合体以及保险经纪人等保险机构的再保险业务经营要求，包括直保公司分出业务的份额比例以及集中度管理要求等，同时规定了保险公司关于其再保险业务经营情况的报告义务。后经三轮更新完善，中国银保监会于2021年7月发布最新修订的《再保险业务管理规定》。

在细分领域，2012年1月，原中国保监会发布《财产保险公司再保险管理规范》，对财产保险公司的再保险业务管理提出详细要求，涉及财产保险公司再保险业务的战略管理、运营管理、资信管理、评估以及合规审计等方面。《财产保险公司再保险管理规范》强调再保险是财产保险公司风险管控的重要手段，财产保险公司应本着"最大诚信原则"开展再保险业务，合理分散风险，优化业务结构，实现公司的稳健经营和可持续发展。2014年9月，原中国保监会发布《关于加强财产保险公司再保险分入业务管理有关事项的通知》，进一步细化财产保险公司开展再保险分入业务的规范要求。

（三）加强再保险业务安全保障

基于再保险行业专业化强、国际化程度高的特点，再保险行业监管注重对再保险业务安全性的监管，包括建立再保险关联交易信息披露和再保险登记机制以及要求离岸再保人提供符合要求的担保等，以防范保险机构通过再保险交易规避监管以及金融风险通过再保险交易跨境传递。

1. 建立再保险关联交易信息披露机制

2006年11月，为提高再保险交易安全性，防范金融风险跨境传递，原中国保监会发布《关于加强外资保险公司与关联企业从事再保险交易信息披露工作的通知》，要求外资保险公司应向监管机构报告其与关联企业发生的再保险交易。后经两次修订，原中国保监会于2015年4月发布《关于加强保险公司再保险关联交易信息披露工作的通知》，一方面放开前端，废止此前对外资保险公司再保险关联交易的审批规定；另一方面管住后端，明确中资、外资保险公司都需要对关联交易进行事后披露，强化了再保险监管的针对性和有效性。

2．建立再保险登记机制

鉴于再保险分入人的偿付能力、财务状况以及盈利能力等因素对分出人的健康稳定运营影响重大，为提高保险行业抗风险能力，原中国保监会于2007年11月发布《关于再保险业务安全性有关问题的通知》，要求再保险分出人强化对再保险业务的风险管理，并设定再保险分入人应满足的国际评级等资质条件。此后为进一步规范再保险信用风险管理，原中国保监会于2015年3月修订发布《关于实施再保险登记管理有关事项的通知》，在更新对再保险分入人资质要求的同时，规定包括转分保接受人和转分保经纪人在内的所有参与中国境内再保险业务的再保险分入人和再保险经纪人都应当在再保险登记系统进行注册登记。

3．要求离岸再保人提供符合要求的担保

为提高离岸再保险交易的安全性，防范离岸再保险人的信用风险，保护境内保险公司作为再保险分出人的合法权益，原中国保监会于2017年2月发布《关于离岸再保险人提供担保措施有关事项的通知》，规定境内保险公司可以要求离岸再保人就应收分保款项和应收分保准备金的风险暴露提供担保措施，并明确离岸再保人可以提供的担保措施类型以及所提供的担保措施应满足的要求。

截至2021年末，上述制度和系统运行良好，增强了国内再保险市场透明度，防范国际金融风险通过再保险传递，降低了再保险业务的信用风险和经营风险，提高了国内再保险业务安全水平。

三、再保险行业 2021 年重要监管政策

（一）优化偿付能力监管机制

2017年9月，原中国保监会启动"偿二代"二期工程建设；2021年12月，中国银保监会正式修订发布《规则Ⅱ》，标志着"偿二代"二期工程顺利完成。《规则Ⅱ》作为国内（再）保险行业偿付能力监管的基础性制度规范，延续"偿二代"框架，对再保险公司资本计量规则做了专门规定，同时新增《市场风险和信用风险的穿透计量》、《资本规划》以及《劳合社（中国）》三项规则。

《规则Ⅱ》对原规则进行了全面优化升级，其绝大部分规则同时适用于再保险公司和直保公司。一是对于第一支柱定量资本要求，严格规定资本认定标准，实施风险穿透监管，全面校准风险因子，完善财务再保险和长期股权投资监管标准以及利率风险计量方法，并特别明确中国内地直保公司向合格的香港再保险机构分出业务以及境内保险机构在香港发行巨灾债券形成的再保险业务的交易对手违约风险因子适用规则，从而夯实保险公司资本质量，实现更加准确地识别和计量保险公司风险，引导保险公司优化资产负债匹配管理。二是对于第二支柱定性监管要求，完善风险综合评级（IRR）的评级标准、偿付能力风险管理要求（SARMRA）以及流动性评价标准，并明确资本规划监管要求，从而更加科学、全面地反映保险公司风险及其管理情况。三是对于第三支柱市场约束机制，提升市场透明度和信息透明度，扩展偿付能力信息公开披露要求，从而充分发挥保险市场相关各方的监督约束作用。

总体而言，《规则Ⅱ》进一步收紧和细化了对直保及再保险公司

的偿付能力监管要求，提升了对再保险偿付能力监管的科学性、有效性和全面性，有利于引导再保险市场整体稳健发展。

此外，对于偿付能力监管机制的优化完善，在《规则Ⅱ》正式发布之前，中国银保监会先于2021年1月发布《保险公司偿付能力管理规定》，对2008年7月发布且已明显滞后于国内保险市场实际情况的原规定进行了全面修订。《保险公司偿付能力管理规定》明确第一支柱定量监管要求、第二支柱定性监管要求以及第三支柱市场约束机制的偿付能力监管"三支柱"框架体系，确定核心偿付能力充足率、综合偿付能力充足率以及风险综合评级三个有机联系的偿付能力监管指标，并明确保险公司偿付能力达标需同时符合核心偿付能力充足率不低于50%、综合偿付能力充足率不低于100%以及风险综合评级在B类及以上。《保险公司偿付能力管理规定》同时强化保险公司偿付能力管理的主体责任，加强监管机构对保险公司偿付能力的监督检查，并强调监管机构对于偿付能力及风险情况不符合要求的保险公司将根据风险成因和风险程度采取针对性的监管措施。

（二）加强保险机构公司治理监管

近年来，中国银保监会高度重视银行保险机构公司治理监管，将健全公司治理作为推动银行保险机构实现高质量发展的重要着力点，不断优化改革公司治理监管机制。2021年6月，作为落实中国银保监会于2020年8月发布的《全银行业保险业公司治理三年行动方案（2020—2022年）》的重要举措之一，中国银保监会修订发布《银行保险机构公司治理准则》。

《银行保险机构公司治理准则》适用于包括再保险公司在内的银行保险机构，其吸收整合现有监管规则，并借鉴国际经验，全面优化完善了对银行保险机构公司治理机制的规范性要求。一是明确股东的权利义务、股东大会的职权以及运作机制。二是强调董事的选任、职责及履职保障,明确董事会及其专门委员会的组成、职权及运作机制。三是规范监事选任履职以及监事会、高管层的设置和运行。四是要求银行保险机构完善激励约束和信息披露机制,并加强风险管理、内部控制及内外部审计。《银行保险机构公司治理准则》在对银行保险机构公司治理机制提出统一规范的同时,也为实施差异化监管预留了空间。此外,在党的领导与公司治理相互促进方面,《银行保险机构公司治理准则》在监管制度层面提出国有机构应有机融合党的领导与公司治理的总体要求,并推动民营机构积极发挥党组织的政治核心作用。

除《银行保险机构公司治理准则》以外,中国银保监会于2021年同时发布了《银行保险机构大股东行为监管办法(试行)》、《银行保险机构董事监事履职评价办法(试行)》、《关于建立完善银行保险机构绩效薪酬追索扣回机制的指导意见》以及《保险公司董事、监事和高级管理人员任职资格管理规定》等规章制度,涉及公司治理监管多个细分领域。一是进一步规范银行保险机构大股东的持股行为、治理行为、交易行为和责任义务。二是优化完善银行保险机构董监事履职评价机制,明确董监事履职评价内容和重点,强调董监事履职评价闭环管理。三是指导银行保险机构建立符合自身实际情况的绩效薪酬追索扣回机制。四是调整银行保险机构董监高任职资格审批要求、条件以及核准程序。

(三)完善再保险业务管理规范

为规范再保险业务经营,推动再保险市场高质量发展,中国银保监会于2021年7月修订发布《再保险业务管理规定》,删除原规定与现有政策冲突的内容，加强对再保险顶层战略、再保险业务安全性、再保险合同、直保公司开展分入业务以及再保险经纪人等多方面的监管，重点维护再保险市场稳定秩序，强调保险公司应正确使用再保险工具，促使再保险回归"保险的保险"的核心定位。

一是要求保险公司严肃使用再保险工具，强调再保险在风险管理和资本战略管理中的重要作用，引导再保险发挥价格传导和周期平抑作用。二是对直保公司分入业务进行规范，要求开展再保险分入业务的直保公司应具备符合要求的机构配置、人员配置、业务系统和年度计划，明确再保险服务直保发展的职能。三是要求保险公司在与关联企业进行再保险交易时，应当遵循市场化原则确定再保险价格与条件，不得利用再保险转移利润、逃避税收。四是明确预约分保属性，定义临时分保为"逐保单办理再保险"，将临时分保与预约分保区分开来，强调"不得以临时分保名义变相经营合约分保业务"。五是要求保险公司应当按照中国银保监会的规定办理再保险，承接国内再保险分出业务的分入人须符合相关要求（经过再保险登记系统审核）。六是对分保至境外再保人的再保险业务进行监管，要求保险公司开展境外分出业务的，应当建立境外分出业务监测制度，定期分析分出至境外的再保险业务的信用风险和流动性风险，以有效控制境外分出风险。七是提高再保险交易质量，详细规定再保险交易的合同签订、资金结付和再保档案管理等方面要求，以提升再保险交易效率以及再保险合同文本的规范性。八是支持再保险分入人获取信息，强调再保险分出人和保险中介机构对再保险分入人的信息告知义务，并对告知方式进行明确规定，有利于再保险分入人获得更多与保险业务有关的信息，便于再保险分入人进行风险定价和产品开发。九是对临时分保的办理时效提出要求，要求再保险分出人应当在承保前完成临时分保安排,促进再保险分出人和分入人合理、稳妥地分担风险,实现稳健经营。十是加强再保险安全性管理,要求财产险分出人每一危险单位分给同一家再保险分入人的总比例,不得超过再保险分出人承保直保合同保险金额或者责任限额的80%,同时要求保险公司建立再保险业务流动性风险管理制度,加强对再保险应收款项的管理。

除修订发布《再保险业务管理规定》以外,中国银保监会为增加巨灾风险分散路径,于2021年9月发布《关于境内保险公司在香港市场发行巨灾债券有关事项的通知》,允许境内保险公司通过特殊目的保险公司在香港市场发行巨灾债券,以分散地震、台风、洪水等自然灾害事件或突发公共卫生事件的损失风险。其中,境内保险公司通过签订再保险合同的方式,将相关巨灾风险分保给特殊目的保险公司。

(四)推进保险资金市场化运用

2021年,中国银保监会发布多项保险资金运用相关监管政策,不断规范保险资金运用行为,并进一步推进保险资金市场化运用,盘活存量保险资金,以支持社会经济发展。

一是发布《关于保险资金投资公开募集基础设施证券投资基金有关事项的通知》,在制度层面明确保险资金投资公开募集基础设施证券投资基金(以下简称基础设施基金)的投资规范和监管规则,包括明确保险公司投资基础设施基金的资质要求以及投资标的条件等。二是发布《关于保险资金参与证券出借业务有关事项的通知》,允许保险资金参与证券出借业务,要求参与证券出借业务的保险公司应满足一定的资质条件,并加强投资风险管理。三是发布《关于调整保险资金投资债券信用评级要求等有关事项的通知》,取消保险资金可投金融企业(公司)债券的白名单要求和外部信用评级要求,规定不同风险特征的保险公司可投非金融企业（公司）债券的外部信用评级要求，同时明确投资BBB级（含）以下债券的集中度要求和投资债券的大类比例核算。四是修订《保险公司股票资产托管指引（试行）》等14项保险资金运用领域已滞后于监管需求和市场实际的规范性文件，增强市场主体的投资自主权。

四、再保险行业监管趋势展望

随着中国再保险行业逐步发展壮大，再保险监管体系也在不断优化完善，旨在与市场发展相适应，推动再保险行业高质量发展。

一是将坚持服务实体经济，聚焦国家重大战略，面向世界科技前沿、面向经济主战场、面向国家重大需求、面向人民生命健康，提供高质量的风险保障和保险服务，发挥好再保险经济"减震器"和社会"稳定器"功能作用。

二是将进一步推动再保险在风险与资本管理、产品与技术领域的创新引领作用，提高再保险对电子信息、先进制造、生物医药、现代农业、智慧交通、新型能源、航空航天及其他国家重点项目、国家重大科技攻关成果转化应用中大型风险、特殊风险的保险保障能力，为中国再保险行业深度参与并引领全球风险治理夯实基础。

三是将进一步重视再保险业务特点及与直接保险的差异，逐步建立完善适应再保险经营特点的、更为独立的监管制度体系，在保障再保险业务依法合规开展、维护再保险市场正常秩序的同时，提高再保险交易效率。

四是将进一步关注再保险国际化经营特征，重视对境外再保险业务的有效监管,注重防范金融风险跨境传递,同时继续加大对外开放力度,在全球政治经济格局深刻调整中更好地参与国际合作与竞争。

五是积极应对目前全球极端天气频发的局势,推动再保险行业与资本市场的合作发展,通过巨灾债券等金融产品创新协助保险风险在资本市场的分散,提高对巨灾风险的保障能力。

专题报告

再保险助力巨灾风险管理与巨灾保险发展专题报告

中国是世界上受自然灾害影响最严重的国家之一，灾害种类多、分布地域广、发生频率高、造成损失重；有超过70%的城市、50%以上的人口分布在气象灾害和地质灾害较严重的地区。气候变化导致极端天气灾害的发生频率和损失强度正以不断"刷新历史纪录"的方式，冲击生产和生活秩序。在极端天气频现、城镇化程度持续深入、资产密度和资产价值不断提高的背景下，自然灾害的危害与日俱增。建立高效科学的巨灾风险管理体系，提高全社会灾害防治能力，显得越加紧迫。巨灾保险是加强风险治理的重要手段，是社会治理能力的重要标志，也是政府转变职能的重要抓手，在推动巨灾保险发展、助力巨灾风险管理体系建设中，再保险能够发挥至关重要的作用。

一、巨灾保险发展历程

新中国成立以来，国内巨灾风险管理经历了一个从无到有、从弱到强、逐渐完善的过程，正逐步形成一套与自然、社会相适应的巨灾风险管理体系。其中，地震保险在巨灾风险保障制度体系中的地位较为突出。

计划经济时代，国内保险业为国家机关、国营企业等单位都办理了财产保险，责任范围包括地震、台风、洪水等巨灾风险。20世纪六七十年代，由于历史原因，全面停办国内保险业务，直到1979年逐步恢复国内保险业务，此后，财产保险业恢复承保巨灾风险。

1996年云南丽江地震后，基于当时国内地震保险经营缺乏科学的精算基础，为确保保险公司稳健经营，地震保险的经营受到严格限制。而同期，中国人民银行组织地震局地球物理研究所、中国再保险公司、中国人民保险公司共同对地震保险产品进行了深入研究，并根据中国历史地震资料和损失情况，结合建筑物的结构特点，开展了编制中国地震保险费率区划图等工作，对开展地震保险进行了探讨。

2002年，由原中国保监会牵头组织开展了国内地震保险制度建设的专题研究，并完成了《建立我国家庭财产地震保险研究报告》。中央领导高度重视，要求"深入研究地震保险方案，加快推进震灾保险体系建设"。

2008年四川汶川地震后，巨灾保险广受关注，顶层制度设计呼声渐高。

2013年，深圳、云南、宁波等地陆续开展巨灾保险首批试点工作。2013年，党的十八届三中全会《中共中央关于全面深化改革若干重大问题的决定》明确提出"完善保险经济补偿机制，建立巨灾保险制度"。

2014年，《国务院关于加快发展现代保险服务业的若干意见》进一步提出"要将保险纳入灾害事故防范救助体系""以多层次风险分担为保障，建立巨灾保险制度"。

2015年，中国城乡居民住宅地震巨灾保险共同体成立，为全国城乡居民住宅及室内附属设施承保住宅地震险。

2016年5月16日，在第8个全国防灾减灾日之际，由原中国保监会、财政部联合印发《关于建立城乡居民住宅地震巨灾保险制度实施方案》，标志着国内巨灾保险制度建设迈出关键一步。

2016年，《中共中央国务院关于推进防灾减灾救灾体制机制改革的意见》中指出"坚持政府推动、市场运作原则，强化保险等市场机制在风险防范、损失补偿、恢复重建等方面的积极作用，不断扩大保险覆盖面，完善应对灾害的金融支持体系。"

2017年，财政部印发《城乡居民住宅地震巨灾保险专项准备金管理办法》，对于积累灾前资金储备，实现巨灾风险跨期分散，推动建设国家灾害管理的稳定和长久机制具有重要意义。

2020年，中国银保监会发布《中国银保监会关于推动银行业和保险业高质量发展的指导意见》（银保监发〔2019〕52号），指出"进一步扩大巨灾试点范围"。

2020年，中国银保监会发布《推动财产保险业高质量发展三年行动方案（2020—2022年）》，指出"完善巨灾保险制度，推动巨灾保险立法，探索巨灾保险证券化，做好灾害事故保险应急处置工作，服务国家灾害救助体系建设。"

2020年10月，《国家"十四五"规划》指出"发展巨灾保险，提高防灾、减灾、抗灾、救灾能力"。

2021年9月，中国银保监会发布《关于境内保险公司在香港市场发行巨灾债券有关事项的通知》指出"支持有意愿的境内保险公司在香港市场发行巨灾债券"。

二、巨灾保险发展现状

根据巨灾保险的主体不同,巨灾保险通常可分为政策性巨灾保险和商业性巨灾保险两大类。政策性巨灾保险指政府从国计民生的角度出发,在特定的政策制度框架下建立的,为商业保险难以单独开展的领域提供巨灾保障,并提供一定的财政支持。国内最典型的政策性巨灾保险就是中国城乡居民住宅地震巨灾保险,以及各地政府补贴的民生类巨灾保险和政府财政风险巨灾指数保险,这类保险的投保方通常是政府。商业性巨灾保险由商业保险机构以营利为目的,按照平等自愿的交易原则向被保险人提供保单范围内的巨灾保障,投保人和被保险人通常是企事业法人单位。

近年来,在党中央、国务院统一部署下,保险业主动作为、大胆创新、多措并举,积极服务自然灾害防治体系和能力建设。

(一)政策性巨灾保险发展情况

政策性巨灾保险又可分为全国性巨灾保险制度和地方巨灾保险试点。

1. 全国性巨灾保险制度

在原中国保监会的支持和推动下,2015年4月,中国城乡居民住宅地震巨灾保险共同体(以下简称地震共同体)正式成立,由41家财产直保公司和5家再保险公司共同组成。人保财险担任执行机构,中再为理事公司和首席再保人。

地震共同体通过灾后赔付起到了缓解灾后财政救灾压力、平滑财政预算的作用。地震发生概率低,一旦发生,则损失巨大。地震巨灾保险的灾后赔付来源于当期准备金和逐年积累的巨灾保险基金，巨灾保险基金不仅能实现保费盈余的跨年累积，还可以向再保险市场和资本市场进行风险分散。地震发生时，巨灾保险基金可获得再保险摊回赔款、资本市场资金赔偿等，将其释放到地震巨灾保险的赔付中。

2016年5月，原中国保监会、财政部联合印发《建立城乡居民住宅地震巨灾保险制度实施方案》，标志着以地震为突破口的巨灾保险制度开始实践探索。

截至2021年底，住宅地震保险制度已累计为全国超过1 621万户次城乡居民，提供6 291亿元的巨灾风险保障，在历次地震灾害中累计赔付7 037万元。随着包括地震、台风、洪水、强降雨、泥石流等灾害在内的多灾因巨灾保险体系建设的不断发展和完善，巨灾保险在国家应急管理体系中所发挥的作用将越发重要，巨灾保险成果将更好地惠及广大人民群众。

2．地方巨灾保险试点

自2013年开始，保险业积极配合各地政府，从当地保险保障需求出发、开展适合当地实情的地方巨灾保险试点业务。目前，云南、四川、河北、广东、湖南等15个省份巨灾保险试点项目相继落地，在服务地方灾害风险管理方面发挥了重要作用，受到地方政府和人民群众的广泛好评。

地方巨灾保险试点得到了地方政府大力支持。地方政府通过发文、协调、财政支持等方式，推动试点工作落实。如云南省由民政厅牵头协调各相关部门，开展试点工作。大理州民政局统一投保，保费由省、州、县三级政府财政全额承担。深圳市建立巨灾保险工作联席会议制度，召开年度会议，市民政局统一购买政府巨灾救助保险，保险保费由市财政全额承担。宁波市民政局作为宁波巨灾保险制度组织实施的牵头部门，与宁波保监局、市金融办、气象局、保险机构等之间建立了定期会商制度，对工作推进中出现的问题，及时会商研究解决，保费由宁波市财政全额负担。四川省成立试点工作领导小组，各级财政提供60%的保险费补贴，农村散居五保户、城乡低保对象、贫困残疾人涉及的最低档自付保费由财政全额承担。广东省建立由财政支持，以台风、洪涝为主要保障范围，以省政府作为投保人，以地级市政府作为被保险人，按指数保险模式设计的巨灾保险实施方案。

从地方试点的保险产品类型来看，试点产品可分为传统型巨灾保险和指数型保险两大类。传统型巨灾保险是指保险赔付基于被保险人及被保标的实际发生的损失提供赔偿的保险。指数型巨灾保险是依据一种或多种灾害参数的取值确定保险责任触发条件的保险，如地震震级、震中距、气温、降雨量等作为触发参数，确立保险合同。

表 1　　　　　　　　地方巨灾保险试点产品类型概览

巨灾保险类型	特点	典型地区
传统型巨灾保险	1. 以居民住房、人身、室内财产为主要保障对象； 2. 保障灾因广泛，包括自然灾害和非自然灾害等； 3. 以实际发生的损失为依据进行理赔； 4. 保险赔付耗时较长，适合灾后资金时间要求非特别急迫的情形。	四川 山东 湖南 张家口 深圳 宁波 厦门等
指数型巨灾保险	1. 以政府救灾和灾害恢复支出为主要保障对象； 2. 保障灾因须满足一定的指数设计和计算条件（降雨、震级等）； 3. 保险赔付主要满足抢险救灾、生命线恢复的紧急资金需求。	广东 广西 云南 大理 湖北武汉等

资料来源：中再研究整理。

（二）商业性巨灾保险发展情况

商业保险涉及的财产保险、工程保险、农业保险、机动车辆保险等主要险种均涵盖一定的巨灾风险责任，发展速度迅猛，但与巨灾导致的财产损失相比，巨灾保障的责任极不充分。常规来看，保险行业将商业性的巨灾保险聚焦在财产险和工程险。根据中再测算的保险行业巨灾风险暴露情况来看，风险暴露呈逐年增加的趋势，2021年底台风洪水保额达到133万亿元，2016—2020年增长58%；地震保额增长更高，2021年底达到70.4万亿元，2016—2021年，地震保额增长105%，扩展地震责任占比也达到53%。

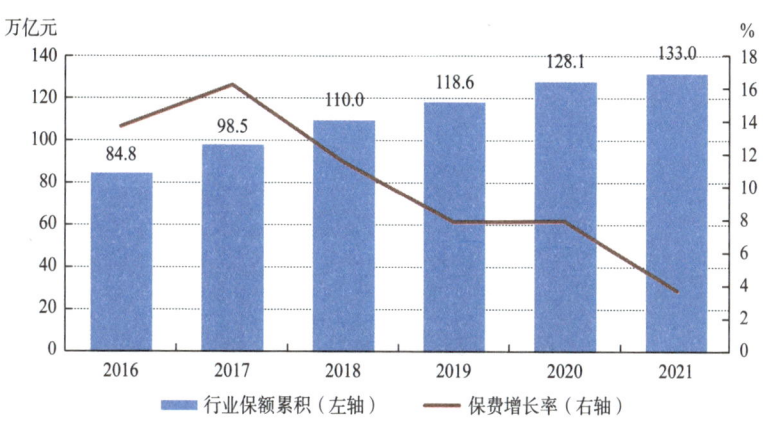

图 1　财产工程险台风/洪水保额

（数据来源：中再研究整理）

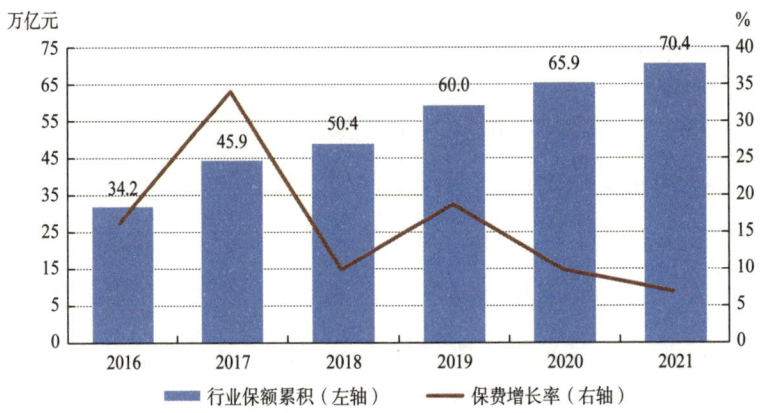

图 2　行业地震风险暴露数据

（数据来源：中再研究整理）

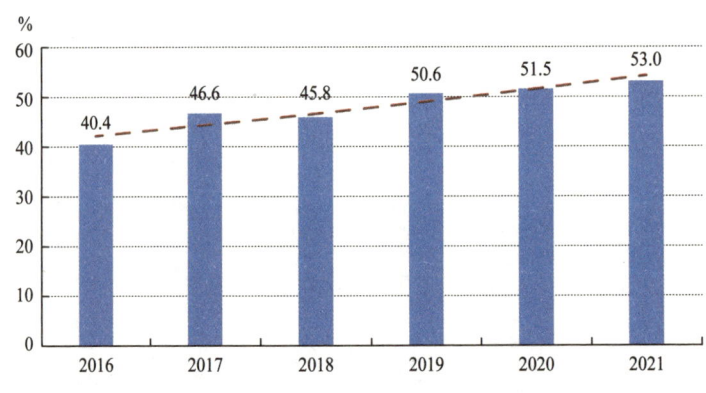

图 3　行业地震风险扩展比例

（数据来源：中再研究整理）

分析自然灾害保险赔付历史数据可以发现，中国灾害损失保障程度极低，目前国内巨灾保险发挥的作用总体有限，近年来保障程度正在逐步提升。2008年汶川地震中，保险业赔付仅为经济损失的0.2%；2021年"7·20"河南暴雨洪涝灾害中，保险业赔付近124亿元，占直接经济损失超过10%，保障程度大大提高。

三、再保险在推动巨灾保险发展中发挥重要作用

巨灾所造成的损失巨大,单一保险公司无力承担全部损失责任。再保险公司是最主要的风险承担者,通过独立承保和交换承保同质巨灾风险,能够达到最大限度地分散风险和分摊损失的目的,有效消除单一巨灾风险对区域经济造成毁灭性打击的潜在威胁。国际上一般都将再保险作为巨灾风险分散机制的核心组成部分,将巨灾赔付风险转移到全球再保险市场乃至资本市场。2010年智利大地震造成85亿美元保险损失,再保险承担了95%的保险损失。2010年和2011年新西兰两次大地震累计保险损失170亿美元,再保险承担了大约70%的保险损失。2011年日本大地震,仅日本地震再保险株式会社(JER)就承担了40%~50%的保险损失。

中国再保险行业在推动巨灾保险发展过程中也发挥了重要作用,积极助力应对重大灾害、保障国计民生、平滑财政收支、支持构建韧性社会。

(一)深度参与全国巨灾保险制度建设和地方巨灾保险试点

再保险凭借在共同体机制建设方面的丰富经验,积极参与筹建地震共同体,其中中再作为理事公司和首席再保人,深度参与地震巨灾保险的顶层制度设计、产品开发与费率测算等工作,牵头参与开发住宅地震巨灾保险产品,形成了《城乡居民住宅地震巨灾保险示范条款》,在国内地震巨灾保险产品设计中发挥了关键作用。在地方巨灾保险试点中,再保险也发挥了积极作用。中再深度参与全国16个省市地区巨灾保险试点,在80%以上的地方政府巨灾保险项目中担任首席

或唯一再保险人，为政府和直保公司提供风险评估、方案设计、定价测算等全方位技术支持，提供年承保能力60亿元。在2021年5月发生的广东韶关特大暴雨及云南大理州漾濞县6.4级地震中，中再作为首席再保人承担赔付均超千万元。

（二）发挥机制优势最大限度分散风险和分摊损失，是最重要的巨灾风险承担者

由于地震、台风等灾害一旦发生，往往在极短时间内造成巨额经济损失，单一保险公司或其他市场主体无力承担全部责任。再保险积极配合各级政府、监管部门以及保险同业为各地区提供风险评估、精算分析、产品设计等重要技术支持以及充足的承保能力，为重大自然灾害提供"第二道"风险保障，是国家巨灾风险管理体系建设中不可或缺的重要组成部分。根据中国保险行业协会分析，针对2016—2020年20场巨灾事件的保险损失和再保险摊回赔款进行统计，再保摊回赔款比例最高的灾害事件为台风莫兰蒂，摊回比例高达81.52%。

表2　　　　　　　　2016—2020年20场巨灾事件

序号	年份	事件
1	2016	2016年第14号台风"莫兰蒂"
2	2016	6月中下旬南方洪涝风雹灾害
3	2016	7月中下旬华北地区暴雨洪涝灾害
4	2016	7月上旬西南至长江中下游地区暴雨洪涝灾害
5	2016	江苏盐城龙卷风冰雹特别重大灾害
6	2017	1713号台风"天鸽"
7	2017	6月下旬至7月初长江中下游5省暴雨洪涝灾害
8	2017	"8·8"四川九寨沟7.0级地震
9	2017	四川茂县"6·24"特大山体滑坡灾害
10	2018	1822号台风"山竹"
11	2018	1818号台风"温比亚"

续表

序号	年份	事件
12	2018	7月上旬渝川陕甘暴雨洪涝灾害
13	2019	1909号超强台风"利奇马"
14	2019	6月上中旬广西、广东、江西等6省（区）洪涝灾害
15	2019	盐城响水"3·21"重特大爆炸事故
16	2019	四川长宁6.0级地震
17	2019	贵州水城"7·23"特大山体滑坡灾害
18	2020	7月长江淮河流域特大暴雨洪涝灾害
19	2020	8月中旬川渝及陕甘滇严重暴雨洪涝灾害
20	2020	2020年第4号台风"黑格比"

资料来源：中国保险行业协会。

整体摊回趋势呈现出"行业巨灾损失越大、再保摊回比例越高"的特点，体现了再保险对于稳定直保公司经营、减少业绩波动性、助力风险分散的重要作用。从国内统计数据来看，目前再保险不仅承担了财产险和工程险约1/3的巨灾损失，也承担了农险40%的巨灾损失。以地震共同体为例，再保险提供了20亿元的地震承保能力。

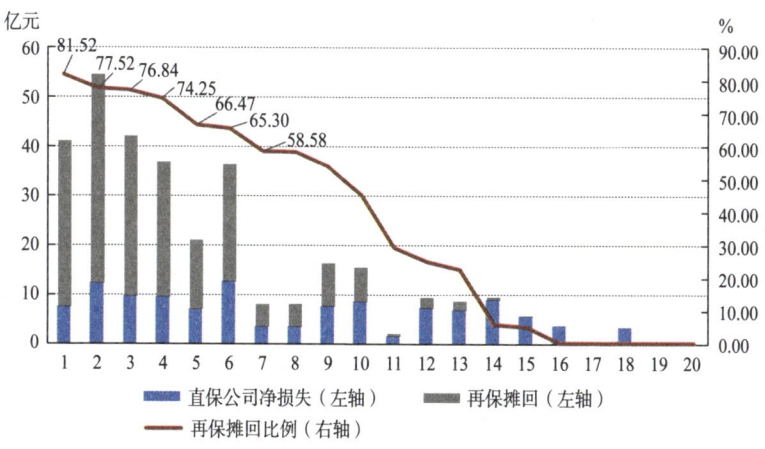

图4　再保险在巨灾保险中的损失分担比例

（资料来源：中国保险行业协会）

（三）创新巨灾风险分散机制

再保险既能将巨灾风险在全球再保险市场进行转移，也能通过证券化方式将巨灾风险转移至资本市场。巨灾债券是多层次巨灾风险分散机制的重要组成部分，是利用资本市场分散巨灾风险、优化保险机制的一种产品创新和制度创新。自1993年汉诺威再保险发行首只巨灾债券以来，发行规模不断攀升、类型不断丰富。最近五年，全球巨灾债券年均发行122亿美元，已成为国际发达市场巨灾风险管理的重要手段。国内巨灾债券起步较晚，保险行业整体仍处于探索阶段。再保险在专业技术、数据模型、人才队伍方面具有突出优势，成为国内巨灾债券探索领域的领头羊。2015年，中再作为发起人，利用特殊目的机构（SPV）Panda Re在百慕大发行了中国首笔巨灾债券，成功向境外资本市场转移了中国地震风险，实现了保险连接资本市场的重大突破。2021年，中再在中国香港成功发行巨灾债券，为内地因台风造成的损失提供保障。巨灾债券的成功发行，不仅为更深入地探索巨灾风险资本市场分散渠道，进一步完善巨灾风险分散转移和补偿机制做出了新的尝试，也对丰富保险行业管理巨灾风险的市场化手段、促进巨灾风险管理制度体系建设、形成多层次巨灾风险分担机制具有积极意义。

（四）发挥巨灾风险管理技术服务优势，强化巨灾风险管理基础设施建设

一是丰富巨灾产品，推动巨灾风险管理创新。再保险公司通过加强基础技术研究，组建专业技术团队，创建巨灾实验室，逐步打造专业化巨灾风险分析团队和平台。巨灾保险的投保人通常为政府及大型企业，再保险公司可着重为其提供系统化、个性化解决方案，并配套

现代化政府治理和城市管理所需要的灾害评估、风险管理、预警预报等科技和数据赋能手段，通过"保险+服务"模式提升政府企业风险管理能力。此外，再保险的平台化优势可有效助推巨灾保险供给侧改革，通过多元化信息收集渠道，实时更新迭代保险产品，增加保险有效供给。二是加强技术研发，提升行业巨灾风险管理能力。由于巨灾风险具有发生概率低、损失巨大的长尾特点，普通精算模型无法对巨灾风险进行有效分析，巨灾模型作为巨灾风险管理与精算评估工具已成为行业共识。为提升行业巨灾风险管理能力，大型再保险公司均持续开展技术研发和数据分析积累，建立了自有的独特巨灾风险数据库和模型。例如慕再的NatCatSERVICE数据库、瑞再Sigma数据库，基于全球灾害历史损失数据而开发的巨灾模型，使得再保险公司拥有专业核心技术，能针对全球巨灾风险建模和分析评估，在提升自身巨灾风险管理的同时，为全行业提供一揽子风险解决方案。太平再（中国）研发"气象灾害风险及保险产品综合分析工具"，涵盖多种气象要素及气象灾害数据，可针对气象要素数据及台风灾害信息提供可视化展示与统计分析，并提供灵活的气象指数保险产品支持服务。中再在"十三五"期间打造巨灾保险的技术优势，针对中国自然灾害风险推出"再·瞰"风险地图，为行业提供免费风险识别服务；2018年推出国内首个拥有自主知识产权的地震巨灾模型"中国地震巨灾模型"；2021年推出自主知识产权的中国台风巨灾模型2.0；持续推进巨灾模型研发，不断迭代升级开发中国地震、台风巨灾模型，加速打造洪水巨灾模型。三是推动行业数据共享，持续加强外部合作。整合相关社会力量开展巨灾保险技术研发，持续加强外部合作，构建巨灾风险管理生态圈，促进跨行业协同，推动建立跨领域、跨部门的沟通合作机制。2018年，中再联合中国地震局、北师大、保险学会等单位，牵头申报国家重点研发项目国家重点研发计划"地震保险损失评估模型及应用研究",获得科技部立项。这是保险业首次获得科技部的资助,开展拥有自主知识产权的地震巨灾模型研发及应用工作,为国内地震保险机制建设提供关键技术支撑。再保险通过科技赋能,正在不断强化巨灾风险管理领域的领先优势,提高防灾防损的抗风险能力。

四、巨灾保险发展的国际经验与启示

(一)主要国家巨灾保险典型实践

面对自然灾害风险,国际普遍注重完善相关机制和运用多样化的金融工具来进行巨灾风险管理,建立了相应的巨灾风险管理体系。

新西兰是世界上最早建立全国性巨灾保险制度的国家。1942年,新西兰中部地区发生里氏7.2级地震,促使新西兰政府成立地震与战争损坏委员会(以下简称EQC),并在此后组建地震保险基金,由EQC专门管理基金和新西兰地震保险事务。新西兰地震保险是在居民购买房屋申请银行贷款时,附加在房屋保险上所必须购买的强制保险。因此,新西兰地震保险投保率非常高,达到了90%以上。2010年9月4日和2011年2月22日,新西兰基督城附近先后发生7.1级和6.3级地震,共造成经济损失约270亿新西兰元。地震发生后,EQC接获理赔报案超过16万件,累积赔付金额约103亿新西兰元,占经济损失比重约38%。

日本是地震多发的国家,1964年,日本中部地区新潟发生里氏7.5级地震,促使日本政府下定决心建立巨灾保险制度。1966年,日本国会通过《地震保险相关法律案》和《地震再保险特别会计法案》,建立日本地震再保险株式会社(JER),正式以立法的形式确立地震保险制度。日本地震保险是自动附加在住宅火灾保险之上的险种,承保住宅及屋内财产损失。经过长达半个世纪的经营,日本地震保险的投保率稳定在30%上下。2011年3月11日,日本本州岛东北部宫城县外海130公里发生9.0级地震(以下简称"3·11地震"),随后引发了强烈的海啸。此次地震是日本有记载以来遭遇的最大震级地震,因此受损的建筑物与公共设施至少超过五年时间才能重建,经济损失高达2 100亿美元。据日本财产保险行业统计数据,"3·11地震"中日本保险业的赔付金额总计达到360亿美元,占直接经济损失比例约为17.1%。地震发生后,日本住宅地震保险累计理赔件数达到74.1万件,赔款金额约160亿美元,占经济损失比重约为8%。

1968年美国国会通过《全国洪水保险法案》,并在此框架下于次年建立了《国家洪水保险计划》(以下简称NFIP),国家洪水保险制度初步建立。NFIP保障风险为洪水风险,以社区为承保对象,当社区申请参加NFIP并采用了NFIP所要求的区划方法和建筑法规后,该社区内的居民才可以购买洪水保险。2017年8月25日,4级飓风"哈维"以130英里(约210公里/小时)的时速登陆美国得克萨斯州,这是美国自2005年以来最强大的"怪兽级"飓风。此次飓风损毁大量房屋汽车,摧毁道路码头,令许多能源厂和化工厂关闭,并且带来了强降雨,造成严重的洪水灾害。据美国国家飓风研究中心报道,哈维飓风造成了1 250亿美元的经济损失,是美国历史上造成损失第二大的自然灾害。此次飓风事件,NFIP共支付损失数量74 065件,赔付84亿美元,占该次灾难经济损失的6.7%。

(二)国际经验借鉴

总结国际经验,有以下共同特点可供借鉴:一是建立了政府主导、商业运作的巨灾风险管理体系;二是建立了巨灾保险制度,由保险、再保险起基础性支撑保障作用;三是建立了多层次的风险分散机制,通过制度安排,保险再保险可承担灾害造成直接经济损失的60%~70%,有效地减轻了受灾地区居民和政府的经济损失,为迅速实现灾后重建、恢复正常生产生活发挥了巨大的作用;四是有统一规范的灾害数据管理,巨灾风险管理涉及许多前沿领域的科技创新,需要强大的底层数据库作为支撑,还需要开发适合本国国情的巨灾模型,为巨灾风险管理决策提供重要的量化信息。

(三)巨灾保险发展面临的主要问题

国内巨灾保险虽然得以快速发展,但仍面临一些问题。一是保险保障程度较低。国内巨灾风险的保险赔付占经济损失平均在10%以下。据国家应急管理部数据显示,2021年中国自然灾害共造成1.07亿人次受灾,直接经济损失3 340.2亿元,保险赔付仅10%,与35%~40%的世界平均水平相比,巨灾保险保障缺口很大。二是巨灾保险缺乏系统性顶层设计。巨灾保险试点仅在部分省市展开,尚未形成体系,依然缺乏更高层次的顶层设计、统筹安排和长效机制。三是风险分散机制比较单一。尚未建立资金跨期积累机制,难以形成巨灾资金的跨期积累和跨区统筹;尚未建立巨灾风险转移至国内资本市场的长效机制,巨灾风险尚不能通过证券化方式进行分散。四是灾害信息数据整合不够。巨灾风险管理涉及应急管理、生态环境、气象水利等多个政府部门,信息缺乏有效整合,影响保险业提升专业技术,不利于进一步扩大巨灾风险保障的覆盖面和普惠性。

五、巨灾保险发展趋势展望

2021年，自然灾害造成的全球经济损失达2 700亿美元，保险损失1 110亿美元，覆盖约40%的经济损失。近年来，全球巨灾风险呈现以下四大发展趋势：一是从"低频高损"向"高频高损"发展；二是受灾最为严重的区域仍以北美、欧洲和亚洲三个地区为主，亚洲新兴市场仍存在大量保险需求；三是次生灾害的损失远远超过原生灾害的损失；四是从供需角度看，巨灾保障缺口越来越大，特别是针对洪水风险。

在全球气候变化加剧的大背景下，在巨灾风险不断凸显的新形势下，在国家碳达峰、碳中和目标要求下，发展巨灾保险已成为当务之急，而有效的巨灾风险管理离不开再保险的支持，在保障国民经济有序发展、保障人民生活、助力政府职能转型中，再保险将发挥越来越重要的作用。

（一）推动巨灾保险积极融入绿色发展理念

在气候变化大背景下，一方面要将巨灾保险纳入绿色金融、绿色保险的整体框架中，进一步深度认识巨灾风险。对巨灾的频率、边界、损失的逻辑进行重新认识；对保险险种的保障范围、价格及其与风险的匹配程度进行重新认识；对巨灾风险产生的次生灾害进行重新认识，再保险将积极助力新理念、新技术的有效传播普及。另一方面，在发挥功能作用上，围绕极端气候变化下对减少碳排放的要求，再保险将大力支持产品和服务创新，在指数保险成功经验的基础上，进一步拓展和探索以改善气候变化为目标，以数据为支撑，以保险交易为载体的机制，鼓励清洁能源利用，促进碳交易，增进社会福利，助力绿色可持续发展。

（二）探索建立财政支持下的多层次巨灾风险分散机制

考虑到巨灾保险的准公共产品属性，坚持"政府推动、商业运作"的原则，不断完善巨灾保险制度，逐步形成中央和地方财政支持下的，包括保险、再保险、巨灾保障基金、巨灾债券等在内的多层次巨灾风险分散机制，让不同保障层次之间各司其职、相互衔接、相互补充。通过保险和再保险为社会提供多样化的保险产品、防灾减灾救灾的技术和服务，承担相应的灾害损失；通过巨灾基金实现保险资金的跨期积累，为罕见巨灾提供足额的赔付资金；通过资本市场，进一步拓宽灾害风险分散渠道。再保险在推动顶层机制设计、利用平台聚合优势、创新开发保险产品、提供专业技术服务方面将发挥核心作用。

（三）加强巨灾保险基础设施建设

再保险将积极助力构建多维度、立体化的自然灾害数据库，加强应急管理、生态环境、气象水利等领域动态监测、灾情记录、理赔记录等数据积累与跨部门、跨领域数据协同共享，推动巨灾风险的多方共治，使保险业不断扩大巨灾风险保障的覆盖面和普惠性。开展巨灾模型的研发，在巨灾数据平台和自主知识产权巨灾模型基础上，以中再为代表的再保险龙头公司将进一步丰富灾害相关数据基础，加强灾害流程管理设计，不断完善巨灾模型，提高模型的精准性。同时形成行业巨灾模型标准，加强模型的使用监督。

专题二

再保险支持农业保险发展专题报告

中国是全球第二大经济体，是拥有14亿人口的发展中大国。农业作为第一产业，是全民生产的根本，是国家发展的基石。粮食安全更是事关国家安全、保障国计民生的重中之重。党的十八大以来，中国提出"确保谷物基本自给、口粮绝对安全"的新粮食安全观，坚持农业农村优先发展，实施乡村振兴战略，保护农民的种粮积极性，让"农民钱袋"鼓起来，让"国家粮袋"更安全。国家对农业发展、粮食安全重视程度与日俱增。与此同时，不可忽视的是，农业安全稳健发展面临的风险挑战正在逐步加大，气象灾害、环境污染、虫灾等多方面挑战一直是农业重点关注的风险点。特别是在全球气候变化背景下，极端天气与自然灾害频发，严重威胁粮食安全，也严重影响农民生产生活。农业领域的风险保障需求显著增大、十分迫切。

农业保险是分散农业主要风险、保障农业产业稳定发展、保护农民利益的重要金融力量，能够有效发挥分散风险、补偿损失、转移支付、防灾防损和风险管理等重要作用，在保障粮食安全、推动农业创新发展、促进农村金融走向成熟等方面扮演重要角色，是保险业服务实体经济和民生发展的重要体现。农业保险具有鲜明的政策性特征，政府对农业保险给予政策支持，使其成为"三农"的重要支撑力量。2019年5月29日，中央全面深化改革委员会第八次会议审议通过了《关于加快农业保险高质量发展的指导意见》，从顶层设计上明确了加快农业保险高质量发展的指导思想、基本原则、主要目标、保障措施等，是今后一段时期开展农业保险工作的根本遵循，其中专设章节对完善大灾风险分散机制作出部署，强调要加快建立财政支持的多方参与、风险共担、多层分散的农业保险大灾风险分散机制，增加农业再保险供给，扩大农业再保险承保能力，完善再保险体系和分保机制。《国家"十四五"规划》指出"我国农业基础还不稳固，城乡区域发展和收入分配差距较大"，作出了"优先发展农业农村、全面推进乡村振兴""健全农村金融服务体系，发展农业保险"的总体部署。2021年中央一号文件提出"扩大三大粮食作物完全成本保险和收入保险试点范围""健全农业再保险制度"。2022年中央一号文件进一步指出要"实现三大粮食作物完全成本保险和种植收入保险主产省产粮大县全覆盖""积极发展农业保险和再保险"。

近年来，农业保险呈蓬勃发展态势。2007年，国内开始推行政策性农业保险，陆续出台相关支持政策，推进农业保险实践创新活动，农业保险制度逐步建立和完善，保险覆盖范围不断拓展，服务能力不断提升。风险保障领域由以生产风险为主扩展到生产与市场两种风险并重，种养殖业面临的主要风险都已纳入保险责任范围。2019年农业保险进入高质量发展阶段后，通过"扩面、增品、提标"，农业保险险种体系趋于完善，险种保障水平和重要农产品保险覆盖面不断提高。从2007年至2021年，国内农业保险参保农户从5 000万户次增加到1.88亿户次，保费收入从51.84亿元增至975.85亿元，相应农业保险风险保障额从1 126亿元增至4.72万亿元，对农业生产总值保障程度从

2.31%增至33.40%。农业保险标的从玉米、水稻、小麦、棉花、大豆、能繁母猪增至种植、养殖和森林等16个大宗农产品和地方优势特色农产品。农作物播种面积承保率从不足10%增至超过60%，其中玉米、水稻和小麦平均承保率超过70%。

再保险行业在助力健全农业保险制度、完善农业大灾风险分散机制等方面发挥了重要作用，为建立适合"三农"特点的多层次、广覆盖、可持续的农村金融体系提供有效支撑，为实现脱贫攻坚战略目标、持续推动乡村振兴战略实施作出了诸多探索实践和积极贡献。

一、中国农业再保险的探索实践

全球气候变化的背景下，再保险是有效分散农业大灾风险、缓冲大灾对国家财政冲击的市场化、专业化机制，是农业巨灾风险管理体系的重要一环。再保险利用平台优势、技术优势，在推动农业保险发展的顶层机制设计方面作出了重要贡献。

（一）中国农共体的设立及贡献

2014年，在原中国保监会的支持下，中再产险与中国境内具有农业保险经营资质的23家非寿险公司共同发起成立中国农共体，专业从事农业保险再保险业务，共同接受成员公司的农业保险分出业务。

中国农共体自成立以来，通过制度化安排和市场化模式，有效整合行业资源，扩大境内农业再保险承保能力，探索完善农业保险风险分散机制，促进行业交流与合作，加强技术研发与服务创新。

中国农共体成立后，先后共有34家成员公司加入；在风险保障水平提升10%~15%、赔付率提高10多个百分点的情况下，维持了农业再保险承保条件的稳定，累计承担农业再保险风险责任1.07万亿元，支付赔款及手续费约296亿元，有力支持了农业"扩面、增品、提标"；特别是为国家推进农业大灾保险、全成本及收入保险和特色农产品保险以奖代补[①]三大改革试点以及地方各类价格保险、气象指数保险、优势特色农产品保险等创新提供了再保险支持，在化解区域性、流域性农业大灾风险以及"非洲猪瘟"等重特大疫情风险方面，有效发挥了大灾风险分散作用，为行业提供了持续稳定的再保险保障。

2019年中国农共体实现保费收入82亿元，同比增长61%，市场份额50.6%；2015—2019年，中国农共体累计实现保费收入272亿元，市场份额50%，为保障国内农业保险体系的稳健运行作出了重要贡献。中国农共体在发展过程中面临着诸多挑战，包括改善运行效率、消除信息不对称、促进稳定运行等。随着外部环境的变化，升级组织运行模式的必要性越发凸显，实体化和更高层级的组织经营模式可以更好服务农业保险和再保险发展。

（二）中国农业再保险股份有限公司成立意义重大

2019年1月29日，中国人民银行、中国银保监会、中国证监会、财政部、农业农村部联合印发《关于金融服务乡村振兴的指导意见》，明确提出要"持续提高农业保险的保障水平，落实农业保险大灾风险准备金制度，组建中国农业再保险股份有限公司，完善农业再保险体系"。2020年，经国务院批准，由财政部牵头并控股，财政部、中再集团、中国农业发展银行、中华联合财产保险股份有限公司、中国人

---

① 2019年，财政部下发《关于开展中央财政对地方优势特色农产品保险奖补试点的通知》（财金〔2019〕55号）。

寿财产保险股份有限公司、北大荒投资控股有限公司、中国太平洋财产保险股份有限公司、中国平安财产保险股份有限公司、中国人民财产保险股份有限公司9家机构共同发起筹建中国农业再保险股份有限公司。组建中国农再是落实中央决策部署的具体举措。按照国务院批复精神，中国农再定位于财政支持的农业保险大灾风险机制的基础和核心，基本功能是分散农业保险大灾风险，推动建立并统筹管理国家农业保险大灾基金，加强农业保险数据信息共享，承接国家相关支农惠农政策。

中国农再主要肩负以下四项职能：一是通过提供农业再保险服务，分散农业保险大灾风险。二是推动建立并统筹管理国家农业保险大灾风险基金。三是加强农业保险数据信息共享，强化信息真实性管理。四是作为国家层面的农业再保险机构，推动完善农业保险制度，有效承接国家相关支农惠农政策，条件成熟时，结合农业价格保险、收入保险等试点情况，探索试点粮食直接补贴改革。

中国农再正式成立之前，财政部与农业农村部于2020年12月16日出台了《关于加强政策性农业保险承保机构遴选管理工作的通知》，要求所有开展农业保险业务的保险公司与中国农再签订《政策性农业保险再保险标准协议》（以下简称《标准协议》）。中国农业再保险自此进入市场主体和运作规则全面升级的新阶段。中国农再正式成立之后，《标准协议》成为农业再保险制度的基础。

与2014年农共体的运作规则相比，《标准协议》在农业再保险的组织治理结构、业务管理、数据整合等方面有明显的突破。中国农再的成立以及《标准协议》的出台，标志着中国农业保险在高质量发展道路上迈出了关键一步。全球著名评级机构A.M.Best在发布的《全球再保险行业展望报告》中认为，中国农再的成立对世界第二大再保险市场产生了巨大影响，保障了农业市场的可持续发展，给中国农险市场带来变革。该报告认为，农业保险约定分保的方式给中国农险市场带来了诸多好处，通过约定分保的方式，能够使业务组合在地理分布与产品种类上更加多样化，形成分散效应，对冲风险，从而有效应对农险大灾风险。同时，约定分保的无差别性有效消除了直保公司逆向选择的可能性，避免了信息不对称产生的道德风险。

二、再保险对推动农业保险发展发挥重要作用

再保险在风险管理、产品创新、技术服务方面具有显著专业优势和独特价值，为农业发展提供了有效的风险保障，切实推动农业保险创新发展，多措并举提升行业服务能力与水平。

（一）提升农业风险保障水平

2021年，中国农再与35家农险经营机构签署了《标准协议》，承担行业20%的农业风险损失，保费规模超过190亿元，为农业生产提供风险保障近1万亿元，服务农户1.88亿户次，全面增强了中国农业再保险保障能力和韧性。2021年河南特大暴雨灾害发生后，中国农再提前对受到较大影响的农险经营公司支付赔款，有效缓解了农险公司经营的赔付压力，大大分散了此次灾害风险，为稳住农业基本盘发挥了重要作用。中再大力拓展商业农险再保险业务，为行业提供风险保障1 100亿元。

（二）发挥战略规划作用

中国农再积极推进农业保险专家委员会组建，设立中国农再研究院，搭建政策研究咨询专业智库。启动研究设立国家农业保险大灾风

险基金工作。承办全国粮食完全成本保险和种植收入保险专题研讨会，相关建议转化为中央和相关部门农业保险政策。围绕粮食完全成本保险和收入保险、农业保险保费补贴政策、农业保险经营费用情况、约定分保数据信息系统建设、特大暴雨灾害警示启示等开展专题研究，形成10余份研究报告，为国家部委提供专业信息速递并多次得到肯定批示，发挥政策研究支撑作用。

（三）推动农业保险创新

再保险机构因地制宜推动农业保险创新。通过对不同地区自然条件、农业发展现状及历史损失等信息的深入调研，再保险有针对性地创新解决方案，扩展保障范围。高标准农田专属保险创新是再保险服务农业发展的重要创新点之一，有利于提高粮食产量、提高农作物质量。中再深入开展实地调研，完成了高标准农田专属保险产品研发，通过保险手段对高标准农田建设项目提供全周期、全链条的风险保障。瑞再针对广东省英德市连樟村现代农业产业园开发了"一揽子创新型农业保险保障方案"并成功落地，保障了当地产业园在发展过程中由于遭受自然灾害导致的人、财、物等相关损失。

（四）提升农业科技化水平

再保险通过开发技术研发平台，从全流程提升服务农业风险管理的技术水平，发挥引领行业技术迭代升级的独特作用。例如，中国农再把约定分保业务信息系统建设作为加强农业保险信息管理的着力点，已实现35家农业保险直保公司、2.5万个分支机构经营数据全覆盖，政策性和商业性保险、270多个种养林险种全覆盖，农业保险全流程保单级和农户清单级数据全覆盖，总体保单数据核验成功率和精准度达99%以上，首次实现了全行业农业保险数据的实时传输。并探索推进农业保险数据治理、加工和共享使用，与有关保险公司共享主要数据，与农业农村部对接达成土地确权数据使用试点方面合作意向并开展数据离线碰撞实验，与民政部对接达成探索行政区划代码共享应用合作意向，开展遥感交叉核验前期准备工作。中再自主开发了农业气象指数保险产品研发平台，为行业提供精准化、自动化和标准化的产品开发工具。瑞再推出其全球首个综合性智能农业风险管理平台"信瑞智农"（SRAIRMP），能够有效解决农险产品创新难、赔付成本高、赔付速度慢等问题，提升农业生产的风险管理能力。截至2021年底，通过"信瑞智农"平台开发超过200款产品，覆盖超过15个省份，产品开发效率提高90%，节约成本10%~15%，有力提升农业科技化水平。

（五）助力低碳农业发展

再保险积极助力打造绿色低碳农业产业链，在践行"双碳"方面起到了保险行业领头羊的作用。农业领域的降碳固碳是完成"双碳"目标的重要路径之一。再保险公司开发了"碳汇+保险"新模式，相比于传统林业保险主要着眼于灾害对于林木本身造成的损失，碳汇保险主要关注森林碳汇价值，即灾害发生造成林木损伤、继而带来的碳汇量下降损失。2021年，中再与广西、江西林业局对接开发森林碳汇保险，助力森林碳汇资源的保护。在慕再支持下，全国首单草原碳汇遥感指数保险成功落地内蒙古包头市，为农牧民提供草原碳汇绿色生态风险保障。瑞再助力全国首个湿地碳汇生态价值保险方案落地宁波，为杭州湾国家湿地公园碳汇等生态价值提供风险保障。

三、面临的风险与挑战

2021年中央经济工作会议对当前经济形势作出了科学研判。世纪疫情冲击下,百年变局加速演进,中国经济运行中面临的困难增多、挑战上升。以习近平同志为核心的党中央坚持把解决好"三农"问题作为全党工作重中之重,坚持农业农村优先发展,走中国特色社会主义乡村振兴道路,扎实推进"三农"各项工作,农业稳产增产、农民稳步增收、农村稳定安宁,为实现"十四五"良好开局奠定了坚实基础。同时必须看到,中国特殊的气候和地理条件,决定了农业灾害多发频发重发是常态化的,随着全球气候变化加剧、极端天气增多,农业生产面临的自然风险在增大;经济下行压力加大将影响农民特别是脱贫群众就业增收,增加巩固拓展脱贫攻坚成果工作难度;全面推进乡村振兴的机制、政策等还有待完善,推动乡村发展建设和治理面临不少困难和制约。总体看,农业保险和再保险高质量发展尚面临一些困难和挑战,与服务"三农"的实际需求相比仍有一定差距。

四、农业再保险发展趋势展望

(一)农业再保险有巨大的发展空间

近年来,政府对农业保险的支持力度不断加大,持续推动农业保险"扩面、增品、提标"。农业保险保费收入增长迅速,从2007年的51.84亿元快速增加至2021年的975.85亿元,连续第二年成为全球最大的农业保险市场。

随着农业保险市场的快速成长,农业保险保费收入占财产保险保费收入的比例也逐步提高,成为市场增量的重要贡献者。中国政府采取了一系列政策支持农业发展,农业保险发展前景广阔。与此同时,尽管2021年国内小麦、水稻、玉米三大粮食作物的承保覆盖率已经达到70%以上的较高水平,但仍然还有很多农户没有投保,特别是在粮食主产省的产粮大县,还有"扩面"的空间。

农业保险规模的迅速壮大,为农业再保险提供了重要的发展机遇。一方面,从风险保障范围来看,专注种植养殖两业保障的"小农险",正在向涵盖农林牧渔和涉农产业风险保障的"大农险"扩展,再保险面临的风险保障也由单一生产风险延伸到全产业链风险,再保险的风险保障需求不断扩大;另一方面,随着乡村振兴战略的不断推进,农业保险保障水平不断提高,涉农保险等产品创新层出不穷,势必会对再保端提出更高的风险分散要求。以国际经验法测算,中国农险保费规模在2025年预计将超过1 600亿元,按照农险平均25%的再保分出率,市场规模将达到400亿元。

(二)再保险成为中国农业大灾风险分散体系的重要支撑

坚持统筹发展和安全,坚持全局理念和系统思维,农业再保险在中国农业大灾风险分散体系中扮演更重要的角色。贯彻落实国务院批复方案,中国农再将会同中再等再保主体不断健全农业再保险制度,充分发挥财政支持的农业大灾风险分散体系基础和核心作用,开展农业大灾风险分散体系战略规划和顶层设计工作,加快推动国家农业保险大灾风险基金的研究设立工作,推动建立"直接保险+再保险+大灾风险基金+紧急融资机制"的多层次大灾风险分散体系。发挥农业保险、再保险、大灾基金和灾害救济、市场价格支持等不同风险管理工具的协同作用,形成合力,共同提升农业大灾风险抵御能力,为防范化解农业大灾风险，稳定农业农村生产，保障国家粮食安全、助力乡村全面振兴提供牢固的安全屏障和风险防火墙。

（三）再保险持续推动农业保险科技水平提升

科技创新和应用为农业保险发展提供了创新驱动力，有效增强了农业保险服务能力，大幅提升了农业保险运营效率。从行业实践看，保险机构也在不断加大科技投入，创新产品助力乡村振兴。随着数据孤岛、农业科技规范化等问题的进一步解决，以及保险公司为适应新险种、新服务需求而不断提升保险产品和服务的质量，农险科技水平有望进一步提升。

再保险具有行业前端的技术优势，在引领农险科技创新，产品和服务的科技赋能方面将发挥更大作用。而农业保险科技水平不断提升，又为再保端发展注入不竭动力。未来，科技将成为农业保险高质量发展的关键驱动力和核心竞争力，加快农业保险科技的战略部署与深度应用，是农险直保端高质量发展的必由之路。再保端可利用其在数据定价、场景应用方面的技术优势，主动服务广大农险直保公司，实现以技术驱动的保险产品创新方案，从而获取以数据为基础的市场价值和客户价值，协同推进农业风险管理与服务平台建设。

（四）再保险成为助力农业绿色发展的重要力量

再保险的风险保障功能是支持绿色发展的重要手段，基于自身在巨灾风险管理、产品精算和国际化等方面的优势，在实现"双碳"目标过程中，将成为绿色农业保险的引领者、探索者、推动者。随着经济发展方式转型加快，中国政府对环境保护问题越加重视，广义范围的农业保险将在产业结构调整、气候治理、绿色技术应用、绿色产品推广等方面发挥较大作用。作为风险兜底端，再保险可在环境污染责任保险、碳保险、种养业保险、森林保险、生态工程保险、巨灾保险等绿色保险产品上发力，进一步支持直保端探索市场化的碳资产管理和碳金融业务，利用市场机制控制和减少温室气体排放，推进绿色低碳发展，助推实现碳达峰、碳中和目标。

专题三

再保险服务"一带一路"建设专题报告

自2013年"一带一路"倡议提出以来,截至2021年底,中国已与145个国家、32个国际组织签署了200多份共建"一带一路"合作文件,中国与"一带一路"沿线国家货物贸易额占中国总体外贸比重的三成,对沿线国家直接投资额占全国对外投资的比重约两成。"一带一路"行动在中国"双循环"新发展格局中占有举足轻重的地位。

习近平总书记在第三次"一带一路"座谈会上提出,"以高标准、可持续、惠民生为目标,继续推动共建'一带一路'高质量发展。"《国家"十四五"规划》指出,要"加快构建以国内大循环为主体、国内国际双循环相互促进的新发展格局","实行高水平对外开放,推动共建'一带一路'高质量发展,积极参与全球经济治理体系改革"。近年来,中国保险业对外开放步伐明显加快,服务"一带一路"建设取得显著成效,但中资保险公司在产品和服务供给方面还存在很多痛点问题。再保险行业作为保险业"走出去"的先行者,把握国家大局需要,发挥好再保险的平台优势、网络优势、技术优势,从推动保险供给侧创新、提升海外风险保障能力等方面,持续助力"一带一路"建设,为推动保险业高水平对外开放贡献积极力量。

一、再保险发挥专业优势，助力解决"一带一路"保险保障痛点

（一）"一带一路"保险保障需求不断增加

中国已是全球第二大经济体、第一大贸易国、第二大对外直接投资国。2021年，中国与"一带一路"沿线国家货物贸易额达11.6万亿元，同比增长23.6%，创8年来新高，占中国外贸总额的比重达29.7%。中欧班列全年开行1.5万列、运送146万标箱，同比分别增长22%、29%。对沿线国家直接投资1 384.5亿元，同比增长7.9%，占对外投资总额的14.8%。中国企业在沿线国家承包工程完成营业额5 785.7亿元，占对外承包工程总额的57.9%。

随着中国经济持续走出去，"一带一路"建设深入推进，中国海外利益持续扩大。然而，"一带一路"建设面临诸多挑战和风险。一方面风险程度高且复杂。凡是政治风险高的国家，基本上都是社会经济发展比较落后的国家，相应的经济、社会等风险都比较高。而且，从未来相当长一段时期看，"一带一路"沿线国家较高的"国家风险"仍将是一个常态，客观上需要保险业提供高质量的风险保障和服务。另一方面政治风险、经济风险、法律风险、安全风险等风险保障仍存在较大缺口。若将上述风险映射到保险业的具体险种上，既包含中国出口信用保险公司经营的出口信用保险和海外投资保险，也包含商业保险公司经营的财产险、工程险、货运险等常规险种，以及政治暴力保险（PV）、工程延期利润损失保险（DSU）、海外医疗保险、并购责任保险、履约保函等特殊险种。而在特殊险种方面，仍然需要保险业加大保障力度。

（二）保险业服务"一带一路"面临的问题与挑战

保险业在服务"一带一路"建设方面已经取得了积极成效。一是政策支持框架已基本形成并逐步完善，政策支持力度逐步加大。二是产品和服务创新不断取得新突破，目前国内保险公司已基本可以覆盖"一带一路"常规险种。三是海外机构和服务网络稳步推进，多家大型中资保险再保险集团逐步拓展海外机构布局，目前主要集中在香港、伦敦、新加坡等全球金融中心。

虽然保险业服务"一带一路"已经初见成效，但是随着合作共建走深走实，传统的粗放式服务模式已经不能适应当前"走出去"企业对风险管理和保障覆盖的新需求，不能适应国际保险公司在"一带一路"业务上竞争加剧的新情况。

一是产品结构单一。相较于"一带一路"项目的保险保障需求，国内保险业提供的保险产品结构较为单一，多集中在跨境车险、工程险、财产险、非保障型寿险等常规型险种，难以与全球性及共建国家本土保险公司竞争。国内公司在常规险种上的承保能力供给过剩，海外项目常见的工程险和财产险长期处于过度竞价状态，不仅导致保险公司承担的风险与价格出现长期背离，还因中资公司的互相竞价扰乱了海外部分险种的市场秩序。

二是整体保障程度偏低。尽管国内公司在常规险种方面的供给能力充足，但相较于中国海外利益保险保障需求来看，覆盖程度依旧偏低。2019年中国境外固定资产规模达3.5万亿元[1]，新签对外直接承包额达1.8万亿元[2]。同期中资保险业对境外财产、工程的保障规模仅为

---

[1] 数据来源：根据商务部中国对外直接投资统计公报测算。
[2] 数据来源：商务部。

8 050亿元[①]，仅占总需求的15%左右。

三是在特殊险种上承保能力和定价能力严重不足。国内保险公司产品开发进度落后于市场需求，"一带一路"沿线不同国别、行业的风险种类程度和客户需求存在差异，保险公司对不同国家客户未有效实行个性化定价策略，部分公司承保特殊风险过于依赖离岸市场，导致保险条款个性化程度不高但定价不低、限制不少，降低了"出海"企业的投保意愿。

四是服务能力亟须提升。一方面保险服务网络不够健全，属地服务能力有待提升。在中国海外利益相对集中的亚非拉发展中国家，国内绝大多数保险公司缺乏分支机构和必要的全球化第三方救援服务网络，一定程度上造成"走出去"企业无法获得专业的风险咨询意见，增大了遭受风险损失和无法获得有效保障的概率。另一方面保险业自身海外风险管理能力有待加强，尚未建立专业的境外标的风险数据库和评估系统，一旦发生巨灾类风险事件，经营海外业务的国内保险公司很容易受到较大冲击。

（三）再保险独特优势能够发挥重要作用

"一带一路"建设存在大量的保险保障和风险管理需求，针对保险业面临的突出问题和挑战，再保险业凭借自身在国际化发展、技术创新与平台连接方面的优势，在服务"一带一路"建设、服务保险业"走出去"中能够发挥重要作用。

一是国际化优势。国际化是再保险的天然属性，经营模式、业务结构、服务模式等均决定了再保险需要在全球范围内分散风险、交流

---

① 数据来源：根据行业统计数据测算。

合作，成为联系国内国际两个市场的桥梁纽带，成为国内保险业"走出去"的先行军。面对国内保险公司境外机构设立数量较少、范围有限的问题，再保险业的海外机构布局和服务网络可以发挥作用。以中再为例，经过多年国际化布局和业务积累，截至2021年已在11个国家和地区拥有经营机构、全球合作服务网络覆盖136个国家和地区，境外业务保费收入占比达18.9%。2018年收购英国桥社保险集团，是迄今为止国有保险公司最大规模的海外主业并购。桥社目前是劳合社市场排名前十的经营单位，在中国海外利益急需保障的政治风险、恐怖主义风险、特殊能源风险、核风险等领域具有一定的全球定价权和话语权。

二是平台化优势。再保险不参与直接保险行业竞争，市场地位较为中立，能够成为连接政府和企业、实业和资本、国内和国际的桥梁纽带，可以推动各方形成利益共享、风险共担的海外利益风险管理命运共同体，实现风险的有效转移与全球分散。2020年，中国"一带一路"再保险共同体正式成立，为建立海外利益风险保障体系迈出了重要一步。再保险凭借在发起、设立和运作保险共同体方面丰富的经验，在"一带一路"共同体设立过程中发挥了关键作用。

三是专业技术优势。再保险是国内较早开展海外业务的专业机构，熟悉各种海外市场的规则和风险，在数据、人才、技术方面拥有较为深厚的储备和专业优势。在产品创新方面，再保险通过海外拓展的技术反哺，在中国海外利益急需保障的政治风险、恐怖主义风险、特殊能源风险、核风险等领域具备一定的全球定价权和话语权。在风险管理方面，基于自身业务组合全球分散特征，再保险也拥有较为成熟的风险管理经验、工具和技术能力。

二、再保险服务"一带一路"建设突出成果

（一）创新体制机制，牵头设立"一带一路"共同体联合体

针对"一带一路"沿线国家风险偏高、"一带一路"保险需求不断增加、在特殊险种上承保能力和定价能力严重不足等痛点问题，2020年7月28日，在中国银保监会支持下，由中再牵头、汇集行业合力，正式成立中国"一带一路"再保险共同体（以下简称共同体），成为国内唯一专门从事"一带一路"风险管理的行业平台。截至2021年底，共同体共有成员公司23家，由中再担任主席单位和管理机构。共同体的宗旨是通过制度化安排和商业化模式，聚焦海外风险管理亟须但国内技术相对薄弱的特殊风险领域，聚集保险业力量，补齐保障短板，深化政策落地，搭建服务平台，增强保险业服务"一带一路"的能力和水平。

2021年，在英国财政部及国际贸易部、劳合社等多方支持下，中再通过旗下桥社集团牵头设立劳合社"一带一路"政治暴力险联合体和政治风险保险联合体，吸引了诸多全球知名保险再保险机构共同支持"一带一路"建设。其中政治暴力险可提供4亿美元承保能力，政治风险可提供6 000万美元承保能力，在中国海外利益政治暴力险领域树立国际首席地位。

2019年，中再牵头在新加坡成立政治暴力险共保体，是亚太市场服务"一带一路"倡议的重要举措，对于推动中国与新加坡保险业互联互通具有重要意义。中再旗下桥社新加坡分支作为首席承保人，联合6家国际保险公司共同组成政治暴力险共保体，可为单一风险单位最

多提供2.5亿美元的承保能力。

（二）中国"一带一路"再保险共同体发挥重要引领作用

共同体成立后，有针对性地缓解和解决了现阶段保险业服务"一带一路"存在的一些迫切问题。一是聚集行业创新能力，提升特殊险种的定价及承保能力，逐步摆脱对离岸保险市场的过度依赖，提升在特殊风险领域的定价权和话语权。二是整合加强配套服务能力，通过搭建行业海外服务平台，提供稳定可靠的海外出单、属地服务和项目风险评估服务，帮助保险业提升属地化服务能力和海外风险管理能力。三是作为政府管理的政策工具和落地抓手，为行业争取相关政策支持，逐步推动将保险纳入"一带一路"制度设计中，提升政策落地效果。四是深化国际政策沟通，代表行业与国际保险监管机构、相关共同体组织、保险公司加强沟通，为监管层面之间的政策沟通协调奠定基础，提升政策协调的效果。

共同体是中国"走出去"企业的强大后盾，在承保能力、稀缺险种方面为"一带一路"保驾护航。自"一带一路"共同体成立至2021年底，共处理询价185笔，共同体报出承保能力累计保障境外资产总规模约1 000亿元。2021年全年，成员公司累计承保中国海外利益项目8 137个，覆盖153个国家和地区，保障境外资产总规模27 382.5亿元，保费收入28.43亿元，其中58%左右的承保能力依靠再保市场提供支持。"一带一路"国家项目数量占比88%，保障规模占比79%，保费收入占比81%，成员公司总赔款金额[①]14.87亿元。在共同体的支持下，国内保险业对"一带一路"重大项目的参与份额提升显著，成员公司对中国能源建设股份有限公司乌兹别克斯坦锡尔燃气发电厂工程险、

---

① 赔款金额含未决。

中国长江三峡集团有限公司巴基斯坦第一风电政治暴力险、中国铁建股份有限公司（以下简称中国铁建）智利5号公路政治暴力险、中国电力建设集团（以下简称中国电建）缅甸皎漂燃气电厂政治暴力险等7个项目的参与份额均超过85%，其中5个项目为成员公司100%承保，充分展现了中资承保能力在"一带一路"项目上所具备的稳定优势。

共同体可以在紧急情况下为"一带一路"项目提供稳定、可靠的保险保障。以中国电建缅甸皎漂电站项目为例，2021年2月缅甸发生政变，国际保险市场停止向缅甸市场投放政治暴力险承保能力，中资在缅项目受到影响，较为典型的是正处于项目融资阶段且于政变当天开工的中国电建皎漂电站项目，其原本计划在劳合社市场排分的政治暴力险无法获得承保能力支持，项目建设面临很大风险暴露。最终，共同体为此项目提供了独家再保险支持，保证了其后续建设的顺利推进，得到客户的充分认可和诚挚感谢。"中国'一带一路'再保险共同体护航'一带一路'倡议"案例获得2021年服贸会最佳实践奖殊荣。

共同体培育政治暴力险自主定价能力，有效填补国内"一带一路"特殊风险保障空白。作为国内近几年的新兴险种，国内直保公司普遍缺乏在政治暴力险领域的承保定价能力。在此背景下，共同体发挥再保险技术优势，加大技术和研发投入，支持成员公司从无到有培育定价能力，汇集承保能力，在已承保的10个政治暴力险项目中，有4个项目采用共同体报价，如在中国电建皎漂电站项目和中国铁建智利5号公路项目中担任首席再保人，在智利5号公路项目中共同体以首席再保人的行业影响力撬动国际保险人以共同体条件承保该项目，报价取得市场广泛认可，在中国海外利益政治暴力险领域确立国际首席地位。

（三）积极推进"一带一路"产品与服务创新

再保险针对目前"一带一路"亟须的保险保障空白和薄弱环节提供创新产品。中再联合相关数据方和技术方，搭建专门针对"一带一路"的"再医"、"再通"平台，为海外企业、国人长期提供风险保障服务。"国人国医"海外保险保障方案，服务中国红十字总会及12省市卫健委，为中国在21个国家、地区近40%的援外医疗队队员提供专业保障。"国人国保"综合风险解决方案为中铁建、中石油等逾两万名海外员工提供绑架勒索保险保障及救援等特色服务。2021年，中再不断拓展"一带一路"沿线服务，累计为"一带一路"范围内超过11个国家的30余家保险公司提供再保服务，复制境内特药保障成功经验到中国台湾、中国香港，以及泰国等海外市场，全年实现保费过百亿港元，荣获"大湾区保险业大奖2021—香港站杰出再保险公司"表彰。太平再（中国）研发"'一带一路'项目风险分析平台"，能够有效识别和评估中资海外利益所面临的自然风险。

三、再保险服务"一带一路"建设趋势展望

当前，百年变局不断演进、新冠肺炎疫情仍在延续、世界加速动荡变革，国际环境日趋复杂严峻，全球经济不确定性因素显著增加，"一带一路"建设面临的海外风险更加复杂多变，海外风险保障需求大、特殊风险保障有缺口、风险机制更复杂，这对"走出去"的中国企业提出巨大挑战，也对服务保障中国海外利益的中国保险业提出更高要求，特别是在提升承保能力、专业技术和风险控制能力等方面，仍然任重而道远。

风险管理能力是再保险的核心竞争力，是再保险服务"一带一路"的核心着眼点。国际环境日趋复杂，政治风险、经济风险、违约风险、法律风险等都是需要考虑的重要因素，这正是再保险大有可为的领域。通过保险服务的延伸，可以有效化解"一带一路"核心区和节点城市建设中出现的各类风险，扩大政府和企业应对风险的选择空间，有效保障中资企业海外利益。

一是围绕保险保障新需求，积极探索创新风险解决方案。伴随"一带一路"建设不断深入，实体企业"走出去"形式也在发生变化。后疫情时期，"一带一路"国家主权担保项目收紧，政策性保险保障已无法满足市场需要，商业保险公司需要提出更多既符合国际商业惯例又适合中国企业经营特点的商业保险解决方案。再保险需要深入了解当前阶段"一带一路"建设企业的境外保险保障需求，特别是加强对市场普遍需求的保函保险、工程设计责任险和政治风险保险产品的研发和技术储备，同时探索针对中国企业海外融资项目的保险解决方案。

二是积极推动绿色转型。中国是全球煤电装机容量最高的国家，也是全球最大的海外煤电项目投资国。根据全球环境研究所（GEI）2017年的报告，2001—2016年，中国在"一带一路"沿线国家参与的煤电项目共计240个。中国于2021年9月宣布将大力支持发展中国家能源绿色低碳发展，不再新建境外煤电项目。再保险将围绕服务"双碳"发展目标，积极应对绿色转型需要，逐步拓展绿色能源相关保险业务，为中国境外绿色能源项目提供有力支持。目前，中国"一带一路"共同体承保的12个发电项目中，有11个为绿色能源项目，超总项目数量的57%，为绿色能源项目提供的保障规模占共同体保障的境外资产总规模的45%，为推动保险业绿色转型持续提供助力。

三是强化国际沟通合作。再保险将进一步发挥行业"聚合器"作用和平台效应,发挥海外网络优势,聚合更多保险公司力量,共同开拓互利共赢的增量市场,不断加大对重点企业、重点项目的保险保障支持力度,为中央企业提供"保险+服务"一揽子解决方案。同时,积极担负起与国际监管沟通、保险同业合作的桥梁纽带作用,联动多方资源、优化沟通渠道、完善合作机制,织密中国海外利益保障网,推动中国保险业服务"一带一路"的"中国实践"向世界交流展示,推动中国保险业加快融入全球保险价值链,增强中国保险业在国际保险市场的话语权。

专题四

再保险推动绿色保险发展、助力实现碳中和目标专题报告

应对气候变化，实现碳中和目标是人类可持续发展的客观需要。保险行业是受到气候变化趋势直接影响和冲击的行业之一，气候变化导致的极端气候灾害（物理风险）和经济结构转型（转型风险）为保险行业带来诸多挑战，同时也带来了新的业务机遇。再保险作为保险行业中的风险知识专家，能够在应对气候变化，实现碳中和的人类事业中发挥重大和独特的作用。

保险业助力实现碳中和目标，关键是要积极对接绿色发展的风险保障需求，推动绿色保险业务发展。但绿色保险属于新兴领域，保险行业承保经验及数据有限，放眼全球市场，再保险行业正在发挥技术与数据优势，加强与直保公司协同合作，推进再保险前置到条款开发、产品定价、风控预案等环节，积极引领保险行业创新绿色保险产品和服务方式，支持绿色产业发展，为本国乃至全球实现碳中和目标贡献力量。

一、国内绿色保险发展背景

《国家"十四五"规划》指出,要"构建生态文明体系,推动经济社会发展全面绿色转型,建设美丽中国",并提出"提升生态系统质量和稳定性、持续改善环境质量、加快发展方式绿色转型"等具体要求。绿色金融是金融业更好服务中国"双碳"目标实现,支持绿色低碳循环经济发展的重要抓手。绿色保险是绿色金融的重要组成部分,能够为绿色产业发展与传统产业转型提供风险管理服务与风险保障,有力助推经济社会绿色发展。

(一)国内绿色保险发展政策背景

2015年9月,中共中央、国务院印发《生态文明体制改革总体方案》(中发〔2015〕25号),首次明确提出"建立绿色金融体系"的总体目标,这标志着中国成为全球首个由政府部门制定系统性绿色金融政策框架的国家。2016年8月,为加强绿色金融支持实体经济转型力度,中国人民银行等七部门联合发布《关于构建绿色金融体系的指导意见》(银发〔2016〕228号),明确了中国绿色金融发展的总体思路,并将发展绿色保险作为独立章节并提出指导意见。以此为起点,中国绿色保险发展迎来具有历史意义的新阶段。2020年中国作出碳达峰、碳中和承诺后,绿色金融政策频发、举措丰富,绿色保险在政策文件中出现的频次也逐渐提升,在支持低碳减排、绿色发展中发挥着越来越大的作用。2021年1月,中国银保监会首次将发展绿色保险列入2021年度重点工作。2021年6月,中国保险行业协会发布《保险业聚焦碳达峰碳中和 助推绿色发展蓝皮书》,对保险业对绿色发展的贡献做了详尽介绍。

表 1　　　　　　　　　　　绿色保险相关政策

时间	政策
2016年8月	中国人民银行与原保监会等七部委联合印发《关于构建绿色金融体系的指导意见》，将发展绿色保险作为独立章节并提出指导意见。
2020年1月	中国银保监会印发的《关于推动银行业和保险业高质量发展的指导意见》（银保监发〔2019〕52号）提出"探索碳金融、气候债券、蓝色债券、环境污染责任保险、气候保险等创新型绿色金融产品"。
2021年1月	中国人民银行年度工作会议将"落实碳达峰　碳中和重大决策部署，完善绿色金融政策框架和激励机制"列入2021年度重点工作，特别提及要"增强金融体系管理气候变化相关风险的能力"。
	中国银保监会年度工作会议将"积极发展绿色信贷、绿色保险、绿色信托，为构建新发展格局提供有力支持"列入2021年度重点工作。
2021年2月	《国务院关于加快建立健全绿色低碳循环发展经济体系的指导意见》（国发〔2021〕4号）印发，在大力发展绿色金融方面明确提出，"发展绿色保险，发挥保险费率调节机制作用"。
2021年6月	中国银保监会举办"保险业聚焦碳达峰　碳中和目标助推绿色发展"工作推进会，中国保险行业协会发布《保险业聚焦碳达峰碳中和　助推绿色发展蓝皮书》。
2021年9月	中共中央办公厅、国务院办公厅印发《关于深化生态保护补偿制度改革的意见》，明确"鼓励保险机构开发创新绿色保险产品参与生态保护补偿。"中国保险行业协会组织召开保险业聚焦碳达峰　碳中和目标助推绿色发展专家委员会第一次（扩大）会议，强调要推进绿色保险产品、服务、技术等标准化建设。

资料来源：中再研究院整理。

（二）国内绿色保险发展实践

在政策指引和支持下，为满足日益增长的绿色转型发展保障需求，同时学习借鉴国际先进经验，中国绿色保险的市场实践在探索中日益丰富，服务路径拓宽。一是支持绿色产业发展，国内保险行业为绿色能源、绿色建筑、绿色交通、绿色农业等绿色产业提供财产险、工程险、新能源汽车保险、责任险、保证险等保险产品，为绿色技术创新提供了首台（套）装备保险、知识产权险等保险产品，以及在碳保险领域逐步开拓森林碳汇保险、碳交易履约保证保险、碳配额质押贷款保证保险等产品。二是围绕适应气候变化，国内保险行业重点发展了以巨灾保险和天气指数保险为代表的绿色保险产品。三是聚焦环境污染防治，国内保险行业推出了环境污染责任险、水污染清理费用保险等产品。四是保护生物多样性，国内保险行业开发了野生动物肇事责任保险、生态系统保护修复类保险等绿色保险产品。五是鼓励消费者实施环境友好行为，国内保险行业正在探索研发类UBI车险产品，以及鼓励绿色出行的人身险产品，全力保障绿色出行。

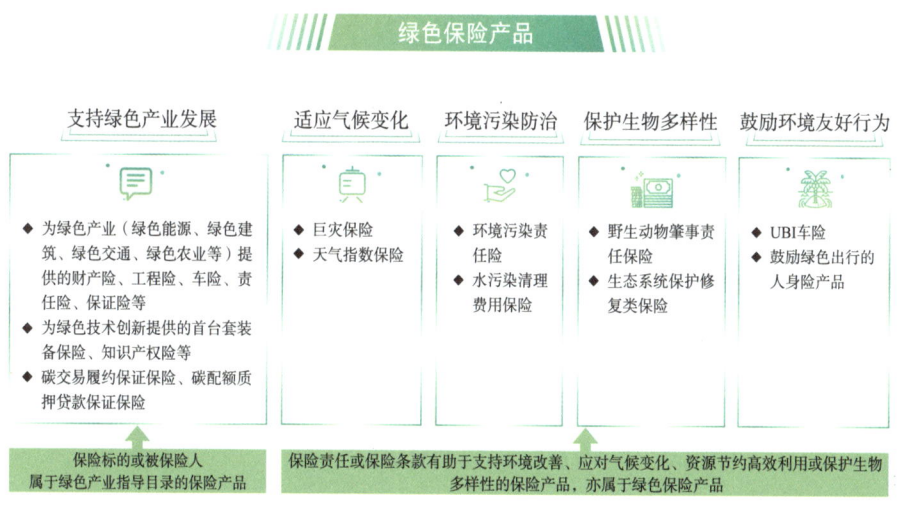

（资料来源：中再研究院整理）

据保险行业协会统计，2018—2020年，保险业累计为全社会提供45.03万亿元保额的绿色保险保障，支付赔款533.77亿元，有力发挥了绿色保险的风险保障功效。2020年绿色保险保额18.33万亿元，较2018年增加6.30万亿元，年均增长23.43%；2020年绿色保险赔付金额213.57亿元，较2018年增加84.78亿元，年均增长28.77%，高于保费年均增长6.81个百分点[①]。

---

① 数据来源：中国保险行业协会，《保险业聚焦碳达峰碳中和 助推绿色发展蓝皮书》。

二、再保险服务绿色保险发展的国际经验借鉴

绿色保险能为氢能、储能、新能源汽车等大量绿色技术创新提供保障，并服务保障传统产业低碳转型。围绕大量产品创新需求，直接保险公司面临着数据积累不足、风险认识不够、定价能力不足等发展痛点，直接影响到绿色保险产品创新的进度。再保险公司的介入有助于解决上述痛点问题，有效助力推进绿色保险的推广普及与健康发展。从国际经验来看，在绿色保险发展过程中，再保险行业发挥着核心主导作用，积极参与国际合作机制建设，引领产品服务创新。

（一）积极建设绿色保险国际合作机制

在共同应对气候变化、发挥金融保险作用迈向净零未来的大背景下，绿色保险相关国际组织及多边合作活跃，国际影响力持续提升。由于再保险行业具有天然国际化特征，在目前运转的绿色保险国际合作机制中，再保险公司均发挥着核心作用。

2021年7月11日，德国安联集团、法国安盛集团、意大利忠利保险、英国英杰华集团、苏黎世保险集团、慕再、法再和瑞再八家全球性保险和再保险公司成立"净零保险联盟"（Net-Zero Insurance Alliance，NZIA），以实现碳中和共同目标，加速向净零排放经济的过渡。发起设立NZIA的8家创始机构中，有3家为再保险公司，分别是慕再、法再和瑞再。NZIA是全球保险行业的集团联盟。联盟成员目前包括25家保险、再保险公司，覆盖超过11%的全球保费。NZIA联盟成员提出将通过倡导企业和行业行动以及支持低碳转型，寻求实现其净零承诺。NZIA通过负责任的保险实践，承诺将全球气温上升幅度控制在

不超过1.5摄氏度,并致力于在2050年前将NZIA成员的承保组合转向净零排放。

在第26届联合国气候变化大会等国际会议上,再保险公司也踊跃发声,用行动支持大会顺利召开。英国劳合社宣布将引入计量框架,监测各辛迪加承保组合的碳强度。劳合社主席布鲁斯·卡内基-布朗表示,衡量各机构温室气体净零排放进展的框架预计将在2023年全面推开。法再等金融机构承诺到2025年结束对与森林砍伐相关的农业大宗商品活动的投资,例如为生产棕榈油、大豆、牛肉和皮革、纸浆和纸张等大宗商品而砍伐森林的活动。

(二)引领绿色保险产品创新

国际市场上大量绿色保险产品与服务创新均由再保险公司肇始,或担任核心角色。

1. 电化学储能保险产品案例

以风能、光能为代表的新能源具有安全、环保、清洁等特点,在碳中和背景下,提升新能源渗透率势在必行。但风能和光能等新能源发电存在突出的间歇性和波动性特点,导致弃风弃光现象,对电网的稳定性也产生影响。在新一轮能源革命中,电化学储能技术具有成本低、灵活性高等优势,成为未来发展储能系统的重要技术路线,将成为提升新能源渗透率的重要装备基础和支撑技术。

然而,电化学储能技术及储能系统产品的发展与大规模应用在国际国内市场均属于新鲜事物,相关技术及产品仍处于不断升级换代的快速变化过程中,技术成熟度有限,因此涉及较多的安全风险、电池产品效能衰减等风险因素,格外需要保险工具保驾护航。

为回应上述保险需求,慕再于2019年为美国制造商ESS公司的液流电池储能系统创新提供了长期电池性能保险，保单为期10年，涵盖重大储能项目。这是全球第一个针对储能系统推出的保险产品。该产品有助于电池制造商更有效地管理质保及索赔事项，扩大储能技术和产品的生产制造规模，加快电池储能系统部署速度，以及提升大型电化学储能项目的可融资性，满足项目融资需求。在承保过程中，为更好地管理风险，确保业务可保，慕再积极引入第三方专业检验认证机构，开展储能系统产品及储能系统工程建设的安全认证工作，以通过认证作为保险合约成立的前提条件。

2. 碳保险案例

随着绿色金融和碳交易市场的不断成熟完善，以及高碳企业低碳转型的迫切度不断提升，碳金融领域受到了更多关注。碳保险可以被界定为与碳信用、碳配额交易直接相关的金融产品[①]，以《联合国气候变化框架公约》和《京都议定书》为前提、以碳排放权为基础，或是保护在非京都规则中模拟京都规则而产生的碳金融活动的保险，主要承保碳融资风险和碳交付风险。

早在2006年，瑞再与私募基金RNKCapital合作开发了国际碳市场的首个清洁发展机制（CDM）支付风险保险产品，该产品能够承保投资人投资于清洁发展项目时有关《京都议定书》机制的投资风险，覆盖了CDM项目中项目注册及核证减排量（CERs）核证失败或延误等风险。如果CDM项目投资人因CERs核证或发放问题受损，保险公司将提供赔偿。此后，瑞再又与联合国环境署等机构合作开发了碳交易信用保险等系列产品。

---

① 资料来源：中央财经大学绿色金融国际研究院。

三、再保险服务绿色发展主要实践

为积极支持国家"双碳"战略以及产业端和保险市场的风险管理需求,与国际市场经验类似,国内再保险行业在国内绿色发展过程中也正在发挥日益凸显的作用。

(一)助力绿色能源产业蓬勃发展

1.支持核能安全发展,助力构建清洁低碳安全高效能源体系

再保险发挥平台优势,通过中国核保险共同体(以下简称中国核共体)平台为核能安全发展保驾护航。核能是低碳、稳定的能源形式,是实现"双碳"目标的重要能源选择,也是最为现实的战略选择之一。中国核共体经原中国保监会批复,于1999年正式成立,聚合国内29家成员公司(占国内财产保险市场份额合计超过90%),连接全球26个核保险共同体,共同为中国核能和平利用提供保险保障和风险管理服务,是践行命运共同体理念、管理分散核巨灾风险的重要平台,中再集团是中国核共体主席单位,中再产险是执行机构管理公司,积极发挥保单设计、费率厘定、国际再保安排等核心作用。中国核共体成员还包括瑞再、汉再、太平再(中国)、法再等再保险公司。截至2021年底,中国核共体承保能力达10.77亿美元,是全球第二大核共体,累计为国内全部53台核电机组提供了全面保险保障和风险管理服务,保障财产总价值近万亿元,其中包括中国具有完整自主知识产权的第三代核电技术项目"华龙一号"和国家科技重大专项——华能石岛湾高温气冷堆核电站示范工程。

中国核共体2021年为境内所有17座运行核电厂的53台运行核电机

组提供全方位保险保障，涉核财产近万亿元、涉核企业一线人员2.4万人。与燃煤发电相比，这些核能发电减排量相当于减少燃烧标准煤1.15亿吨、减少二氧化碳排放3.02亿吨、二氧化硫98万吨、氮氧化物85万吨。核能也为全球提供了约10%的电力，2021年，中国核共体承保了境外300余座核电机组，为全球碳中和作出了贡献。此外，核共体积极支持山东海阳核电厂的核能供暖改造项目，助力推动海阳市成为全国首个冬季"零碳"供暖城市。

2. 为国内大型清洁能源项目提供长期稳定的承保支持

再保险为风电、水电、光伏等清洁能源提供可靠再保险支持。电力工程项目属于投资巨大、施工工期长、工程地质条件复杂、技术难度大的高风险项目，需要再保险业在保险行业身后提供有力可靠的再保险支持。截至2021年底，在全国新能源电力资产的保险保障中，中再承担的风险保额占财产保险行业承保保额的15%左右，承担再保险分出责任超过20%。太平再（中国）为风电、核电、水电、光伏等清洁能源项目提供总保额约50亿港元的保障；为新疆哈密伊州区天山乡的抽水蓄能电站工程项目提供再保险支持，装机容量120万千瓦，以220千伏电压接入新疆电网，工程投资82.3亿元，为稳定当地电网、风能光能消纳起到了重要作用，项目保额达61亿元。慕再为正泰新能源等领先光伏组件制造商提供质量保证、功率保证等再保险服务与保障，有效降低了产品召回时光伏组件制造商面临的财务风险，提高了国内光伏组件产品的可融资性以及整体竞争力。人保再积极保障国内以风电、核能为代表的清洁能源项目，五年来累计提供风险保额超过100亿元；人保再还为被誉为"北极圈上的能源明珠"的亚马尔天然气建设项目提供再保险保障支持，2018—2020年为整个项目累计提供风险保额超过22亿元。

（二）支持绿色交通与绿色建筑产业开拓创新

1．服务新能源汽车产业发展

新能源汽车的风险特征与传统燃油车有较大差异，传统车险产品难以满足新能源汽车消费者的需要。2021年12月，国内市场正式推出新能源汽车专属保险产品，在这一产品诞生的过程中，再保险行业发挥了重要作用。中再参与中国银保监会新能源车险费率测算项目，构建新能源汽车商业保险费率模型并完成项目测算；与中国汽研签署战略合作协议并建立联合车险实验室，建立远程安全数据交互环境，对千万级数据进行深度挖掘，目前已研发得出车辆电池热失控定价风控模型，并开始运用于业务实践。慕再通过提供完整的风险管理解决方案和再保险保障，支持新能源汽车专属保险的创新和落地，推动新能源车在民用和商用物流车队领域的应用与发展；同时通过调研前装自动驾驶技术和后装物联网风险管理技术，为车险市场提出创新型科技保险解决方案。瑞再设计推出新能源汽车延长保修责任保险产品，并于2021年发起新能源车动力电池修换理赔评估项目，引领行业内外共同探索电池故障、事故及自然灾害下的修换理赔规范，为理赔定损和产品定价工作提供参考。

2．提升城乡建设绿色低碳发展质量

在绿色建筑保险领域，再保险行业为多家直保公司提供专业再保技术及承保能力支持，为绿色建筑保险的高质量发展打下坚实基础。中再积极在绿色建筑领域开展相关产品的研究及创新工作，为政府、企业提供综合保险解决方案，积极推动搭建建筑业安责险平台和维修金平台，已为约1.5亿平方米建筑提供保险服务，截至2021年底已为湖州市约30万平方米绿色建筑提供6 000万元保额的风险保障，为北京市

约30万平方米高标准住宅提供4 000万元保额的风险保障。法再已启动专项课题积极跟进市场动态和客户需求,旨在为绿色建筑全生命周期提供专业的保险保障和增值服务,并推进后续研究成果转化。

(三)服务污染防治与生态文明建设

1. 深度参与多地环境污染责任保险项目顶层设计与制度建设

再保险行业承担环境污染责任保险的"先行者"和"推动者"的角色,积极助力国家环境污染治理体系建设。中再整合自身在数据分析、环境风险评估和精算技术等方面的专业优势,提升保险行业精准定价能力,积极推动环责险生态圈建设,与生态环境部政研中心、循环经济协会危废专委会、清华大学环境学院等环境监管、行业及技术方建立广泛联系,积极参与相关顶层政策设计和研讨,为北京、贵州、深圳、山西、大连等地环责险项目提供再保支持。法再积极承保突发意外污染的环责险业务,还调动整合在美国和欧洲责任险市场的承保经验和技术专家,开展渐进污染环责险承保、定价工具的研发,旨在为国家强制环责险的进一步推行和落地提供承保能力和技术支持。

2. 创新开发污染防治与环境保护相关保险产品

再保险行业发挥技术数据优势,助力保险行业创新开发污染防治与环境保护相关保险产品,为污染治理工作提供保险支持。2021年,中再自主创新开发了"污水处理系统"环保绿色责任险产品,支持智能远程污水处理检测系统的推广应用工作。为支持地方政府农业污染防治工作,2018年中再联合中国大地保险自主创新开发了"粪肥还田"环保绿色责任险产品,极大推进了粪肥施用项目落地实施,推动环境治理和生态农业同步发展。

四、再保险支持绿色保险发展趋势展望

一是再保险引领绿色保险产品创新。为满足绿色保险不断升级的新需求，再保险公司将充分利用自身数据技术优势，投入更多资源开发风险曲线、风险定价模型、巨灾风险管理模型等多种工具，充分将大数据、区块链、人工智能、遥感等新科技运用于定价风控、查勘理赔等环节，开拓清洁能源保险、储能保险、碳保险、天气保险、生物多样性保护保险等新业务领域，引领保险行业绿色保险产品创新趋势。

二是再保险为绿色保险承保能力提供有力支撑。绿色保险主要集中于非车险，分保需求比较旺盛，即使是车险领域的新能源车险，也因涉及较多新兴风险，分保需求较传统燃油车保险更强。再保行业能够通过合约、临分等传统再保险产品，以及创新的保险连接证券产品，为直保公司提供稳定的承保能力支撑，支持直保公司拓展绿色保险新领域。其中，利用保险连接证券为绿色保险产品分散风险的趋势在国际市场更加突出，目前除巨灾债券外，国际市场已出现ESG相关保险连接证券产品。

三是再保险机构携手产业端构建生态圈。为更好地发挥绿色保险产品创新与风险管理等独特作用，巩固既有的数据技术优势，挖掘新风险池，再保险机构正在越来越多地与绿色产业端直接建立合作关系，构建绿色产业生态圈，推动产业链和合作网络建设，升级经营模式与服务模式，除了与保险公司联合提供保险再保险服务，还联合相关专业机构提供风险预警、安全认证等风险减量管理服务，以打造风险综合解决方案。

四是再保险行业将在绿色保险国际合作中发挥不可或缺的重要作用。中国参与国际气候变化谈判以来，身份角色由积极参与者向积极引领者转变，对《巴黎协定》签署及COP26的成功召开均作出重大贡献。目前，参与气候变化全球治理的绿色保险国际合作机制仍以欧美保险机构为主导，未来，发展中国家保险机构将越来越多地参与到相关机制建设中。2020年6月，中再正式加入保险发展论坛（IDF）[①]，与其他保险机构一道推动保险及保险相关的风险知识服务于联合国可持续发展目标的实现，相信未来以中再为代表的中资再保险机构，将进一步发挥国际化优势，积极参与绿色保险国际机制建设，发出中国保险业的声音，增强中国在全球气候治理中的规则制定权和话语权，为人类命运共同体建设贡献力量。

---

① 保险发展论坛是由联合国国际减灾战略署（UNISDR）和国际保险学会（International Insurance Society）共同发起，于2016年由联合国、世界银行和相关保险机构正式成立的国际组织，旨在通过运用保险及相关风险管理能力，为个人和企业等遭遇巨灾导致的经济损失提供更有效的防护。中再集团是唯一一家参与IDF指导委员会的中国保险机构。

附录

中国再保险行业发展大事记

(1949—2021年)

附录

时间	类别	大事记
1949年10月	重大事件	中国人民保险公司在北京成立，专设海外业务室经营国际保险和再保险业务
1951年	重大赔案	"海后轮"事件，98%左右的损失从国际再保险市场摊回，为国家减轻了外汇补偿的负担
1963年	重大赔案	"跃进轮"事件，仅用65天即从伦敦市场摊回赔款（保额125万英镑，获赔104万英镑），为国家挽回83%的财产损失
1985年3月	重大制度	国务院颁布《保险企业管理暂行条例》，规定国内保险公司应当将其承保的保险业务按照规定比例办理再保险，国内由此进入到法定分保时期
1988年	市场要闻	中国人民保险公司开始办理国内再保险业务
1995年6月	重大制度	《中华人民共和国保险法》颁布，再保险第一次通过法律的形式得到了界定和规范，确立了再保险的行业地位
1996年8月	重大事件	中国人民保险公司拆分，新中国首家专业再保险公司中保再保险有限公司成立
1999年3月	市场要闻	在中保再保险公司的基础上，中国再保险公司成立
1999年9月	市场要闻	经原中国保险监督管理委员会批准，中国再保险公司牵头，与中国人民保险公司、中国太平洋保险公司、中国平安保险公司共同发起设立中国核保险共同体
2001年12月	重大事件	中国正式加入世界贸易组织（WTO），再保险市场向外资开放；根据承诺，法定分保比例逐年递减并于2006年取消
2002年9月	重大制度	原中国保监会发布《再保险公司设立规定》，明确了入世开放新格局下再保险公司设立的条件

时间	类别	大事记
2002年10月	重大制度	针对中国加入WTO对保险业的要求，对《中华人民共和国保险法》进行修正
2003年9月	市场要闻	瑞士再保险股份有限公司北京分公司成立
2003年10月	市场要闻	慕尼黑再保险公司北京分公司成立
2003年12月	市场要闻	中国再保险公司完成股份制改造，成立中国再保险（集团）公司
2004年1月	重大制度	原中国保监会发布《外国保险机构驻华代表机构管理办法》，加强对外国再保险机构驻华代表机构的管理
2004年7月	市场要闻	原德国科隆再保险股份有限公司上海分公司成立，后更名为通用再保险股份公司上海分公司
2005年10月	重大制度	原中国保监会发布《再保险业务管理规定》，这是国内第一部全面系统地规范再保险市场的法规
2005年12月	市场要闻	香港中国国际再保险有限公司设立北京代表处（已注销）
2006年7月	市场要闻	德国利富世再保险公司设立北京代表处，后更名为法国再保险全球人寿公司北京代表处（已注销）
2006年7月	重大制度	原中国保监会发布修订后的《外国保险机构驻华代表机构管理办法》
2006年11月	重大制度	原中国保监会发布《关于加强外资保险公司与关联企业从事再保险交易信息披露工作的通知》，提高了相关信息披露要求
2007年3月	市场要闻	劳合社再保险（中国）有限公司成立

时间	类别	大事记
2007年5月	市场要闻	中国人民财产保险股份有限公司、中华联合财产保险公司和安华农业保险股份有限公司等国内主要经营农业保险的保险公司共同与中国再保险集团公司签订了政策性农业再保险框架协议
2007年6月	重大制度	原中国保监会发布《中国再保险市场发展规划》，进一步明确了国内再保险市场的发展方向、预期目标和政策措施
2007年12月	市场要闻	百慕大博纳再保险有限责任公司设立北京代表处
2007年10月	市场要闻	中国再保险（集团）股份有限公司整体改制为股份公司
2007年11月	重大制度	原中国保监会发布《关于再保险业务安全性有关问题的通知》，细化对再保险接受人的要求，强化了对再保险业务的风险管理
2007年12月	重大制度	原中国保监会发布《再保险数据交换规范（JR/T 0036—2007）》，明确了再保公司与直保公司的数据交换原则
2008年3月	市场要闻	法国再保险公司北京分公司成立
2008年5月	重大赔案	四川省汶川县发生8.0级地震，截至2009年5月10日，保险业合计支付保险金16.6亿元
2008年5月	市场要闻	汉诺威再保险股份公司上海分公司成立
2008年9月	市场要闻	突尼斯伊盛再保险公司设立北京代表处（已注销）
2008年12月	市场要闻	中国国际再保险有限公司北京分公司成立，后更名为太平再保险有限公司北京分公司
2009年2月	重大制度	《中华人民共和国保险法》第二次修正
2009年4月	重大制度	原中国保监会发布《保险公司偿付能力报告编报规则第15号——再保险业务》及其实务指南，进一步完善了再保险偿付能力监管制度

时间	类别	大事记
2010年5月	重大制度	原中国保监会根据《保险法》修改情况修订《再保险业务管理规定》
2011年3月	市场要闻	信利保险（中国）有限公司成立
2012年1月	重大制度	原中国保监会发布《财产保险公司再保险管理规范》，首次对财产保险公司的再保险业务管理提出了明确的规范化要求
2012年9月	重大制度	原中国保监会发布《保险稽查审计指引第7号——再保险业务分册》，系统地提出了对再保险业务开展稽查审计工作的主要方法和实务操作规范
2013年9月	重大赔案	江苏无锡SK海力士半导体（中国）有限公司发生厂房爆炸事故，再保险人向保险人摊回赔款53亿元，约占保险赔付责任的97%
2014年9月	市场要闻	RGA美国再保险公司上海分公司成立
2014年11月	市场要闻	中国农业保险再保险共同体成立，这是中国农业保障体系建设的一次重大创新，标志着国内农业保险发展进入新阶段
2015年2月	重大制度	原中国保监会发布《保险公司偿付能力监管规则（1—17号）》，规范了再保险公司保险风险最低资本的计量要求
2015年3月	重大制度	原中国保监会发布《中国保监会关于实施再保险登记管理有关事项的通知》
2015年4月	市场要闻	在原中国保监会支持推动下，中国城乡居民住宅地震巨灾保险共同体正式成立，由41家财产直保公司和5家再保险公司共同组成，标志着国内巨灾保险制度建设迈出坚实一步
2015年4月	重大制度	原中国保监会发布《中国保监会关于加强保险公司再保险关联交易信息披露工作的通知》
2015年4月	重大制度	《中华人民共和国保险法》第三次修正
2015年7月	市场要闻	中再集团在百慕大成功发行以国内地震风险为保障对象的巨灾债券

时间	类别	大事记
2015年7月	市场要闻	全国首家再保险经纪公司江泰再保险经纪有限公司成立
2015年8月	重大赔案	天津市滨海新区天津港的瑞海公司危险品仓库发生火灾爆炸事故,再保险人向保险人摊回赔款81.3亿元,约占保险赔付责任的83%
2015年10月	市场要闻	中国再保险(集团)股份有限公司在中国香港上市
2015年10月	重大制度	原中国保监会根据行政审批制度改革要求修订《再保险业务管理规定》
2015年12月	市场要闻	美国奥德赛再保险公司设立北京代表处
2015年12月	市场要闻	太平再保险有限公司北京分公司改建为太平再保险(中国)有限公司
2016年2月	市场要闻	西班牙曼福再保险公司设立北京代表处
2016年11月	重大制度	原中国保监会发布《再保险数据交换规范(JR/T 0036—2016)》
2016年12月	市场要闻	前海再保险股份有限公司成立
2017年2月	市场要闻	人保再保险股份有限公司成立
2017年6月	市场要闻	英国佰仕富人寿再保险有限公司设立上海代表处
2017年12月	重大制度	中国保险行业协会发布再保险业首批团体标准《人寿比例再保险合同规范》和《人寿巨灾超赔再保险合同规范》,这是中国保险业首次以团体标准的形式对合同文本进行规范
2018年2月	重大制度	中国保险行业协会发布《财产再保险临时分保业务操作指引》和《财产再保险合约分保业务操作指引》,这是财产再保险领域第一批团体标准
2018年2月	市场要闻	上海保险业完成国内首个再保险区块链技术应用实验
2018年12月	市场要闻	中国再保险(集团)股份有限公司成功收购英国桥社保险集团

时间	类别	大事记
2019年4月	市场要闻	太平再保险（中国）有限公司上海分公司成立
2020年1月	市场要闻	大韩再保险公司上海分公司成立
2020年6月	重大制度	中国保险行业协会发布《财产再保险合同行业范本——比例合约》和《财产再保险合同范本——非比例合约》，并于2021年11月10日发布中文版，减少了因对再保险合同理解差异而引发的合同纠纷
2020年7月	重大制度	中国银保监会发布《财产保险公司、再保险公司监管主体职责改革方案》，落实了监管主体责任，完善再保险公司监管工作体制机制
2020年7月	市场要闻	中国"一带一路"再保险共同体成立，标志着保险业高质量服务"一带一路"迈出了坚实的一步
2020年12月	市场要闻	中国农业再保险股份有限公司成立
2020年7月	市场要闻	信利保险（中国）有限公司变更为信利再保险（中国）有限公司，成为首家外资再保险法人机构
2021年6月	市场要闻	中再集团旗下桥社牵头设立劳合社"一带一路"政治暴力险共保体
2021年7月	重大赔案	河南中北部发生特大暴雨，保险业损失估计约为124亿元
2021年7月	重大制度	中国银保监会修订《再保险业务管理规定》
2021年8月	重大制度	中国银保监会发布《中国银保监会 上海市人民政府关于推进上海国际再保险中心建设的指导意见》，推进上海国际再保险中心建设
2021年10月	市场要闻	中再集团旗下中再产险在中国香港成功发行首只粤港澳大湾区巨灾债券
2021年10月	市场要闻	中国集成电路共保体成立，为国家集成电路产业高质量发展提供保障，中再产险作为首届理事会中唯一的再保险公司参与发起

后　记

再保险是"保险的保险",在应对全球气候变化、保障国家金融安全、完善社会治理体系、分散经济运行风险等方面都具有独特作用。中再集团是中央金融企业,与中华人民共和国同生共长,勇担中国再保险行业主力军、中国保险市场风险分散主渠道和中国保险企业走出去先行者。

2021年9月29日,中再集团在承办的首届北京国际再保险高峰论坛上正式揭牌成立中国再保险研究院,旨在打造"聚焦再保、深耕中国、纵览全球、开放共享"的行业一流再保险风险管理智库。在中国银保监会和中国保险行业协会指导下,在国内保险和再保险同业支持下,中国再保险研究院聚合中再系统力量组织编写了首份《中国再保险行业发展报告（2022）》。

本报告在编写过程中,始终得到中国银保监会财产保险监管部（再保险监管部）李有祥主任的悉心指导,在此致以诚挚的谢意!

本报告出版发行,离不开所有编写人员的辛勤付出。撰写人员分别是:第一章马晓静、何占峰、任复兴、顾飞,第二章孙涛、彭昕宇,第三章李非、金笑权,第四章薛源、刘爽,第五章郑利娜、范令箭,四个专题和大事记史鑫蕊、马晓静、傅若兰、周俊华、李超、窦健。马晓静、史鑫蕊负责中文版统稿,王少康、寿振炜负责英文版审校。此外,柳桉、常春、刘国乾、方春银对报告编写提出了专业意见。

本报告出版发行，离不开中国保险和再保险行业相关单位领导和专家同仁的大力支持。感谢中国银保监会财产保险监管部（再保险监管部）再保险公司监管处王君、金学群、郑琬冬，在报告体例框架、监管内容把关等方面的指导！感谢中国保险行业协会统计研究部尹博、付盛麟，在行业调研安排和意见征求等方面的协调！感谢中国农再、人保再、太平再、前海再四家中资再保险公司以及瑞再、慕再、法再、汉再、美国再、通用再、大韩再等在华机构，提供报告编写基础素材并在行业报告研讨会上反馈专业意见。

万事开头难，本报告填补行业空白，虽经数易其稿，也有多方把关，但尚有诸多不足，恳请大家指正！

一起向未来，衷心期待与各方携手，持续做好报告编写工作，用文字记录中国再保险行业高质量发展的绚丽篇章！

中国再保险（集团）股份有限公司

2022年12月

Appendix   Major Events in the Development of China's Reinsurance Industry (1949—2021)

Time	Category	Events
December 2020	Market news	China Agriculture Reinsurance Corporation was established.
July 2020	Market news	XL Insurance (China) Company Limited was transformed into XL Reinsurance (China) Company Limited, the first foreign reinsurance corporation (artificial person).
June 2021	Market news	Chaucer, a subsidiary of China Re Group, took the lead in setting up Lloyd's BRI political violence insurance pool.
July 2021	Major claim	An extraordinary rainstorm hit central and northern Henan, and the loss of the insurance industry was estimated at about RMB 12.4 billion.
July 2021	Important regulation	The CBIRC revised the *Regulations on the Administration of the Reinsurance Business*.
August 2021	Important regulation	The CBIRC issued the *Guiding Opinions of the CBIRC and Shanghai Municipal People's Government on Promoting the Construction of Shanghai International Reinsurance Center* to promote the construction of Shanghai as an international reinsurance hub.
October 2021	Market news	China Re P&C, a subsidiary of China Re Group Corp, issued the first GBA catastrophe bond in Hong Kong.
October 2021	Market news	China IC Reinsurance Pool was founded to safeguard the high-quality development of the national IC industry. As the only reinsurance company in the first council, China Re P&C participated in the founding of the pool.

Time	Category	Events
June 2017	Market news	Pacific Life Reinsurance Limited set up its representative office in Shanghai.
December 2017	Important regulation	The Insurance Association of China issued the first group standards of the reinsurance industry, that is, the *Norms for Life Proportional Reinsurance Contracts* and the *Norms for Life Catastrophe Overcompensation Reinsurance Contracts*. This is the first time that the Chinese insurance industry has standardized the contract text in the form of group standards.
February 2018	Important regulation	The Insurance Association of China issued the *Operational Guidelines for Temporary Reinsurance of Property Reinsurance* and the *Operational Guidelines for Reinsurance of Property Reinsurance Contracts*, the first batch of group standards in the field of property reinsurance.
February 2018	Market news	The insurance industry in Shanghai completed the first experiment as to the application of reinsurance blockchain technology in China.
December 2018	Market news	China Re Group Corp successfully purchased Chaucer Group.
April 2019	Market news	Taiping Reinsurance (China) Company Limited set up its branch in Shanghai.
January 2020	Market news	Korean Reinsurance Company set up its branch in Shanghai.
June 2020	Important regulation	The Insurance Association of China issued the *Model of Property Reinsurance Contract: Proportional Contract* and *Model Property Reinsurance Contract: Non-proportional Contract* and published the Chinese versions on November 10, 2021, which reduced contract disputes caused by different understandings of reinsurance contracts.
July 2020	Important regulation	The China Banking and Insurance Regulatory Commission (CBIRC) issued the *Reform Plan for the Responsibilities of Regulators of Property Insurance Companies and Reinsurance Companies*, which specified the responsibilities of regulators and improved the regulatory system and mechanism of reinsurance companies.
July 2020	Market news	China's Belt and Road Initiative (BRI) Reinsurance Pool was founded, paving the way for the insurance industry to provide BRI with high-quality services.

Appendix Major Events in the Development of China's Reinsurance Industry (1949—2021)

Time	Category	Events
April 2015	Market news	With the support of the former CIRC, the China Urban and Rural Residential Earthquake Catastrophe Insurance Community was officially founded, composed of 41 property primary insurance companies and five reinsurance companies, marking a solid step in the construction of a domestic catastrophe insurance system.
April 2015	Important regulation	The former CIRC issued the *Notice of China Insurance Regulatory Commission on Strengthening the Information Disclosure of Connected Reinsurance Transactions of Insurance Companies*.
April 2015	Important regulation	Third amendment of the *Insurance Law of the People's Republic of China*.
July 2015	Market news	China Re Group successfully issued domestic earthquake risk catastrophe bonds abroad.
July 2015	Market news	Jiang Tai Reinsurance Brokers Limited, the first reinsurance brokerage company in China, was established.
August 2015	Major claim	A fire and explosion occurred at Ruihai International Logistics Company Limited's hazardous articles warehouse in Tianjin Port, Tianjin Binhai New Area. The reinsurer paid RMB 8.13 billion to the insurer, which was about 83% of the liability for the insurance indemnity.
October 2015	Market news	China Reinsurance (Group) Corporation was listed in Hong Kong.
October 2015	Important regulation	The former CIRC revised the *Regulations on the Management of the Reinsurance Business* in accordance with the requirements of the reform of the administrative authorization system.
December 2015	Market news	Odyssey Reinsurance Holdings Corporation set up its representative office in Beijing.
December 2015	Market news	Taiping Reinsurance Company Limited Beijing Branch was transformed into Taiping Reinsurance (China) Company Limited.
February 2016	Market news	MAPFRE S.A. set up its representative office in Beijing.
November 2016	Important regulation	The former CIRC issued the *Norms for Reinsurance Data Exchange (JR/T 0036—2016)*.
December 2016	Market news	Qianhai Reinsurance Company Limited was established.
February 2017	Market news	PICC Reinsurance Company Limited was established.

Time	Category	Events
April 2009	Important regulation	The former CIRC issued the *Reporting Rules for Insurance Company's Solvency Report No. 15: Reinsurance Business* and its practical guide, further improving the reinsurance solvency regulation system.
May 2010	Important regulation	The former CIRC revised the *Regulations on the Administration of the Reinsurance Business* according to the amendment of the *Insurance Law of the People's Republic of China*.
March 2011	Market news	XL Insurance (China) Company Limited was established.
January 2012	Important regulation	The former CIRC issued the *Regulations on Reinsurance Management of Property Insurance Companies*, which put forward clear and standardized requirements for the reinsurance business management of property insurance companies for the first time.
September 2012	Important regulation	The former CIRC issued the *Guidelines for Insurance Inspection and Auditing No. 7: Reinsurance Business*, which systematically put forward the main methods and practical operating standards for the inspection and audit of the reinsurance business.
September 2013	Major claim	An explosion happened to a factory of SK Hynix Semiconductor (China) Company Limited in Jiangsu and the reinsurer paid RMB 5.3 billion to the insurer, which accounted for about 97% of the liability for the insurance indemnity.
September 2014	Market news	Reinsurance Group of America, Incorporated set up its branch in Shanghai.
November 2014	Market news	The China Agricultural Insurance Pool was founded, which is a major innovation in the construction of China's agricultural protection system, indicating that the development of domestic agricultural insurance has entered a new phase.
February 2015	Important regulation	The former CIRC issued the *Rules for Regulation of Insurance Company Solvency (No.1-No.17)*, which standardized the measurement requirements for the minimum insurance risk capital of reinsurance companies.
March 2015	Important regulation	The former CIRC issued the *Notice of China Insurance Regulatory Commission on the Implementation of Reinsurance Registration Management*.

Appendix   Major Events in the Development of China's Reinsurance Industry (1949—2021)

Time	Category	Events
March 2007	Market news	Lloyd's Insurance Company (China) Limited was established.
May 2007	Market news	PICC Property and Casualty Company Limited, China United Property Insurance Company Limited, Anhua Agricultural Insurance Company Limited, and other large domestic insurance companies engaged in agricultural insurance signed a policy-oriented agricultural reinsurance framework agreement with China Re Group.
June 2007	Important regulation	The former CIRC issued the *Development Plan of China Reinsurance Market*, which further specified the development direction, expected objectives, and policy options of the domestic reinsurance market.
December 2007	Market news	Partner Reinsurance Company Limited set up its representative office in Beijing.
October 2007	Market news	China Re Group was restructured into a joint-stock company.
November 2007	Important regulation	The former CIRC issued the *Notice on Issues Related to the Security of Reinsurance Business*, which detailed the requirements for reinsurance recipients and strengthened the risk management of the reinsurance business.
December 2007	Important regulation	The former CIRC issued the *Norms for Reinsurance Data Exchange (JR/T 0036—2007)*, which specified the principles of data exchange between reinsurance companies and primary insurance companies.
March 2008	Market news	SCOR SE set up its branch in Beijing.
May 2008	Major claim	An 8.0-magnitude earthquake struck Wenchuan County, Sichuan Province. As of May 10, 2009, the insurance industry had paid a total of RMB 1.66 billion in insurance claims.
May 2008	Market news	Hannover Re set up its branch in Shanghai.
September 2008	Market news	Best Re set up its representative office in Beijing (now closed).
December 2008	Market news	China International Reinsurance Company Limited set up its branch in Beijing, later renamed Taiping Reinsurance Company Limited Beijing Branch.
February 2009	Important regulation	Second amendment to the *Insurance Law of the People's Republic of China*.

Time	Category	Events
September 2002	Important regulation	The former CIRC issued the *Regulations on the Establishment of Reinsurance Companies*, which specified the conditions for establishing reinsurance companies under the new pattern of China's entry into the WTO.
October 2002	Important regulation	Based on the requirements of China's entry into the WTO for the insurance industry, the *Insurance Law of the People's Republic of China* was amended.
September 2003	Market news	Swiss Reinsurance Company Limited set up its branch in Beijing.
October 2003	Market news	Munich Reinsurance Group set up its branch in Beijing.
December 2003	Market news	China Re Corp. completed the reform of its shareholding system, and China Reinsurance (Group) Company ("China Re Group") was established.
January 2004	Important regulation	The former CIRC issued the *Measures for the Administration of Representative Offices of Foreign Insurance Institutions in China* to strengthen the management of representative offices of foreign reinsurance institutions in China.
July 2004	Market news	The former Cologne Reinsurance Company set up its branch in Shanghai, later renamed General Reinsurance Corporation Shanghai Branch.
October 2005	Important regulation	The former CIRC issued the *Regulations on the Management of Reinsurance Business*, the first comprehensive and systematic regulation of the reinsurance market in China.
December 2005	Market news	China International Reinsurance Company Limited in Hong Kong set up its representative office in Beijing (now canceled).
July 2006	Market news	RRAG set up its representative office in Beijing, later renamed SCOR Global Life SE Beijing Representative Office (now canceled).
July 2006	Important regulation	The former CIRC issued the revised *Measures for Administration of Representative Offices of Foreign Insurance Institutions in China*.
November 2006	Important regulation	The former CIRC issued the *Notice on Strengthening the Information Disclosure of Foreign-Insurance Companies and Connected Enterprises in Reinsurance Transactions*, which set higher requirements for information disclosure.

Appendix Major Events in the Development of China's Reinsurance Industry (1949—2021)

Time	Category	Events
October 1949	Major event	The People's Insurance Company of China was established in Beijing with an overseas business office dedicated to international insurance and reinsurance business.
1951	Major claim	In the Haihou Ship incident, the international reinsurance market recovered approximately 98% of the losses, which reduced the country's burden of foreign exchange compensation.
1963	Major claim	In the Yuejin Ship incident, it took only 65 days to recover the indemnity from the London market (the sum insured was 1.25 million pounds, and the indemnity was 1.04 million pounds), which recovered 83% of the country's property losses.
March 1985	Important regulation	The State Council issued the *Provisional Regulations on the Administration of Insurance Enterprises*, which stipulated that domestic insurance companies should cede their insurance business in accordance with the prescribed proportion, marking China's entry into the statutory reinsurance era.
1988	Market news	The People's Insurance Company of China (PICC) started underwriting the domestic reinsurance business.
June 1995	Important regulation	*The Insurance Law of the People's Republic of China* was promulgated, and reinsurance was legally specified and regulated for the first time, establishing reinsurance's industry status.
August 1996	Major event	The PICC was divided, and the People's Insurance Company of China Reinsurance Co., Ltd. ("PICC Re") was established as the first professional reinsurance company in China.
March 1999	Market news	On the basis of PICC Re, China Reinsurance Corporation ("China Re Corp.") was established.
September 1999	Market news	With the approval of the former China Insurance Regulatory Commission (CRIC), China Re Corp. took the lead and jointly initiated the founding of the China Nuclear Insurance Pool with PICC, China Pacific Insurance Company, and Ping An Insurance Company.
December 2001	Major event	China officially joined the World Trade Organization (WTO), and foreign investment was permitted in the reinsurance market. According to the commitment, the statutory reinsurance share decreased year-by-year and was terminated in 2006.

Appendix

Appendix

Major Events in the Development of China's Reinsurance Industry

(1949—2021)

of the reinsurance business, attach importance to effective regulation of overseas reinsurance, focus on guarding against cross-border transmission of financial risks, and continue to be open to the outside world to better participate in international cooperation and competition in the profound adjustment of the global political and economic landscapes.

Fifth, the system will proactively respond to the current frequency of extreme weather events across the world, bolster the cooperative development of the reinsurance industry and the capital market, assist in the diversification of insurance risks throughout the capital market via innovation in financial products such as catastrophe bonds, and improve the ability to protect against catastrophe risks.

adapt to the market development and promote the high-quality development of the reinsurance industry.

First, the system will continue to serve the real economy, focus on major national strategies, and provide high-quality risk protections and insurance services for the global scientific and technological frontiers, the main economic arenas, prioritized national needs and people's life and health. It will give full play to the functions of reinsurance as an economic "shock absorber" and "social stabilizer".

Second, the system will further foster the innovative and leading role of reinsurance, both in risk management and capital management, and in products and technologies, and enhance the underwriting capacity for large risks and special risks in the fields of electronic information, advanced manufacturing, biomedicine, modern agriculture, smart transportation, new energy, aerospace and other prioritized national projects, and the transformation and application of major national achievements in scientific and technological research, which lays a solid foundation for in-depth participation and leading of China's reinsurance industry in the global risk governance.

Third, the system will pay more attention to the characteristics of the reintegration business and its difference from primary insurance, gradually establish and improve a more independent supervision system that suits the characteristics of reinsurance, to ensure that the reinsurance business is carried out in accordance with the law and the reinsurance market is kept in good order and improve the efficiency of reinsurance transactions.

Fourth, the system will further eye the international characteristics the development potential of the Chinese market in the future and actively explore the business opportunities of related lines as they expedite the implementation of major prioritized national strategies such as "Carbon Peaking and Carbon Neutrality" goals, Green Finance, Rural Revitalization, Health China Initiative, and addressing the aging issue. Second, foreign reinsurance companies have been operating in the international market for many years, and they have mature product lines and are experienced in the development of innovative products, and they can provide a variety of customized risk solutions for domestic customers, to further improve their capabilities of serving customers in Chinese market. Third, foreign reinsurance companies are ahead of their counterparts in digital transformation and have basically conducted online and intelligent business. In the future, they will continue to integrate digitalization into customer business scenarios in all aspects to further better customer experience. Fourth, foreign reinsurance companies attach great importance to cooperation with governments and professional institutions, and place much emphasis on investing in health insurance, agricultural insurance and liability insurance and providing professional services in such fields as medical care, agriculture, rural areas and farmers, environmental pollution, and food safety that Chinese governments are concentrating on.

V. Prospects of the Regulation Trend of the Reinsurance Industry

With the gradual development of China's reinsurance industry, the reinsurance regulation system is constantly being optimized and improved to to death rates, incidence rates, and lifestyles of the insured despite the growing demand for some life products in the context of the aging issue. China's life reinsurance business has long been confronted with challenges.

(II) Prospect

In terms of the overall strategy of foreign reinsurance companies in China:

The medium and long-term development strategies of foreign reinsurance companies in the Chinese market have certain similarities. First, they insist on making a long-term investment in the Chinese market. Foreign reinsurance companies are generally optimistic about the tremendous development potentials of the Chinese market in the medium and long term and make a long-term sustained investment based on the concept of "long-termism". Second, they generally increase their capital investment in the Chinese market. From 2019 to 2021, foreign reinsurance companies increased their capital by a total of RMB 3.67 billion in their Chinese branches, far exceeding the capital supplement of Chinese reinsurance companies in the same period. After the capital addition, foreign reinsurance companies have all maintained a high solvency adequacy level, leaving more room for them to explore markets, expand their business, and hire more employees. Third, they continuously make full use of internal retrocession to balance business development and capital efficiency and increase their competitive competence.

In terms of the business strategies of foreign reinsurance companies in China:

First, foreign reinsurance companies will continuously pay attention to rate unsurpassed in other markets and can sustain a higher growth rate in two or three decades to come. Second, the Chinese market continues to be open to the outside world, with a friendly regulatory environment. In recent years, China has kept opening wider. From 2018 to 2019, China Banking and Insurance Regulatory Commission successively introduced 14 measures for opening up pertinent to the insurance industry, including loosening and abolishing the restrictions on foreign-invested companies' shareholding ratio, loosening the restrictions on total assets, operating years and shareholder qualifications of those foreign-invested institutions and encouraging foreign-invested companies with distinctive and professional characteristics to enter the Chinese market to bolster the overall high-quality development of the industry. Meanwhile, China's market has strongly supported the insurance industry and foreign-invested insurance companies, and can provide them with incomparable national treatment and stable policy expectations, which is almost unseen in other emerging markets.

Challenges: First, due to insufficient rates, poor underwriting quality of commercial property insurance, and increasingly frequent extreme weather, the property insurance contract business of foreign-invested reinsurance companies in China underperformed, and a package of Quota Share Reinsurance Treaties' profit margin has diluted by factors such as comprehensive motor insurance reform, excessive competition, the founding of China Agriculture Re, and participation of offshore reinsurers. Some foreign-invested reinsurance companies have suffered underwriting losses in recent years. Second, due to the impacts of inflation and demographic changes, the traditional model may not be applicable to assumptions relevant enrich the big data storage of the health sector, actively carry out data fusion and co-creation projects and accelerate cross-border data concentration, desensitization and sharing. Third, they will strengthen technological advantages and improve core technologies such as risk modeling, actuarial pricing, and risk assessment. They will also combine technical research with data analyses to enhance accurate underwriting and pricing capabilities, deeply understand the effects of advances in medical technologies, accurately divide responsibilities, define and classify diseases, gain insight into claims trends, thereby improving business tracking and quality testing. In the future, life reinsurance companies will further concentrate on making the best of product innovation and data advantages, improving their own expertise and service, boosting the development of health insurance, driving business growth, expanding their own strategic distribution, and fostering their own core competence.

IV. Prospects of Development of Foreign Reinsurance Companies in China

With the deepening insight into the Chinese market and the rising strategic status of the Chinese market, foreign reinsurance companies are optimistic about the future development of the Chinese market.

(I) Opportunities and Challenges

Opportunities: First, China's reinsurance market turns out to be a tremendous market with sustainable development potential. After years of rapid development, China's reinsurance market has maintained a growth insurance. In other reinsurance business, it is necessary to fully consider the impact of IFRS17 and C-ROSS Phase II and continuously formulate comprehensive solutions to improving the efficiency of capital use and enriching the means of serving clients. Moreover, it is necessary to further improve the ability to match assets with liabilities and to be competent in countercyclical management. In the future, the short-term challenge of life insurance will be transferred to the reinsurance market, and the life insurance companies' reinsurance demand is expected to fluctuate with the rapid development of traditional and non-traditional business.

(III) Prospects for changes in underwriting strategies of professional reinsurance companies

On the supply side, life reinsurance companies will vigorously implement the Health China strategy and steadfastly promote the innovation and development of health insurance to cater to people's livelihood. First, they will give full play to product advantages and push forward supply-side reform, fully demonstrate the role of life reinsurance as an engine in the field of life insurance product innovation, and start from the principle "based on the entire population and the full life cycle" proposed in the Health China strategy to continuously make sweeping efforts to meet the people's yearning for a better life and fill the gap in the domestic medical care system. Second, they will create data advantages, keep pace with the times to meet the demands of the digital era, promote the standardization of internal data, and enhance data security and circulation efficiency. They will also select segmentation scenarios such as medicine and medical services to is restricted, and business expansion and team building are confronted with some difficulties. In 2021, there were 6.419 million domestic agents in China, decreasing from 8.428 million at the end of the previous year to 2.521 million, which is down nearly 30% year-on-year, putting pressure on the reinsurance business. Third, the new detection technology has greatly improved the detection rate of diseases, which poses challenges for the critical illness insurance business based on past experience with pricing. Long-term medical insurance also resulted in greater uncertainties in their own operations.

(II) Prospects for the Changes in Demand for Reinsurance

On the demand side, health insurance is an essential source of growth for life insurance in traditional business and faces challenges in the short term. Since its inception in 2013, health insurance has earned more than RMB 840 billion in premiums, with an average annual growth rate of 32.8%. The proportion of commercial health insurance in the life insurance business has been increasing year by year, reaching 25.4% in 2021, becoming the main driving force for the growth of the life insurance market. Besides, health insurance products play an irreplaceable role in the insurance companies' product line. Critical illness insurance is the traditional "safety product" (i.e., the most basic profitable product) of the agent channel, and is also the main tool to stabilize the agent team. The Million Medical Insurance has become the most important product for agents to secure clients and for popular Internet platforms to turn their traffic into cash. Meanwhile, *huiminbao* is a successful model for integrating medical insurance into commercial

Reinsurance can provide vital support and play a leading role in product innovation and risk management. Second, against the background of industrial channel upgrade and supply-side reform of products and services, insurance companies' demand for comprehensive services from reinsurance companies in data, products, services, sales support and other aspects has continued to increase, and the value output of reinsurance in new risk definition, product development, as well as risk pricing and management has become increasingly important. Third, in the practice of integrating the insurance industry into the health industry, the market urgently needs reinsurance companies to rely on their own professionally neutral position to connect all parts of the service chain and provide product-based operational support. Fourth, completing the insurance industry's infrastructures, such as critical illness tables, accident tables, and life tables, requires reinsurance to give full play to the advantages of data and technologies and contribute to the overall development of the industry. Fifth, under C-ROSS Phase II, the solvency of insurance companies, in general, has declined while the reinsurance demand has increased, which implies certain business opportunities.

In terms of challenges: First, the macro-economy is faced with triple pressures, and the financial environment tends to be more intricate. In terms of interest rate, the long-term interest rate showed a downward trend in 2021. In terms of investment, the volatility of the stock market and bond market increased. Second, the primary insurance industry has been up against increasing pressure to transform itself. Due to the ongoing impacts of the COVID-19 pandemic, the insurance companies' offline business frequency of non-model catastrophes and severe inflation, the headquarters of international reinsurance companies generally require themselves to reduce the release of underwriting capacities for the catastrophe reinsurance business.

Concerned about the impact of price competition at the primary insurance on the adequacy of risk pricing, reinsurers are partially tightening underwriting conditions to control risk exposure. First, the market situation tends to be complicated due to several factors, such as the comprehensive reform of motor insurance and the implementation of C-ROSS Phase II. Second, the catastrophe losses are high, and the market has suffered from the heavy rain and flood disasters in Henan and a series of large claims losses. Third, affected by price competition in the primary insurance market, the underpricing of the primary insurance business is common, further putting the underwriting profits of reinsurers under pressure.

III. Prospects of Life Reinsurance Development

(I) Opportunities and Challenges

In terms of opportunities: First, the implementation of national strategies, such as Health China, Rural Revitalization, and Belt and Road Initiative, has made increased demand for innovative insurance products such as "*huiminbao*"[①], rare disease insurance, and anti-poverty insurance.

[①] "Huiminbao", also known as urban customized commercial medical insurance, has the characteristics of low price, low threshold and high security, which effectively makes up for the gap of multi-level medical security system.

insurance, reinsurance companies have stepped up their participation in risk research and product R&D in emerging fields, which has further boosted the transition from risk diversification demand to reinsurance business collaboration in the supply side.

(III) Prospects for Changes in Underwriting Strategies of Professional Reinsurance Companies

Overall, the reinsurance market's underwriting capacity is in short supply, and the conditions of insurance quotes are increasingly stringent. The property reinsurance market will remain to be stable but rigorous, and reinsurers will pay more attention to risk consideration. Strictly controlling the accumulated responsibilities for natural catastrophes, the risk exposure in some specific areas, and the further release of excessive underwriting capacities remains to be the common demand of the mainstream reinsurance market.

Offshore reinsurers continue to transfer their underwriting capacities to countries and regions where prices increase sharply, thereby somewhat reducing the attractiveness of the Chinese market. First, the catastrophe losses have taken on a high-frequency and high-loss trend in recent years, coupled with the impacts of massive catastrophes such as the winter storms and Hurricane Ida in the US, as well as the floods in European countries, which have continuously eroded the underwriting profits of the international reinsurance market. Second, there is limited growth in reinsurance capital supplies, and the continuous loss forces reinsurers to raise prices, shrink their underwriting capacities, and choose the best option. Third, due to the catastrophe risks and the smoothing of business fluctuations are the main tasks for reinsurance arrangements. First, the overall reinsurance rate of traditional insurance is kept within an appropriate range. Second, property insurance companies can, to a certain extent, accept the market's reasonable adjustment of reinsurance contract terms. Third, in the reinsurance arrangement to protect EXL treaties, the property insurance companies can raise the expense budget to a certain extent to ensure that they can obtain full risk protections during hard markets.

In terms of emerging insurance and innovative products, demand for reinsurance cession from property insurance companies remains high. First, the rapid development of emerging strategic industries has stimulated demand for risk protection. In recent years, emerging industries such as integrated circuits and offshore wind energy have developed rapidly, and the demand for risk protections and relevant reinsurance protections is high. Second, the policy-supported insurance business has developed rapidly, driving up the reinsurance demand. This business is represented by Inherent Defect Insurance (IDI) which enhances the quality of buildings, the project performance guarantee insurance which replaces the security deposit by insurance and thus reduces the cost of enterprises, the mid-range health insurance which serves the Health China strategy, the urban affordable health insurance, etc. and they all maintain a high reinsurance rate. Third, reinsurance companies are more active in outputting data and expertise and collaborating with primary insurance companies to develop innovative insurance products and risk solutions. In terms of insurance related to new energy vehicles and industrial chains, cyber insurance and other types of challenges. Reinsurance companies will collaborate more actively with primary insurance companies to conduct risk research and risk reduction management to manage risks and improve underwriting performance. Second, non-motor insurance is still in the incremental market stage. Large insurance companies willing to comprehensively transform into business models of customer groups are expected to expedite research and application of innovative products and maintain strong demand for reinsurance in the fields of emerging insurance and innovative products. Third, there is a rapid increase in the amount of business as to policy-supported insurance, government administration scenarios, and personal line insurance. It has become a consensus to control risks and continuously improve underwriting performance, and reinsurance protection is indispensable.

In terms of challenges, first, the catastrophe loss brought by the extreme weather has been exacerbated, the accumulated risks of the reinsurance are obvious, and the catastrophe loss is faced with the risk of significant volatility. Second, the demand for reinsurance, both in emerging risks and innovation, has risen sharply, and the reinsurers' underwriting pricing is encountering great uncertainties. Third, due to price competition in the primary insurance market, it is common for the insurance business to be undervalued, which puts greater pressure on the reinsurers' underwriting profits.

(II) Prospects for the Changes in Demand for Reinsurance Cession From Property Insurance Companies

In terms of traditional insurance, demand for reinsurance cession from property insurance companies is generally stable. The diversification of technologies, and drive innovation of green insurance products such as new energy vehicles, weather risks, and forest carbon sinks. It will also speed up the innovation of commercial agricultural insurance products and proactively promote the development of innovative agricultural insurance products such as index insurance, price insurance, and agriculture-related insurance; encourage innovation of science and technology insurance products and service in emerging fields such as integrated circuits, software quality, and intellectual property rights; develop and promote new liability insurance products and solutions for the new social governance needs. In terms of life reinsurance, it will focus on serving the strategy to build a Health China and addressing the aging issue, driving product innovation in fields including healthcare, nursing, and medical devices, proactively serving the third pillar of pension insurance, integrating high-quality health management service resources, and boost the transformation and modernization of the insurance industry by way of product innovations.

II. Prospects of P&C Reinsurance Development

(I) Opportunities and Challenges

In terms of opportunities, first, the comprehensive reform of motor insurance reshapes the industry's business models. The market gradually absorbed the adverse impacts of the decline in premium scale, followed by pressure from underwriting earnings. In terms of segmentation, exclusive insurance for new energy vehicles takes the lead in breaking the ice, but the slogan, namely "High growth means high claims" exacerbates the technical and capital strengths, reinsurance will transform from a pure provider with underwriting capacity to a wholesaler offering a package of new risk management products and a comprehensive provider of capital and technologies, and function as the intermediary for the capital market, drive the transfer of reinsurance value chain to supply chain, channel, and customer value chain, and capture high points of the value chain. Collaborations with government organs, insurance companies, science and technology platforms, and other organizations will be deepened, an ecosystem featuring reinsurance will be built, industrial chains and cooperation networks will be constructed with sweeping efforts, and business models and service models will be upgraded. Besides, reinsurance's functions like risk management and technology transmission will be strengthened, and the coverage and penetration of reinsurance in the primary insurance market will also be improved to play a greater role in promoting the healthy development of the insurance market. The reinsurance industry will give full play to its professional advantages in data, technology, and talents, strengthen the R&D of business models, and leverage product innovation as a breakthrough to provide more comprehensive insurance protections for property loss and life health, particularly for a wide range of emerging risks, such as insurance for intangible assets (e.g., patents, data, and algorithms), insurance specially designed for the Belt and Road Initiative, such as terrorism risk insurance and political violence risk insurance, and various innovative products such as catastrophe insurance, cyber insurance, and special risk insurance. In terms of property reinsurance, it will conduct more risk research related to new energy, green buildings, and carbon reduction global natural disasters caused by climate change are frequent, the COVID-19 pandemic remains resurgent, the international situation is complex, and the insurance industry is stepping into the most challenging phase. Due to the factors above, the volatility of reinsurance operations will increase significantly, which has placed higher requirements on the reinsurance industry's ability to operate prudently as well as its risk management and control ability.

Second, serving the real economy will become a key focus of the reinsurance industry's mid- and long-term development. At present, China's economy is transitioning from the rapid growth phase to the high-quality development phase. As an important "safety valve" and "stabilizer", reinsurance will innovate and expand business opportunities by safeguarding the development of the real economy. In the process of stepping up efforts to implement key national strategies such as carbon neutrality, rural revitalization, empowering the country through science and technology, building a Health China, addressing the aging issue, and in the process of expanding the size of the middle-income group, and raising the public's awareness of insurance, reinsurance can leverage its distinctive advantages in expertise, resources and talents to explore new strategic opportunities and business increments through serving our national strategies and engaging in national governance and social services.

Third, reinsurance will give full play to its value in the insurance industry chain by focusing on innovation. Reinsurance will gradually adapt to the expansion of its functions in underwriting catastrophe risks, adapt to the new situation of fierce global competition, and expedite technological innovation and business model innovation. Based on enhancing its the agent's capacity will continue to expand, and the product margin will be basically stable. After achieving business goals in the short term of this year, the life insurance companies have paid more attention to medium-and long-term transformation and reform. The health and pension insurance markets will be the priorities for future development.

Fourth, acceleration of digital transformation. The insurance industry is in an important period of transition to digitalization. In the next step, the regulators and industry's organizations will beef up stronger support in establishing data connectivity and sharing mechanisms, eliminating the data cocoon effect of insurance companies and promoting global data collection in the industry. The insurance industry will focus on "data + new scenarios" and create a new online system providing digital solutions for fine management, precise services and optimizing traditional financial and insurance business.

In terms of reinsurance industry:

First, reinsurance will continue to maintain a steady and progressive development trend in the future, but operational risks and volatility caused by uncertainties will increase significantly. The increasingly steady trend of China's economic development remains unchanged, and the insurance industry still has tremendous potential for development and more diversified market demands. The development of the reinsurance market is closely related to the development of the national economy and insurance industry, and will continue to maintain a steady and progressive development trend, and the income from ceded premiums and reinsurance ceded premiums by insurance companies will maintain a good growth trend. Meanwhile, of insurance companies. This helps promote the insurance companies to optimize the matching of assets and liabilities and pay attention to long-term value investment, and also contributes to promoting the insurance industry back to its original aspiration, i.e. risk protections.

Second, the reform of motor insurance will be further deepened, and the development of property insurance will gradually return to stability. Since the comprehensive reform of motor insurance, insurance companies have actively adjusted their strategies in the fierce competition to enhance their development capabilities, and the monthly premium of motor insurance has gradually achieved positive growth since the fourth quarter of 2021. Under the influence of China's incentive policies for car consumption, the industry is expected to see recovery growth in the premium of motor insurance. The competitiveness of leading insurance companies in the field of motor insurance will be more outstanding, and the business concentration will be further improved.

Third, the adjustment and transformation of life insurance are continuing. As a result of changes in the business environment of the industry, the growth rate of new business value for life insurance core indicators has been in negative growth since 2018 and has accelerated its decline in the two years of the COVID-19 pandemic. Life insurance in 2021 witnessed the largest loss of agents in history, indicating that the transformation of agents steps into the toughest phase. The life insurance channel is faced with the problem of reduced personnel and increased difficulty in developing the industry. The downward trend of the industry' sales end will continue, but the most severe adjustment period has passed, insurance companies, which makes higher demands on the speed of product innovation, efficiency for customer service, and platforms' operational capability of traditional insurance and reinsurance companies. Therefore, it is increasingly challenging to realize high-quality development.

Fourth, the international reinsurance market is faced with uncertainties. At present, the international balance of power is undergoing a profound adjustment, along with the long-standing Sino-US competition, prevalent trade protectionism, and gradually rising geopolitical risks. The major global reinsurance markets are continually raising market access standards for offshore reinsurance business.

(II) Development Prospects

In terms of insurance industry:

First, as the C-ROSS Phase II is implemented, the regulatory rules will be fully optimized and upgraded. The risk factor of the C-ROSS Phase II has been increased, and the risk control system of the insurance industry has ushered in new changes. On the one hand, as the future surpluses of new policies are grouped in the C-ROSS Phase II, the limits are included in core capital, and the risk factors are generally increased, it is expected that the solvency adequacy ratio of the industry will generally decline in the short term, and the demand for future capital replenishment, such as capital increases or bond issuances, may increase. On the other hand, the C-ROSS Phase II solves the problems such as fraudulent capital, false data and unclear underlying assets, which can more scientifically assess the demand for capital occupation and more accurately reflect the risk exposure proves to be more complex and uncertain. As the impact of the COVID-19 pandemic continues, global economic uncertainty has significantly increased, market volatility is becoming unknown, and severe disasters have often occurred due to climate change. Besides, the low-interest-rate environment poses major risks for the management of insurance assets and liabilities and asset allocation, and the increase in economic and social complexities has led to an increase in difficulties as to the risk management. External risk factors that insurance companies are faced with have also increased significantly.

Second, policy requirements have changed considerably. Relevant policies like the International Financial Reporting Standard (IFRS17), the comprehensive reform of motor insurance, and C-ROSS Phase II will be implemented one after another, which will dramatically affect the business behavior of insurance companies, and pose great challenges to the product form, service mode, service scope, and technical level of reinsurance companies. The constraints and rules confronting the companies' reform and development will also significantly increase.

Third, competition in the insurance market has become increasingly fierce. China's financial and insurance industries have gathered pace in their two-way opening up, the growth rate of the primary insurance market has slowed, and the Matthew effect that "strong leading enterprises become stronger and stronger" has become increasingly conspicuous. Besides, foreign-invested reinsurance companies, top insurance companies, and Internet technology platforms have enriched the levels of the reinsurance market players and diversified the means of market competition. Insurance technology accelerates the digitization and industrial integration of for significant development in insurance asset management, and the third-party asset management business is expected to become a critical profit growth point in the future.

Fourth, insurance technology has brought about new revolutions, and the digital economy has become the main battlefield of the international arena and has led the industrial transformation. The development of the insurance market calls for the in-depth involvement of the insurance industry in industrial development through platforms and ecosystems. The application of new technologies represented by BASIC[①] will gather pace, and the insurance industry's risk management will extend from post-payment to pre-risk prediction and prevention. Science and technology will become the impetus for digitization, business model transformation, and high-quality development of the insurance industry, and reinsurance is expected to reshape the insurance value chain through the empowerment of ecological platforms.

Fifth, the international market is faced with development opportunities. Due to the impact of the catastrophe loss and COVID-19, the global insurance premium rate has risen significantly, and the international property reinsurance market has shown a significant escalating trend, creating good conditions for the high-quality development of international business. As the internationalization of RMB continues, the demand for savings transactions in the international life reinsurance market continues.

Development challenges: First, the macro environment in China

---

① BASIC refers to new technologies represented by Blockchain, AI, Security, IoT and Computing.

and technology, improving social governance, tackling the country's aging problem, and creating a Health China have been accelerated. The size of the middle-income population expands; the public's awareness of insurance increases. Insurance, especially reinsurance, has tremendous potential and space to serve our national strategies and participate in our national governance and social services.

Third, the business structure of China's insurance market has experienced accelerated changes. Strong regulation has become a primary focus, creating a favorable environment for the high-quality development of the industry. With China's in-depth implementation of strategic plans such as developing a strong manufacturing country, rural revitalization and modernization of social governance, non-motor insurance, such as agricultural insurance and liability insurance, are expected to grow rapidly. The realization of "carbon peaking and carbon neutrality" goals will give rise to systemic changes in the economy and society, and green development will become a significant force to improve the benefits of economic development and people's quality of life and to increase development opportunities for innovative products represented by green insurance. As the in-depth reform of China's medical system progresses, health insurance has overtaken motor insurance as the second largest type of insurance in China, and its premium income is expected to reach RMB 2 trillion in 2025. As tackling the aging problem becomes a national strategy and with the accumulation of residents' wealth, commercial endowment insurance is expected to usher in rapid development. Benefiting from the growth in demands for insurance guarantee, wealth management, and pension management, there is still room

Chapter V Prospects of China's Reinsurance Industry Development

I. Prospects of Overall Market Development

(I) Opportunities and Challenges

Opportunities: First, China's economy has robust resilience and strong momentum. In 2021, China's GDP reached RMB 114.4 trillion, up 8.1% year-on-year, ranking first among the world's major economies. According to the *Proposal of the Central Committee of the Communist Party of China on Formulating the Fourteenth Five-Year Plan for National Economic and Social Development and the Long-term Objectives for 2035* (hereinafter referred to as the 14th Five-Year Plan), the average annual growth rate of GDP in the next 15 years will be about 4.74% and will maintain a good growth momentum during the implementation of the 14th Five-Year Plan. The new dual-cycle development pattern will reposition China's growth role in the world economy, and the fundamentals of stable and long-term economic growth will remain unchanged, laying a solid foundation for the high-quality development of the insurance industry.

Second, China's insurance industry remains a vast space for development. In 2021, China's premium income was RMB 4.5 trillion, accounting for about 10% of the world's total, much lower than the proportions of China's GDP and population in the world's GDP and population. China will remain the most important growth market for the world's insurance industry in the next 10 to 15 years. As "insurance" has been mentioned 35 times in China's 14th Five-year Plan, national strategies for revitalizing rural areas, developing a strong country in manufacturing

Chapter V

Prospects of China's Reinsurance Industry Development

I. Prospects of Overall Market Development
II. Prospects of P&C Reinsurance Development
III. Prospects of Life Reinsurance Development
IV. Prospects of Development of Foreign Reinsurance Companies in China
V. Prospects of the Regulation Trend of the Reinsurance Industry

the *Notice on Adjusting the Credit Rating Requirements of Use of Insurance Funds in Bonds and Other Related Matters*, canceling the requirements for the white list and external credit rating for use of insurance funds in the bonds of financial enterprises (companies), specifying the external credit rating requirements for the investment by insurance companies with different risk characteristics in the bonds of non-financial enterprises (companies). Furthermore, the notice stipulated the concentration requirements of investment in bonds with or below BBB level and the accounting of the proportion of large categories of investment bonds. Fourth, it revised the *Guidelines for the Custody of Stock Assets of Insurance Companies (Draft)* and 14 other regulatory documents on the use of insurance funds that have lagged current regulatory needs and market situation, with the aim to enhance the investment autonomy of market players.

In addition to the Provisions, CBIRC issued the *Notice on Issues Related to Catastrophe Bonds Issued by Domestic Insurance Companies in the Hong Kong Market* in September 2021 to add ways to spread catastrophe risks, allowing domestic insurance companies to issue catastrophe bonds in the Hong Kong market through special insurance companies, thereby diversifying the loss risks of natural disasters such as earthquakes, typhoons, floods, or public health emergencies. Domestic insurance companies cede reinsurance catastrophe risks to special insurance companies by signing reinsurance contracts.

(IV) Promote Market-oriented use of Insurance Funds

In 2021, CBIRC issued several regulatory policies on the use of insurance funds, constantly standardized the use of insurance funds, further promoted market-oriented use of insurance funds, and revitalized the stock of insurance funds to support socioeconomic development.

First, it issued the *Notice on Matters Related to the Investment of Insurance Funds in Real Estate Investment Trusts*, stipulating the investment norms and regulatory rules of investment of insurance funds in Real Estate Investment Trusts (hereinafter referred to as "REITs") at the institutional level, including qualifications of insurance companies to invest in REITs and the conditions of investment targets. Second, it issued the *Notice on Matters Related to the Use of Insurance Funds in Securities Lending Business*, allowing insurance funds to be used in securities lending business, and requiring that insurance companies participating in securities lending business meet certain qualifications and strengthen investment risk management. Third, it issued in China shall meet the relevant requirements (verified by reinsurance registration system). Sixth, regulate the reinsurance business ceded to overseas reinsurers—where insurance companies need to carry out overseas reinsurance business, a monitoring system for overseas reinsurance business should be established, and the credit and liquidity risk of reinsurance business ceded to overseas reinsurers should be regularly analyzed to effectively control overseas reinsurance risks. Seventh, improve the quality of reinsurance transactions—specify detailed requirements of contract signing, fund settlement, and reinsurance file management of reinsurance transactions, to improve the efficiency of reinsurance transactions and standardization of reinsurance contracts. Eighth, support reinsurers' access to information—emphasize the obligation of reinsurers and insurance intermediaries to inform reinsurers, and specify the notification method, to help reinsurers access more information related to insurance business and facilitate reinsurers' risk pricing and product development. Ninth, requirements for the time limit of facultative reinsurance—require cedants to complete the facultative reinsurance arrangement before underwriting, to promote reasonable and steady risk sharing between the cedants and the reinsurers, and secure sound operation. Tenth, strengthen reinsurance safety management—total proportion per risk unit of property insurance ceded to the same reinsurer should not exceed 80% of the insured amount or liability limit of the primary insurance contract underwritten by the cedant, and insurance companies must establish a liquidity risk management system for reinsurance business and strengthen the management of reinsurance receivables.

original regulations and the existing policies. The Provisions strengthened the regulation of top-level reinsurance strategies, reinsurance business security, reinsurance contracts, reinsurance business of primary insurance companies and reinsurance brokers, focus on maintaining the stable order of the reinsurance market, emphasizing that insurance companies should correctly use reinsurance as tools, and prompt reinsurance to return to its core function as the "Insurance for Insurers."

The Provisions require insurance companies to follow certain regulations and policies. First, use of reinsurance as a tool by insurance companies—emphasize the important role of reinsurance in risk management and strategic capital strategic, and guide reinsurance to play a role in price transmission and cycle stabilization. Second, standardize the reinsurance business of direct insurance companies—require primary insurance companies with reinsurance business to deploy qualified entities, staff, business systems, and annual plans, and clarify the functions of reinsurance that serve primary insurance. Third, determine reinsurance prices and conditions under the market-oriented principle—particularly when conducting reinsurance transactions with connected enterprises, and ensure reinsurance is not misused to transfer profits or evade taxes. Fourth, obligatory-facultative reinsurance—temporary reinsurance defined as "reinsurance by policy," temporary reinsurance distinguished from obligatory-facultative reinsurance and emphasize that "insurance companies cannot operate contract reinsurance business disguised in the form of temporary reinsurance." Fifth, conduct reinsurance business according to the provisions of CBIRC—the reinsurer who undertakes reinsurance business and Supervisors in Bancassurance Entities (Draft)*, the *Guiding Opinions on Establishing and Improving the Performance Compensation Recovery and Deduction Mechanism of Bancassurance Entities*, and the *Regulations on the Administration of the Qualifications of Directors, Supervisors and Senior Managers of Insurance Companies* (hereinafter referred to as these Measures) in 2021, which involved many sub-sectors of corporate governance regulation. First, these Measures further standardize the shareholding behavior, governance behavior, transaction behavior, and responsibilities of major shareholders of bancassurance entities. Second, these Measures optimize and improve the performance evaluation mechanism of directors and supervisors of bancassurance entities, clarify the contents and focus of performance evaluation of directors and supervisors, and emphasize the closed-loop management of performance evaluation of directors and supervisors. Third, these Measures guide bancassurance entities to establish a performance-based compensation recovery and deduction mechanism in line with their actual situation. Fourth, these Measures adjust the requirements, conditions, and approval procedures for the qualification examination and approval of directors and supervisors of bancassurance entities.

(III) Reinsurance Business Management Standard Improvement

To standardize the reinsurance business and promote the high-quality development of the reinsurance market, CBIRC revised and issued the *Provisions on the Management of Reinsurance Business* (hereinafter referred to as the Provisions) in July 2021, deleting contradictory content between the reinsurance companies. It absorbs and integrates existing regulatory rules, draws lessons from sound international experience, and comprehensively optimizes and perfects the normative requirements for bancassurance entities' corporate governance mechanism. First, it specifies the rights and obligations of shareholders, the powers and functions of the shareholders' general meeting, and the operating mechanism. Second, it emphasizes director selection and duties and guarantees directors' performance, and clarifies the composition, powers, and operation mechanism of the board of directors and its special committees. Third, it standardizes supervisor appointment and performance and the establishment and operation of the board of supervisors and senior management. Fourth, it requires banks and insurance entities to improve incentive and restraint mechanisms and information disclosure mechanisms, and strengthen risk management, internal control, and internal and external audit. The Guideline not only proposes a uniform standard for the corporate governance mechanisms of bancassurance entities, but also has scope for implementing differentiated regulation. In addition, in terms of the mutual promotion between the Party's leadership and corporate governance, the Guideline sets out for the first time at the level of the regulation system, the general requirements that state-owned entities should systematically incorporate the Communist Party's leadership into corporate governance and inspire private entities to give full play to the political core role of the Party organizations built within them.

In addition to the *Guideline*, CBIRC issued the *Measures for the Regulation of Major Shareholders' Behavior in Banking and Insurance Entities (Draft)*, the *Measures for the Performance Evaluation of Directors* determines the solvency regulation indicators for the core solvency adequacy ratio, the comprehensive solvency adequacy ratio and the integrated risk rating, which are organically correlated , and prescribes that the solvency of insurance companies must meet both the standards and requirements that the core solvency adequacy ratio is not less than 50%, the comprehensive solvency adequacy is not less than 100%, and the integrated risk rating (IRR) is B or above. The provisions also strengthen the primary responsibility of insurance companies with respect to solvency management and regulation and inspection of insurance companies' solvency by regulatory agencies, and emphasize that regulatory agencies will take targeted regulatory measures for insurance companies whose solvency and risk don't meet the requirements based on the causes and degree of risk.

(II) Enhancing Insurance Entities' Corporate Governance Regulation

In recent years, CBIRC has attached immense importance to the regulation of corporate governance of bancassurance entities. It has taken sound corporate governance as an important highlight to promote the high-quality development of bancassurance entities, and continuously optimized and reformed the corporate governance regulation mechanism. In June 2021, as one of the important measures to implement the *Three-year Action Plan for Corporate Governance of Insurance Companies in the Banking Industry (2020-2022)* issued by CBIRC in August, 2020, CBIRC revised and issued the *Guideline for Corporate Governance of Bancassurance Entities* (hereinafter referred to as the Guideline).

The Guideline applies to all bancassurance entities, including identification and measurement of insurance companies' risks, and guide insurance companies to optimize asset-liability matching management. Second, in terms of the second pillar—qualitative regulation requirements, it improves IRR rating standards, solvency risk management requirements (SARMRA), and liquidity evaluation standards, and specifies the capital planning regulation requirements, to more scientifically and comprehensively reflect the risks and management of insurance companies. Third, in terms of the third pillar—market restraint mechanism, it is necessary to improve market transparency and information transparency, as well as expand the requirements for the public disclosure of solvency information, to give full play to the regulation and restraint role of all parties involved in the insurance market.

In general, Rule II tightens and refines the solvency regulation requirements for primary insurance and reinsurance companies, as well as improves the scientific, effective, and comprehensive regulation of reinsurance solvency, thereby guiding the overall stable development of the reinsurance market.

Furthermore, prior to the official release of Rule II, CBIRC issued the *Provisions on the Administration of the Solvency of Insurance Companies* in January 2021, which comprehensively revised the original regulations issued in July 2008 that significantly lagged the actual situation of China's insurance market.

The *Provisions on the Administration of the Solvency of Insurance Companies* specifies the "three-pillar" (first pillar—quantitative regulation requirements; second pillar—qualitative regulation requirements; and third pillar—market restraint mechanism) framework for solvency regulation,

III. Important Regulatory Policies for the Reinsurance Industry in 2021

(I) Solvency Regulation Mechanism Optimization

In September 2017, the former CIRC started the construction of Phase II of the "C-ROSS" project, and in December 2021, CBIRC officially revised and issued the Rule II, which marked the successful completion of Phase II of the "C-ROSS" project. As the basic institutional norm of solvency regulation of China's (reinsurance) industry, Rule II includes additional provisions on the capital measurement rules of reinsurance companies under the "C-ROSS" framework and adds three new rules: Penetrative Measurement of Market Risk and Credit Risk, Capital Planning, and Lloyd's (China).

Rule II comprehensively optimizes and upgrades the original rules, the majority of which apply to both reinsurance companies and primary insurance companies. First, in terms of the first pillar—quantitative capital requirements, it strictly stipulates capital recognition standards, requires risk penetration regulation, comprehensively calibrates risk factors, improves financial reinsurance and long-term equity investment supervision standards and interest rate risk measurement methods, and specifies the applicable rules for risk factors of default of counterparts of reinsurance business ceded by primary insurance companies in the Chinese mainland to qualified Hong Kong reinsurance entities and the reinsurance business arising out of catastrophe bonds issued by insurance companies in Chinese mainland, to consolidate the capital quality of insurance companies, realize more accurate insurance industry. It requires reinsurers to strengthen risk management of reinsurance business and established qualifications such as the international rating level that reinsurers need to meet. Since then, to further standardize reinsurance credit risk management, the former CIRC revised and issued the *Notice on the Implementation of Reinsurance Registration Management* in March 2015, updating the qualification requirements for reinsurers and stipulating that all reinsurers and reinsurance brokers involved in reinsurance business in China should register in the reinsurance registration system.

Offshore reinsurer's qualified guarantee requirements

To improve the safety of offshore reinsurance transactions, mitigate offshore reinsurers' credit risks, and safeguard the legitimate rights and interests of domestic insurance companies as cedents, the former CIRC issued the *Notice on the Relevant Matters Concerning the Provision of Guarantee Measures by Offshore Reinsurers* in February 2017, stipulating that domestic insurance companies may require offshore reinsurers to provide guarantees for the risk exposure of reinsurance receivables and reinsurance reserves. The notice also specified the types of guarantees that offshore reinsurers can provide and the requirements that they should meet.

The aforementioned systems have been fully operational as of the end of 2021, increasing the transparency of the Chinese reinsurance market, preventing the transmission of international financial risks through reinsurance, reducing credit risk and operational risk, and enhancing the security of China's reinsurance industry.

from evading regulation through reinsurance transactions and cross-border transmission of financial risks through reinsurance transactions.

Establish information disclosure mechanism for reinsurance connected transactions

To intensify the security of reinsurance transactions and prevent cross-border transmission of financial risks, in November 2006, the former China Insurance Regulatory Commission issued the *Circular on Intensifying the Information Disclosure of Reinsurance Transactions between Foreign-invested Insurance Companies and Connected Enterprises*, which required foreign insurance companies to report their reinsurance transactions with connected enterprises to the regulatory authorities. After undergoing two revisions, the former China Insurance Regulatory Commission issued the *Notice on Intensifying the Information Disclosure of Connected Reinsurance Transactions of Insurance Companies* in April 2015. On the one hand, it relaxed the front end and did away with the previous regulations on the approval of connected reinsurance transactions of foreign insurance companies, and on the other hand, it strengthened the back end and clarified that both Chinese and foreign insurance companies needed to disclose connected transactions, which improved the accuracy and effectiveness of reinsurance regulation.

Establish reinsurance registration mechanism

Considering that the solvency, financial conditions, and profitability of reinsurers have a significant impact on the sound and stable operation of reinsurers, the former CIRC issued the *Notice on Issues Related to the Safety of Reinsurance Business* in November, 2007, to improve the resilience of China's

In terms of sub-sectors, in January 2012, the former China Insurance Regulatory Commission issued the *Regulations on the Administration of Reinsurance of P&C Insurance Companies*, which provided detailed requirements for the administration of reinsurance business of P&C insurance companies, covering strategic management, operation management, credit management, evaluation, and compliance audit of the reinsurance business. The regulations stressed that reinsurance is an important means of risk management and control of P&C insurance companies, and that P&C insurance companies should carry out reinsurance business in accordance with the "Doctrine of Utmost Good Faith," spread risks reasonably, and optimize their business structure to achieve steady operation and sustainable development. In September 2014, the former China Insurance Regulatory Commission issued the *Circular on Matters Related to Tightening of the Administration of Reinsurance Ceded Business of P&C Insurance Companies*, which further specified the normative requirements for P&C insurance companies to conduct reinsurance ceded business.

(III) Reinsurance Business Security Enhancement

Reinsurance is a highly professional and global industry, so regulations for the reinsurance industry are concentrated on ensuring the safety of the reinsurance business. These regulations include the establishment of mechanisms for the information disclosure of reinsurance connected transactions and reinsurance registration, as well as the requirements that offshore reinsurers offer qualified guarantees, to prevent insurance entities reinsurance business through their branches, joint ventures, or wholly-owned subsidiaries without geographical restrictions or limitations of the number of business licenses. Therefore, compared with the primary insurance industry, China's reinsurance industry was opened to foreign-invested companies earlier and faster. In September 2002, to clearly define the conditions for the establishment of reinsurance companies after China's entry into the WTO, the former China Insurance Regulatory Commission issued the *Regulations on the Establishment of Reinsurance Companies*, which provides specific requirements for the establishment approval, business scope, capital, and staffing of domestic reinsurance companies.

(II) Specific Regulations on the Administration of Reinsurance Business

In October 2005, the former China Insurance Regulatory Commission issued China's first comprehensive and systematic regulation on the administration of reinsurance business—*Regulations on the Administration of Reinsurance Business*, which provided a preliminary clarification on reinsurance business requirements for insurance companies, insurance consortiums, insurance brokers, and other insurance entities involved in reinsurance business, including the share of business ceded by primary insurance companies and requirements for the administration of concentration. In addition, it also states the obligation of the insurance companies to report the operation of their reinsurance business. After 3 rounds of modifications, CBIRC issued the latest revised *Regulations on the Administration of Reinsurance Business* in July 2021.

of Reinsurance Business, the *Rules on the Compilation of Solvency Reports of Insurance Companies No. 15: Reinsurance Business*, and the *Regulations on the Administration of Reinsurance of P&C Insurance Companies*, during the subsequent five years, and made the first revision of the *Regulations on the Administration of Reinsurance Business* issued in October 2005, which gradually improved reinsurance market regulation and ensured the sound and stable development of the reinsurance industry.

II. Special Policies Regulating the Reinsurance Industry

In addition to the regulatory policies that apply to the entire insurance industry, the policies of regulators overseeing the reinsurance industry also include special regulatory policies formulated in accordance with the characteristics of the reinsurance industry, particularly its international characteristics.

(I) Regulations for Establishment of Reinsurance Companies

China officially joined the WTO in December 2001. In March 2002, the former China Insurance Regulatory Commission issued the *Circular on Printing and Distributing the Contents of the Legal Documents of China's Entry into the WTO Concerning Insurance Industry*, which reported on China's commitment to open the insurance industry to the outside, including policies such as: foreign insurance companies being permitted to engage in cross-border reinsurance business after China's entry into the WTO and foreign insurance companies being permitted to provide life and non-life accounting system, and its Accounting Standard No. 25 for Enterprises-Reinsurance Contracts comprehensively regulates the recognition, measurement of insurance contracts, and presentation of relevant information, including reinsurance contracts, which affected the premiums written and operational strategy of reinsurance business.

At the same time, the guiding opinions and development plans issued by the Central Committee, the State Council, and relevant regulatory agencies with respect to national economic and financial work also have a far-reaching impact on the reinsurance industry and the policies regulating it. For example, to fulfill its WTO commitments, China completely abolished the compulsory reinsurance in January 2006, and issued the *Several Opinions of the State Council on the Reform and Development of the Insurance Industry* in June of that year, which specified the guiding philosophy, objectives, tasks, and policies for the reform and development of the insurance industry in the future. Furthermore, it required the insurance industry to strengthen the regulation of solvency, further advance the regulation of the governance structure of insurance companies and reinforce the regulation of market practices. To implement the opinions and to meet the needs of a fast-growing and highly competitive reinsurance market after China's entry into WTO, in June 2007, the former China Insurance Regulatory Commission issued the *China Reinsurance Market Development Plan*, which further clarified the general guidelines, objectives, and policies for the development of China's reinsurance market. Based on the above guiding opinions and development plans, the former China Insurance Regulatory Commission issued rules and regulations such as the *Notice on the Relevant Problems Concerning the Safety* regulations like the *Measures on the Regulation and Administration of Anti-money Laundering and Anti-terrorist Financing of Financial Entities*, which clearly stipulate that financial entities should establish internal control and risk management mechanisms for anti-money laundering and anti-terrorist financing that meet the requirements, and fulfill their obligations such as carrying out of due diligence investigations on clients, maintaining identity and transaction records of clients, and reporting large and questionable transactions. However, in the reinsurance business, as both the reinsurers and cedants are strictly regulated insurance entities and no natural persons and cash transactions are involved, the risk of money laundering and terrorist financing is relatively small. Therefore, with respect to the reinsurance industry, some policies regulating anti-money laundering and anti-terrorist financing are somewhat flexible. For example, the *Measures on the Administration of Financial Entities for Carrying Out Due Diligence on Clients and Maintaining Client Identity Data and Transaction Records* issued by the PBC in January 2022 specifically states that "when insurance companies conduct reinsurance business, fulfilling the obligation of due diligence on clients is not applicable."

The Ministry of Finance fulfills its duties as an investor of state-owned financial capital in accordance with the authorization of the State Council. The requirements for the administration and disposal of pertinent assets of financial enterprises holding state-owned assets are laid forth in the rules and regulations published by the Ministry, such as the *Measures on the Administration of the Transfer of State-owned Assets of Financial Enterprises*. In addition, the Ministry formulated and implemented a unified national concerning insurance sales, intermediaries, services, and anti-fraud. The specific manner of regulating market practices depends on the characteristics of market practices of regulated entities. Due to the differences between P&C insurance, life insurance, and reinsurance in terms of trading entities, business nature, and risk characteristics, regulators handle each industry differently and typically develop unique regulations for various insurance entities and insurance firms. For example, to regulate insurance terms and premium rates, regulators issued the *Measures on the Administration of Terms and Premium Rates of Life Insurance Companies* (latest revision in 2015) and the *Measures on the Administration of Terms and Premium Rates of P&C Insurance Companies* (latest revision in 2021).

In general, national authorities rigorously control the organizations in the primary insurance and reinsurance businesses as well as their operations. The reinsurance and primary insurance businesses are regulated similarly in many respects under the same three-pillar structure that governs solvency, corporate governance, and market practices of the insurance industry, but differently in some respects due to their differences.

(II) Regulation of Other Important Aspects

In addition to CBIRC's professional regulation, authorities like the PBC and the Ministry of Finance also regulate financial entities, including reinsurance companies with respect to anti-money laundering, anti-terrorist financing, and state-owned assets management.

The PBC is responsible for regulating financial entities with respect to anti-money laundering and anti-terrorist financing. It issued rules and insurance entities to strengthen the obligations of major shareholders, improve the development of the board of directors, give full play to the role of the board of supervisors, regulate the operation of the management, and reinforce connected transactions and information disclosure management. Thus, corporate governance regulation was officially introduced to China's insurance industry. In June 2021, CBIRC revised and issued the *Rules on the Corporate Governance of Bancassurance Entities*, establishing the leadership of the Party Committee in all aspects of corporate governance of insurance entities, and further clarified the composition, responsibilities, and operation mechanism of the governing bodies in the corporate governance structure. It comprehensively and systematically strengthened the normative requirements for corporate governance of insurance entities. Furthermore, to continuously optimize and improve the regulation system of corporate governance, regulators also issued several policies governing the subdivision of corporate governance regulation, including the code of conduct for shareholders of insurance entities, the evaluation of directors' and supervisors' performance, and the management of directors', supervisors', and senior executives' qualifications.

Regulation of market practices

Regulation of market practices guarantees orderly operation of the insurance market. This regulation primarily focuses on protecting the rights and interests of customers and maintaining the regular operation of the insurance market by regulating the market practices of insurance entities. It primarily covers aspects like insurance terms and premium rates, practices solvency adequacy ratio to three organically inter-relatedly indicators—core solvency adequacy ratio, comprehensive solvency adequacy ratio, and risk comprehensive rating. In April 2012, the former China Insurance Regulatory Commission initiated the development of a risk-oriented C-ROSS, establishing a three-pillar system to regulate solvency, consisting of quantitative capital requirements, qualitative regulatory requirements, and a market discipline mechanism. In September 2017, CBIRC initiated the development of C-ROSS II to comprehensively optimize and upgrade the solvency regulation system. In December 2021, it officially issued Rules II, indicating the fulfillment of phase II of C-ROSS.

Corporate governance regulation

Corporate governance is the cornerstone of the modern enterprise system. Its purpose is to constantly improve the governance of an enterprise through the establishment of a corporate governance framework that includes governing bodies like the (general) meeting of shareholders, board of directors, board of supervisors, and senior management, determining the scope of roles and requirements of performing duties for these bodies, and improving mechanisms like risk control, the balance of power, and incentives and restraints. Effective corporate governance plays a vital role in the sound and stable operation of insurance entities. In January 2006, Chinese insurance companies were restructured before being listed and gradually established a modern enterprise system, and the former China Insurance Regulatory Commission issued the *Guiding Opinions on the Regulation of Governance Structure of Insurance Companies (Draft)*, requiring such as the PBC and the Ministry of Finance with respect to anti-money laundering, anti-terrorist financing, and management of state-owned financial assets.

(I) Three-pillar Framework Regulation the Insurance Industry

China's insurance regulation has gone through three stages since the development of the sector fully resumed: first, market practice-focused regulation; second, regulation of both market practices and solvency; and third, the current three-pillar regulatory framework, which consists of solvency regulation (core), corporate governance regulation (foundation), and market practice regulation (starting point).

Solvency regulation

Solvency regulation lies at the core of regulating the modern insurance industry. It involves comprehensive evaluation, supervision, and inspection of the solvency adequacy ratio, comprehensive risk, and risk management ability of insurance companies, to ensure that the solvency level of insurance companies meets the risk protection requirements. In March 2001, the former China Insurance Regulatory Commission issued the *Regulations on the Administration of Minimum Solvency and Regulatory Indicators of Insurance Companies (Draft)*, which specifies the requirements for minimum solvency of property insurance companies, life insurance companies, and reinsurance companies, as well as the calculation methods of relevant regulatory indicators. After undergoing three rounds of modifications, CBIRC issued the *Regulations on the Administration of Solvency of Insurance Companies* in January 2021, which expanded the single indicator of

I. Current Regulatory Framework of the Reinsurance Industry

In a legal sense, the Insurance Law of the People's Republic of China (also known as the Insurance Law) governs China's reinsurance and primary insurance sectors, with CBIRC serving as the regulatory agency. CBIRC's reinsurance industry regulations are mainly divided into two categories: Regulations that apply to the insurance industry, such as those that control corporate governance, solvency, and how insurance funds are used. These regulations, which are typically applicable to both reinsurance companies and primary insurance companies, or to primary insurance companies only, but to reinsurance companies as reference regulations, are developed based on the shared characteristics of the reinsurance and primary insurance industries. Special regulations that apply to the reinsurance industry are mainly reflected in the regulation of reinsurance market practices and special regulation with respect to the international characteristics of the reinsurance industry.

CBIRC combines on-site regulation with off-site regulation to ensure the effective implementation of the aforementioned regulations. It regulates insurance entities by formulating regulatory standards, conducting capacity assessments, and enforcing administrative penalties for legal violations. This is done to encourage the entities to maintain a reasonable level of solvency, raise the bar for corporate governance, and carry out market operations in accordance with the law.

In addition, China's reinsurance industry is also regulated by entities

Chapter IV Overview of China's Reinsurance Regulation in 2021

In 2021, CBIRC actively promoted the high-quality development of the insurance industry and issued several regulatory policies that have an impact on the reinsurance industry. First, optimized regulatory mechanism for solvency: CBIRC revised and issued the *Rules on the Regulation of the Solvency of Insurance Companies (II)* (hereinafter referred to as Rules II) and *Regulations on the Administration of the Solvency of Insurance Companies*, which further improved the regulatory mechanism for the solvency of insurance companies. Second, stricter regulation of corporate governance of insurance entities: CBIRC issued several policies regulating corporate governance like the *Code for Corporate Governance of Bancassurance Entities* and increased corporate governance requirements. Third, improved regulations for the administration of reinsurance business: CBIRC revised and issued the *Regulations on the Administration of Reinsurance Business* to further regulate business conducted by reinsurance companies. The regulations stress that the core function of reinsurance is to be the insurance for insurers, and allow domestic insurance companies to issue catastrophe bonds in Hong Kong SAR's insurance market through special-purpose insurance companies, to spread the risk of catastrophic events and natural disasters. Fourth, use of insurance funds in a more market-oriented manner: CBIRC expanded the scope of use of insurance funds and revised some normative documents pertaining to fund use, to reduce restrictions on fund investment and direct funds toward economic and social development.

Chapter IV

Overview of China's Reinsurance Regulation in 2021

I. Current Regulatory Framework of the Reinsurance Industry

II. Special Policies Regulating the Reinsurance Industry

III. Important Regulatory Policies for the Reinsurance Industry in 2021

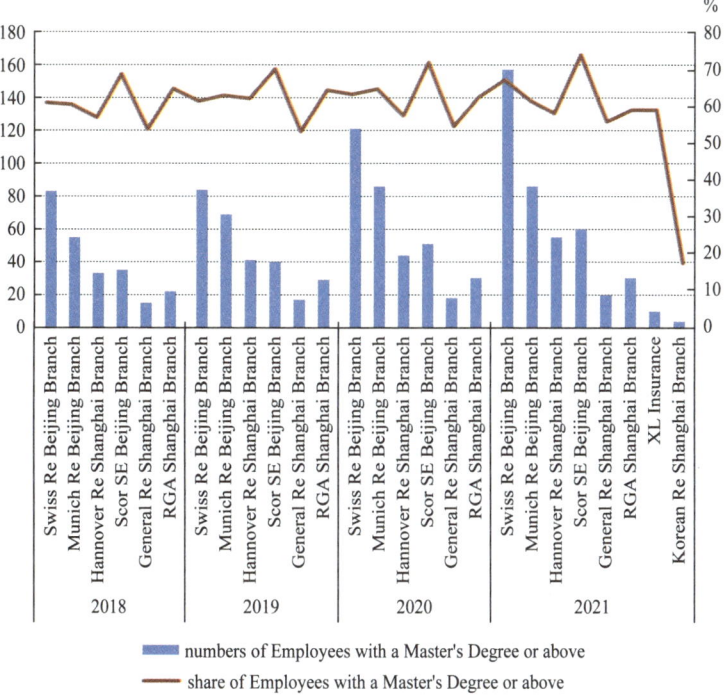

Figure 5   Employees with a Master's Degree or above in Foreign Reinsurance Companies

(Source: 2018–2021 Yearbook of China's Insurance)

3. Educational background structure

Regarding the educational background structure, employees with a master's degree or above account for 50%–70% of the total number of employees. Some of the foreign reinsurance companies attach importance to market research as well as product innovation and development, and have more employees with doctoral degrees.

Table 9 Staff Structure of Major Foreign Reinsurance Companies

Company	Total number			Education background				Age		
	Total	Male	Female	Doctor	Master	Bachelor	Associate or below	Under 35	36-45	Above 46
Munich Re Beijing Branch	140	56	84	3	83	53	1	70	50	20
Swiss Re Beijing Branch	234	84	150	17	140	73	4	98	107	29
Scor SE Beijing Branch	81	31	50	0	60	21	0	41	30	10
Hannover Re Shanghai Branch	95	36	59	3	52	38	2	52	38	5
Korean Re Shanghai Branch	23	11	12	0	4	19	0	9	13	1

Source: 2021 Yearbook of China's Insurance.

2. Age and gender structure

Regarding the age structure, in recent years, employees of foreign reinsurance companies have tended to be younger. Among major foreign reinsurance companies, employees under the age of 35 account for about 47%, and employees over the age of 45 account for about 12%.

Regarding the gender structure, the proportion of female employees in foreign reinsurance companies is high—the proportion of female employees in Munich Re Beijing Branch, Swiss Re Beijing Branch, Scor SE Beijing Branch, and Hannover Re Shanghai Branch is over 60% respectively.

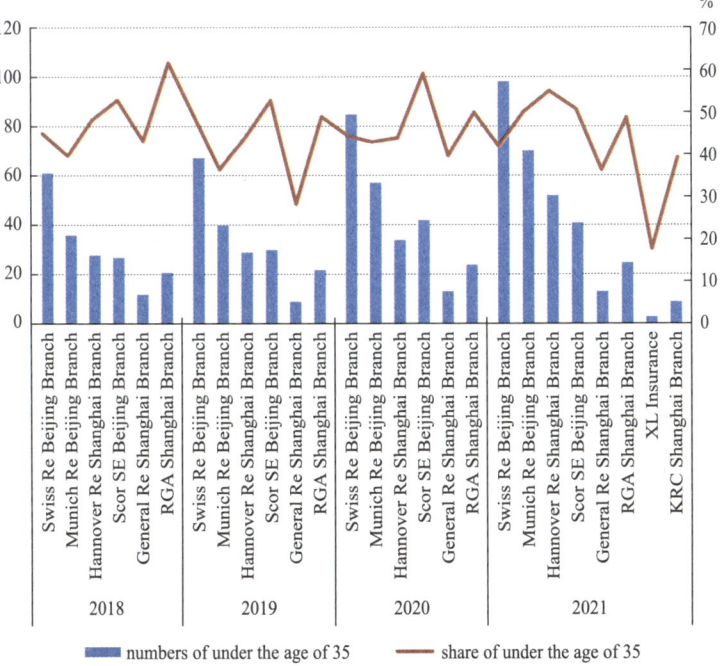

Figure 4　Employees under the Age of 35 in Foreign Reinsurance Companies

(Source: 2018-2021 Yearbook of China's Insurance)

collaborative projects.

(II) Development of Foreign Reinsurance Companies' Human Resources in China

1. Growth in number of employees

The number of foreign reinsurance companies' employees in China has significantly increased in recent years as a result of their increased focus on creating a Chinese market team to drive business development with talents. For long-term development in China, some foreign reinsurance companies have established a fairly complete talent team, and the scale of their workforce is comparable to that of Chinese reinsurance firms.

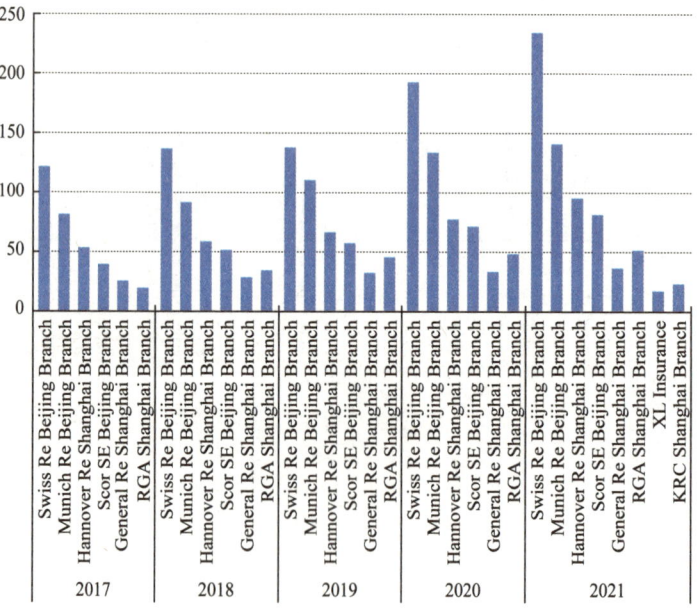

Figure 3　Staffing growth of foreign reinsurance companies

(Source: 2017–2021 Yearbook of China's Insurance)

to overseas entities, as this effectively broadens the international vision and intensifies loyalty of outstanding employees and helps create a reserve of management talents. Common departments for exchanging these talents include the business department, financial department, human resources department, etc. The headquarters are responsible for selecting, assessing, and hiring these employees.

3. Emphasizing cultural communication

First, they provide short-term (one month) exchanges (lectures, forums, etc.) and visits (training, etc.) to promote communication and understanding between the headquarters and entities in China. Second, they hold collaborative activities on cultural communication and interaction, conduct cultural workshops, discuss cultural differences, enhance the understanding of different countries' cultures, and promote cultural integration.

4. Establishing collaboration mechanism

First, they set up a dialogue committee that included senior anagement, and the entities in China hold a direct dialogue with the Group's senior management on key points. This enables them to reach a consensus efficiently and promote its implementation. Second, they set up a contact group within the entities in China. The contact group is responsible for collecting information of functional departments horizontally, communicating with relevant functional departments on daily operation issues, and communicating with the corresponding departments of the group vertically. Third, they set up a temporary collaborative working group and establish a project mechanism to promote gradual implementation of

(I) Main Measures of Foreign Reinsurance Companies to Develop Their Human Resources in China

1. Strengthening the vertical management of lines.

First, by improving the vertical management of lines, they can obtain better information of their entities in China, and improve the comprehensive and visible management of these entities in China; Second, they stress that foreign companies and entities in China should learn from each other to form complementary advantages or strong alliances, laying a solid foundation for expanding business in the future.

2. Strengthening the secondment of personnel

First, they second senior executives to important positions and functions in China, to ensure effective control and decision effectiveness of their entities in China. They also second senior executives to important positions such as CEO and CFO. The parent company is responsible for the selection, assessment, and employment of those executives. Second, they second the middle management in an effort to obtain the actual operation information of entities in China and toughen the middle-ranking backbones while controlling key functions and departments. They also second them to those common departments such as Business Department, Financial Department, Legal & Compliance Department, Audit Department, Risk Management Department, etc. The headquarters are responsible for selecting, assessing, and hiring the seconded senior management. Third, they establish a system of secondment and rotating their outstanding employees

(III) Solvency

The four foreign reinsurance companies mentioned above had significantly higher solvency ratios in 2021 than their Chinese counterparts. Among them, Swiss Re Beijing Branch had the highest solvency ratio, reaching 392%. Foreign reinsurance companies had robust overall capital strength, and great potential to underwrite high-quality business, laying a solid foundation for them to further tap into China's reinsurance market.

Table 8 Solvency of Foreign Reinsurance Companies in China

Reinsurance Group	Solvency Ratio in 2021	Branches in China	Solvency Ratio in 2021
Munich Re Group	227%	Munich Re Beijing Branch	305%
Swiss Re Group	223%	Swiss Re Beijing Branch	392%
Hannover Re Group	243%	Hannover Re Shanghai Branch	285%
Scor Group	226%	Scor SE Beijing Branch	276%

Source: Annual reports of reinsurance companies.

IV. Human Resources of Foreign Reinsurance Companies in China

Foreign reinsurance companies attach great importance to the planning and training of market managers in China. To improve their understanding of the Chinese market, they initially chose managers who were familiar with the local market. Over time, they dispatched key personnel with extensive management experience and long-term training to ensure that the Group's crucial strategies could be successfully implemented in the local market. In addition, foreign reinsurance companies also took the training of local talents seriously.

Table 6 Business Structure of Munich Re Beijing Branch

Business lines	Premium Income in 2021 (RMB 100 million)	Proportion
Property Insurance	77.54	58.41%
Life and Health Insurance	55.22	41.59%
Total	132.76	100.00%

Source: Annual report of Munich Re Beijing Branch.

(II) Profitability

The overall profitability of foreign reinsurance firms in China in 2021 was quite favorable. Some foreign reinsurance firms have diversified product lines. The internet and mid-range medical insurance business started quite early, and the critical illness insurance business accounted for a relatively small proportion but with good profitability. Profits for some foreign reinsurance companies fell as a result of intense pressure to cut back on their critical illness business. The profitability of foreign reinsurance entities will be somewhat impacted by their high retrocession rate, so the net profit index does not accurately reflect their operational circumstances.

Table 7 Net profit of Foreign Reinsurance Companies in China

	Net profit in 2021 (RMB 10,000)	ROE in 2021
Swiss Re Beijing Branch	8,069	1%
Munich Re Beijing Branch	37,700	9%
Hannover Re Shanghai Branch	−2,940	−1%
Scor SE Beijing Branch	18,113	8%

Source: Annual report of reinsurance companies.

Business lines	Premium Income in 2021 (RMB 100 million)	Proportion
Agricultural Insurance	7.83	4.76%
Credit Insurance	15.50	9.42%
Property Insurance	15.96	9.70%
Engineering Insurance	6.96	4.23%
Cargo Insurance	2.55	1.55%
Hull Insurance	1.00	0.61%
Health Insurance	1.23	0.75%
Casualty Insurance	0.54	0.33%
Others	0.68	0.42%
Total	164.54	100.00%

Source: Annual report of Hannover Re Shanghai Branch.

4. Munich Re Beijing Branch

The total premium income of Munich Re Beijing Branch in 2021 was RMB 13.276 billion, nearly the same as it was in the same period last year. The premium income from life reinsurance and health reinsurance shows a downward trend, with a significant decrease of proportion in the total premium income, with non-life reinsurance becoming the main business.

Property reinsurance makes up roughly 60% of Munich Re Beijing Branch's business structure, while life reinsurance and health reinsurance make up roughly 40%. In 2021, premium income from property reinsurance was RMB 7.754 billion, a year-on-year increase of 14.75%, accounting for 58.41% of the total premium income; premium income from life reinsurance and health reinsurance was RMB 5.522 billion, down 15.27% year-on-year, accounting for 41.59% of the total premium income.

3. Hannover Re Shanghai Branch

Hannover Re Shanghai Branch's insurance business income was RMB 16.454 billion in 2021, down 8.9% year-on-year, and the business began to shrink in 2021. Nevertheless, the premium income of Hannover Re Shanghai Branch in 2021 was second only to that of Swiss Re Beijing Branch, ranking second among foreign reinsurance companies.

Regarding its business structure, the life reinsurance and property reinsurance business of Hannover Re Shanghai Branch account for about half of the total insurance, respectively. Health reinsurance accounts for the highest proportion in life reinsurance business, i.e., 35.51%; liability reinsurance accounts for a relatively high proportion in property reinsurance business, i.e., 9.81%; property reinsurance accounts for 9.70%; credit reinsurance accounts for 9.42%; and motor reinsurance accounts for 8.85%.

Regarding the business growth rate, credit premiums increased significantly in 2021, with an increase of 21.41%; liability, motor, property, engineering, and cargo premiums increased slightly; agricultural dropped sharply, with a decrease of 65.98%.

Table 5 Business Structure of Hannover Re Shanghai Branch

Business lines	Premium Income in 2021 (RMB 100 million)	Proportion
Life	81.58	49.58%
Health Insurance	58.43	35.51%
Life Insurance	16.37	9.95%
Casualty Insurance	6.78	4.12%
Non-life	82.96	50.42%
Liability Insurance	16.15	9.81%
Motor Insurance	14.56	8.85%

increase of 397.5%. This growth has mainly come from financial reinsurance business.

Regarding its business structure, Scor SE Beijing Branch's life reinsurance business has increased every year and has overtaken property reinsurance as the largest line of business, accounting for 64.41% of total premium income. Premium income of property reinsurance business was RMB 3.667 billion, increasing by 23.2% year-on-year, accounting for 35.59% of total premium income. The main growth points of property reinsurance business were agricultural, cargo, and specialty, and the related reinsurance premium's growth rates were 140.42%, 96.84%, and 86.66%, respectively, in 2021.

Table 4 Business Structure of Scor SE Beijing Branch

Business lines	Premium Income in 2021 (RMB 100 million)	Proportion
Short-term Health Insurance	15.30	14.85%
Motor Insurance	4.32	4.19%
Credit & Guarantee Insurance	7.02	6.81%
Life Insurance	40.05	38.88%
Long-term Health Insurance	11.00	10.68%
Liability Insurance	7.14	6.93%
Enterprise Property Insurance	5.49	5.33%
Engineering Insurance	2.03	1.97%
Casualty Insurance	2.64	2.56%
Agricultural Insurance	4.80	4.66%
Hull Insurance	0.88	0.85%
Cargo Insurance	1.41	1.37%
Specialty Risk Insurance	0.95	0.92%
Total	103.01	100.00%

Source: Annual report of Scor SE Beijing Branch.

higher than life insurance and health insurance.

Regarding its business structure, Swiss Re Beijing Branch's property premium income in 2021 accounted for 72.21% of its total income, wherein, property liability and motor accounted for 41% and 22.3%, respectively (relatively high). Life life reinsurance premium income accounted for 27.79%. The premium income for lifelife reinsurance has increased over the past two years as the life and health insurance market in China turns out to be promising and related industries are less impacted by the COVID-19 pandemic.

Table 3 Business Structure of Swiss Re Beijing Branch

Business lines	Premium Income in 2021 (RMB 100 million)	Proportion
Life	53.41	27.79%
Life Insurance	4.85	2.52%
Health Insurance	48.56	25.27%
P&C	138.78	72.21%
Motor Insurance	42.87	22.30%
Property Liability Insurance	78.80	41.00%
Marine Insurance	12.85	6.69%
Others	4.26	2.22%
Total	192.19	100.00%

Source: Annual report of Swiss Re Beijing Branch.

2. Scor SE Beijing Branch

The premium income of Scor SE Beijing Branch in 2021 was RMB 10.301 billion, a year-on-year increase of 50.4%. Among the different sources of premium income, life insurance premium income was RMB 4.005 billion, accounting for 39% of the total premium income, with a year-on-year steady growth, and they are becoming increasing profitable and capable in competition.

(I) Business Scale

The overall business scale of foreign reinsurance companies increased steadily between 2017 and 2021. With its 2021 reinsurance premium income reaching RMB 19.219 billion, Swiss Re Beijing Branch took the lead among all foreign reinsurance companies, followed by Munich Re, Hannover Re, and Scor SE.

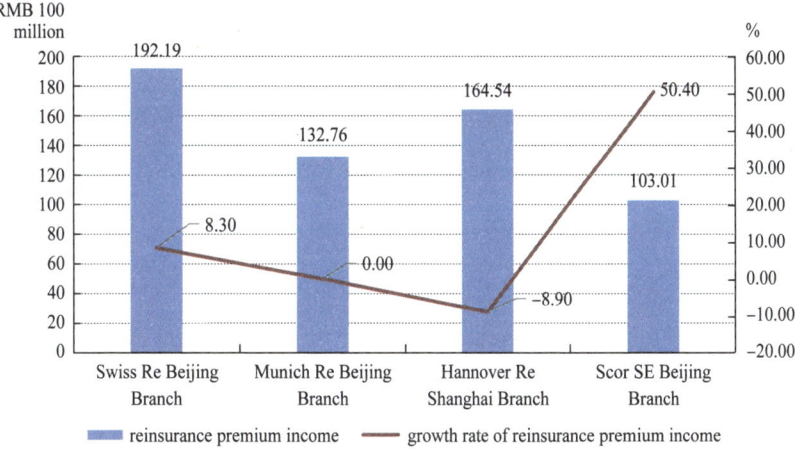

Figure 2　Reinsurance premium income and growth rates of foreign reinsurance companies in 2021

(Source: Annual report of reinsurance companies)

1. Swiss Re Beijing Branch

The total premium income of Swiss Re Beijing Branch in 2021 reached RMB 19.219 billion, an increase of 8.3% year-on-year. In recent years, Swiss Re Group's property business has increased significantly, and has accounted for more than 70% of Swiss Re Beijing Branch's total premium income, much employees at the operational level. The development and changes in foreign reinsurance companies in terms of business scale, employee headcount, age distribution, and educational background further suggest that their core competence is constantly improving.

(V) Risk Management Structure Compatible With Risk Management Culture

In order to uniformly manage the inherent and non-inherent risks that the companies face, foreign reinsurance companies have strong risk management departments in place at their corporate headquarters. These departments also set the ideal risk tolerance level for each risk category. Furthermore, foreign reinsurance companies' risk management governance frameworks emphasize resource integration and sharing and are in line with the culture of risk management. First, the groups' uniform capital model is used to accomplish the capital management and risk management of different regions and markets; Second, the risk preference and risk transmission mechanisms are established and improved, and the preference setting is finally adapted to the requirements of economic capital return, rating capital, and regulatory capital; Third, there is an emphasis on the centralized and standardized building of information systems.

III. Overview of Foreign Reinsurance Companies' Operations in China

In recent years, foreign reinsurance companies have become an integral part of China's reinsurance market. Their overall business scale exhibits

Entities	2017	2018	2019	2020	2021	Accumulated capital increase	Registered capital at the end of the period
RGA Shanghai Branch						—	3.0
Subtotal						49.6	115.4
Total	29.5	7.4	35.1	15.6	0	88.6	204.4

Source: CBIRC.

(III) Complying With Overall Group Strategy and Pursuing Globalization

Foreign reinsurance companies in China have clear business goals consistent with the overall development strategy of their respective group companies. First, foreign reinsurance companies have specific requirements for ROE; Second, foreign reinsurance companies place greater demand on solvency restrictions to ensure that their solvency is within the specified range; Third, foreign reinsurance companies plan their prospective capital in a focused manner; Fourth, foreign reinsurance companies explore alternative capital, making full use of various tools for capital supplement such as catastrophe bonds, subordinated debts, etc.; Fifth, oriented towards risk capital management, foreign reinsurance companies evaluate and allocate capital via internal uniform financial standards.

(IV) Steady Growth in Number of Employees

The number of employees at foreign reinsurance companies have increased from 2 to 10 employees at the representative office level to over 100

(II) Steady Increase in Operating Capital

After Munich Re Beijing Branch increased its working capital by RMB 1.3 billion in 2015 and became the first foreign reinsurance company to increase its capital; other foreign reinsurance companies continued to increase their capital in China, with a total capital increase of RMB 4.96 billion in five years (from 2017 to 2021), including RMB 2.8 billion by Hannover Re Shanghai Branch and RMB 1.05 billion by Swiss Re Beijing Branch. Specifically, from 2019 to 2021, foreign reinsurance companies gathered pace of their capital addition in Chinese branches, with a total increase of RMB 3.67 billion, which was significantly higher than the RMB 1.4 billion increase by Chinese reinsurance companies.

Table 2 Capital Changes by Reinsurance Entities from 2017 to 2021 (RMB 100 million)

Entities	2017	2018	2019	2020	2021	Accumulated capital increase	Registered capital at the end of the period
PICC Re	20.0		10.0			30.0	40.0
Taiping Re (China)	5.0		4.0			9.0	19.0
Qianhai Re						—	30.0
Subtotal						39.0	89.0
Swiss Re Beijing Branch			10.5			10.5	13.1
Munich Re Beijing Branch						—	16.5
Hannover Re Shanghai Branch		2.4	10.0	15.6		28.0	41.0
Scor SE Beijing Branch	4.5	3.6	0.6			8.7	20.7
General Re Shanghai Branch		1.4				1.4	4.4

Report on the Development of Reinsurance Industry in China 2022

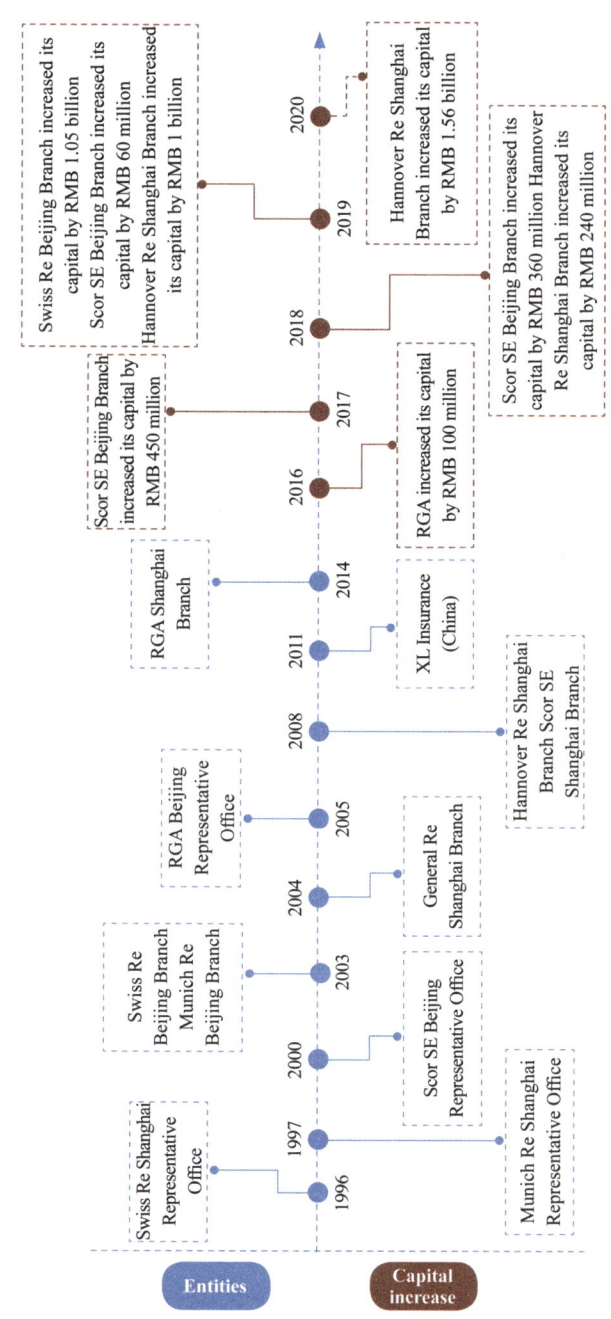

Figure 1 Development Timeline of Foreign Reinsurance Companies in China

(Source: Annual report of reinsurance companies)

(I) Overview of Foreign Reinsurance Companies' Branches in China

Swiss Re and Munich Re were the first major international reinsurance companies to enter China, opening their representative offices in Shanghai in 1996 and 1997, respectively. In 2003, these two companies received the license to open branches in Beijing. The Chinese reinsurance market is open to foreign reinsurance companies. Swiss Re, Munich Re, and other leading reinsurance companies took the initiative in developing their distribution while other reinsurance companies stepped up their efforts to follow suit. They started by establishing representative offices and gradually transitioned to direct operations. With the exception of AXA XL Reinsurance, the seven other foreign reinsurance entities in China are conducting business by setting up branches.

Name of Company	Date of Incorporation	Place of Registration	Nature of Registration
Reinsurance Group of America, Incorporated Shanghai Branch	2014	Shanghai	Subsidiary
Korean Reinsurance Company Shanghai Branch	2020	Shanghai	Subsidiary

Sources: Yearbook of China's Insurance and annual reports of reinsurance companies.

The rapid development of the macro-economy and insurance market has led to a quick rise in China's reinsurance market as well. The domestic market has been highly competitive, and the growth rate of premium income is significantly higher than the average growth rate of mature markets. At present, the property reinsurance market has established a multi-level participation form in terms of the scale of reinsurance premium income and solvency level. Pressurized macroeconomics, switch in regulatory policies such as CROSS II, and transformation and slowdown of the direct insurance market, are all together exerting a triple pressure on the life reinsurance market, which is exhibiting a trend of fluctuations. With continuous investment by foreign reinsurance companies, competition in China's reinsurance market is deepening and becoming increasingly fierce.

II. Development of Foreign Reinsurance Companies in China

The Chinese reinsurance market has paved the way for foreign investment ever since China joined the WTO in 2001. China's reinsurance market has grown from scratch and has become one of the most open and promising reinsurance markets in the world.

I. Outline of Foreign Reinsurance Companies' Development in China

The global reinsurance market's growth rate has slowed down in recent years, but the emerging reinsurance markets represented by China have stood out. Major international reinsurance companies who view the Chinese market as a strategic target are leveraging their professional expertise and capital advantage to increase their investment in the Chinese market.

By the end of 2021, there were 15 professional reinsurance companies operating in China, including 7 China-invested companies (including 1 group company, namely China Re Group) and 8 foreign-invested companies. Of the 8 foreign-invested companies, 7 ranked on the A.M. Best Global Reinsurance Company List. In addition, more than 100 P&C and life insurers or reinsurers are competing in China's reinsurance market. More than 500 foreign reinsurance entities have not set up branches in China, but they accept China-ceded business through offshore transactions.

Table 1 Overview of Foreign-invested Professional Reinsurance Companies in China

Name of Company	Date of Incorporation	Place of Registration	Nature of Registration
Munich Reinsurance Group Beijing Branch	2003	Beijing	Subsidiary
Swiss Reinsurance Company Limited Beijing Branch	2003	Beijing	Subsidiary
General Reinsurance Corporation Shanghai Branch	2004	Shanghai	Subsidiary
Hannover Re Shanghai Branch	2008	Shanghai	Subsidiary
Scor SE Beijing Branch	2008	Beijing	Subsidiary
XL Reinsurance (China) Company Limited	2011	Shanghai	Single company

Chapter III

Development of Foreign Reinsurance Companies in 2021

I. Outline of Foreign Reinsurance Companies' Development in China

II. Development of Foreign Reinsurance Companies in China

III. Overview of Foreign Reinsurance Companies' Operations in China

IV. Human Resources of Foreign Reinsurance Companies in China

reinsurance companies as well as such domestic ones as Qianhai Re, Taiping Re (China), and PICC Re.

In 2021, China had 10 registered professional reinsurance companies engaging in life reinsurance business in the Chinese market. 1 company had a market share of over 50%, 1 with a share between 10% and 15%; 5 with a share between 5% and 10%, and 3 with a share of less than 5%.

stricter industry regulation, and the ongoing quit of insurance agents, life insurance that is a non-obligatory consumer expenditure will also come under pressure, and its growth is expected to slow down.

In terms of demand for reinsurance, although the industry has been under pressure, driven by product innovation and risk spreading, 56 life insurance companies saw a year-on-year increase in ceded premiums in 2021, accounting for 63% of the total, indicating that demand for reinsurance continues to grow; among them, 24 had a year-on-year increase of over 50%, 15 had a year-on-year increase between 20% and 50%, and 17 had a year-on-year increase between 0% and 20%.

In 2021[1], 9 life insurance companies had ceded premiums over RMB 5 billion, totaling RMB 68.82 billion, accounting for 69.1% of the industry's total ceded premiums; 18 had ceded premiums between RMB 1 billion and RMB 5 billion, totaling RMB 43.95 billion, accounting for 44.1% of the total; 29 had ceded premiums between RMB 0.1 billion and RMB 1 billion, totaling RMB 10.85 billion, accounting for 10.9% of the total; 27 had ceded premiums of less than RMB 0.1 billion, totaling RMB 0.72 billion, accounting for 0.7% of the total.

(III) Supply-side Analysis

In terms of supply-side structure, China Re Life has given full play to its role as the main channel of reinsurance in China, and has ranked first in terms of market share. Other major players include large international

---

[1] Data from 2021 suggests that some life insurers in China wrote negative premiums ceded. The total net premiums ceded by China's life insurance companies stood at RMB 99.63bn. If taking this as the basis to calculate different shares of premiums ceded, all shares combined exceed 100%.

companies as a whole recorded a steady increase. The cession rate saw a steady increase to a peak between 2012 and 2014, significant decline in 2015, steady increase between 2016 and 2020, and moderate year-on-year decrease in 2021. Overall, compared with 2012, the reinsurance cession rate in 2021 had doubled over the past 10 years, and was 1.6 percentage points higher than that in 2012. This change was largely due to the rapid development of China's medical insurance market. Compared with the surplus reinsurance for critical illness, medical insurance has mostly adopted quota share reinsurance, which has led to a significant increase in the life insurance companies' demand for reinsurance.

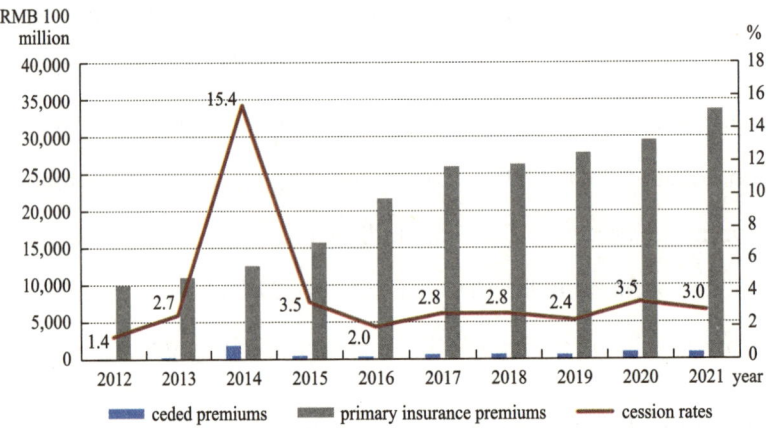

Figure 19 Reinsurance cession rates of life insurance companies (2012-2021)

(Sources: Yearbook of China's Insurance and CBIRC)

(II) Demand-side Analysis

In 2021, the primary premiums of China's life insurance stood at RMB 3.36 trillion, up 6.2% year-on-year. Looking ahead, with COVID-19 putting more pressure on the economy, a slowdown in per capita income growth,

Table 11 Primary insurance premiums, ceded premiums and cession rates of life insurance (2012-2021)

(RMB in 100 million)	Ceded	Growth rate	Primary	Growth rate	Cession rate
2012	140.4		9,957.9		1.4%
2013	298.8	112.8%	11,010.0	10.6%	2.7%
2014	1,937.4	548.4%	12,592.3	14.4%	15.4%
2015	555.6	−71.3%	15,724.0	24.9%	3.5%
2016	435.9	−21.5%	21,662.8	37.8%	2.0%
2017	722.4	65.7%	25,972.7	19.9%	2.8%
2018	736.2	1.9%	26,232.5	1.0%	2.8%
2019	673.9	−8.5%	27,792.6	5.9%	2.4%
2020	1,043.7	54.9%	29,500.7	6.1%	3.5%
2021	996.3	−4.5%	33,636.0	14.0%	3.0%

Sources: Yearbook of China's Insurance and CBIRC.

Cession rates

In 2021, the reinsurance cession rate of China's life insurance companies was around 3%, exceeding 3% for the second year in a row, down 0.5 percentage points year-on-year. At present, China's life reinsurance cession rate is converging towards that of the world, which basically remains at around 3%, mainly due to the business structure and changes in the life primary insurance market. Traditional protection-oriented reinsurance business accounted for a relatively large cession share, while savings-oriented life insurance business has a lower share. Meanwhile, the overseas stock market has been stable, resulting in limited growth. Business changes are mainly influenced by international mergers and acquisitions, annuities, and other bulk transactions.

From 2012 to 2021, the reinsurance cession rate of life insurance against the backdrop of the fact that the Chinese economy faces triple pressures from shrinking demand, disrupted supply and weakening expectations at the macro level, C-ROSS II and other new regulatory policies are being transformed or introduced, and the primary insurance market is undergoing transition and slowdown in growth, the growth of the reinsurance market is encountering certain shocks and challenges.

The ceded premiums of China's life insurance companies increased between 2012 and 2021, from RMB 14.04 billion to RMB 99.63 billion, with an average annual growth rate of about 24.3%, securing a steady increase. The ceded premiums increased rapidly between 2012 and 2014, declined significantly between 2015 and 2016, increased unstably between 2017 and 2020, and decreased slightly year-on-year in 2021.

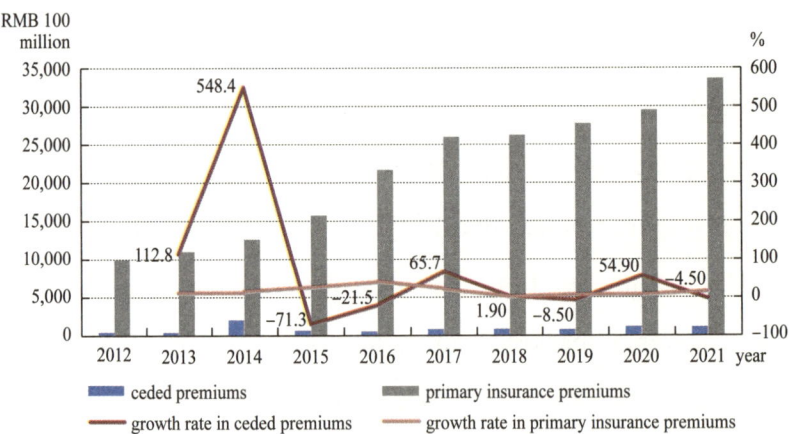

Figure 18 Primary insurance premiums, ceded premiums and growth rates of life insurance (2012-2021)

(Sources: Yearbook of China's Insurance and CBIRC)

(III) Supply-side Analysis

In terms of supply-side structure, China Re P&C gave full play to its role as the main channel of reinsurance in China, ranking first in terms of market share. Meanwhile, new local reinsurance entities have been established in the P&C reinsurance market in recent years, including China Agriculture Re, PICC Re, Taiping Re (China), and Qianhai Re. Foreign reinsurers also attach great importance to China's reinsurance market. In 2021, Swiss Re, Hanover Re, and other foreign reinsurers increased capital to gather pace in China's market.

In 2021, China had 12 registered professional reinsurance companies engaging in P&C reinsurance business (including Lloyd's Insurance Company (China) Limited). 1 company had a market share of over 20%, 1 with a share between 10% and 15%, 3 with a share between 5% and 10%, and 7 with a share of less than 5%.

III. Life Reinsurance

(I) Market Size

Ceded premiums

In 2021, the total ceded premiums of life insurance companies in China stood at RMB 99.63 billion, down 4.5% year-on-year. During the same period, the total primary insurance premium income of life insurance companies was RMB 3.36359 trillion, up 6.2% year-on-year. Overall, the amount of life ceded premium fluctuated from year to year. At present, on-year increase of less than 10%, accounting for 18.2% of the total; 10 had a year-on-year increase between 10% and 20%, accounting for 11.4% of the total; 35 had a year-on-year increase of over 20%, accounting for 39.8% of the total. In 2021, 27 P&C insurance companies saw a year-on-year decline in P&C ceded premiums, accounting for 30.7% of the total; 8 among which had a year-on-year decline of less than 10%, accounting for 9.1% of the total; 7 had a year-on-year decline between 10% and 20%, accounting for 8.0% of the total; 12 had a year-on-year decline of over 20%, accounting for 13.6% of the total.

Distribution of cession rates

In 2021, 39 P&C insurance companies had a P&C reinsurance cession rate of over 20%, accounting for 44.3% of the total, and an increase of 7 companies year-on-year; 5 had a P&C reinsurance cession rate between 15% and 20%, accounting for 5.7% of the total, and a decrease of 5 companies year-on-year; 8 had a P&C reinsurance cession rate between 10% and 15%, accounting for 9.1% of the total, and an increase of 1 company year-on-year; 18 had a P&C reinsurance cession rate between 5% and 10%, accounting for 20.5% of the total, and an increase of 6 companies year-on-year; 18 had a P&C reinsurance cession rate of less than 5%, accounting for 20.5% of the total, and a decrease of 9 companies year-on-year.

Table 10 Distribution of reinsurance cession rates of P&C insurance companies (2016-2021)

Cession Rate	2016	2017	2018	2019	2020	2021
>20%	26	26	28	34	32	39
15%~20%	4	5	8	2	10	5
10%~15%	12	12	11	15	7	8
5%~10%	14	17	15	11	12	18
<5%	24	24	25	25	27	18
Total	80	84	87	87	88	88

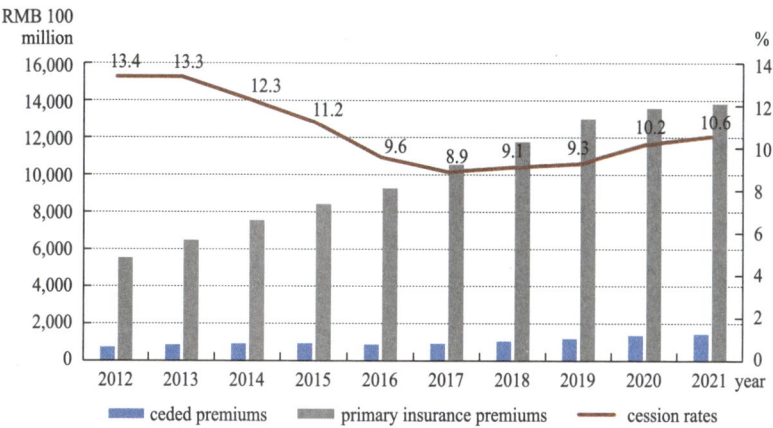

Figure17 Reinsurance cession rates of P&C insurance companies (2012-2021)
(Sources: Yearbook of China's Insurance and CBIRC)

(II) Demand-side Analysis

Distribution of ceded premiums

In 2021, 4 P&C insurance companies had P&C ceded premiums over RMB 10 billion, totaling RMB 92.92 billion and accounting for 63.6% of the industry's total ceded premiums; 14 P&C insurance companies had P&C ceded premiums ranging from RMB 1 billion to RMB 10 billion, totaling RMB 33.57 billion and accounting for 23.0% of the total; 51 P&C insurance companies had P&C ceded premiums ranging from RMB 0.1 billion to RMB 1 billion, totaling RMB 18.93 billion and accounting for 13.0% of the total; 19 P&C insurance companies had P&C ceded premiums of less than RMB 0.1 billion, totaling RMB 0.63 billion and accounting for 0.4% of the total.

Changes in ceded premiums

In 2021, 61 P&C insurance companies saw a year-on-year increase in P&C ceded premiums, accounting for 69.3% of the total; among them, 16 had a year-

Table 9 Ceded premiums, primary insurance premiums and cession rates of P&C insurance (2012-2021)

(RMB in 100 million)	Ceded	Growth rate	Primary	Growth rate	Cession rate
2012	739.0	—	5,529.9	—	13.4%
2013	865.2	17.1%	6,480.9	17.2%	13.3%
2014	929.8	7.5%	7,544.4	16.4%	12.3%
2015	946.0	1.7%	8,423.3	11.6%	11.2%
2016	887.9	−6.1%	9,266.2	10.0%	9.6%
2017	938.8	5.7%	10,541.4	13.8%	8.9%
2018	1,072.3	14.2%	11,755.7	11.5%	9.1%
2019	1,207.7	12.6%	13,016.3	10.7%	9.3%
2020	1,383.4	14.5%	13,583.7	4.4%	10.2%
2021	1,460.5	5.6%	13,816.2	1.8%	10.6%

Sources: Yearbook of China's Insurance and CBIRC.

Cession rates

In 2021, the reinsurance cession rate of China's P&C insurance companies was about 10.6%, exceeding 10% for the second year in a row, up 0.4 percentage points year-on-year.

The reinsurance cession rate saw a year-on-year decline in market performance between 2012 and 2015, but all were above 10%, and showed a falling trend followed by a rising one between 2016 and 2021. In 2016, mainly affected by the implementation of the C-ROSS, the reinsurance cession rate declined sharply to below 10%; in 2017, as the impact of the C-ROSS continued, the rate declined to less than 9%; since 2018, the reinsurance cession rate has increased over time due to the growth of non-motor insurance business; in 2020, the rate increased to over 10%; in 2021, the rate continued to increase, which was nearly 1 percentage point higher than in 2016.

primary insurance premiums over the same period.

The ceded premiums of P&C insurance companies in China increased between 2012 and 2021, from RMB 73.9 billion to RMB 146.05 billion, with an average annual growth rate of about 8.1%. During the same period, the primary insurance premiums of P&C insurance companies increased from RMB 552.99 billion to RMB 1.38162 trillion, with an average annual growth rate of about 10.7%. The average annual growth rate of ceded premiums was 2.6 percentage points lower than that of primary insurance premiums in the same period. Since 2016, the growth of ceded premiums has accelerated. According to data between 2016 and 2021, the average annual growth of ceded premiums of P&C insurance companies was about 10.4%. During the same period, the average annual growth of primary insurance premiums of P&C insurance companies was about 8.3%. The average annual growth rate of ceded premiums was about 2 percentage points higher than that of primary insurance premiums in the same period.

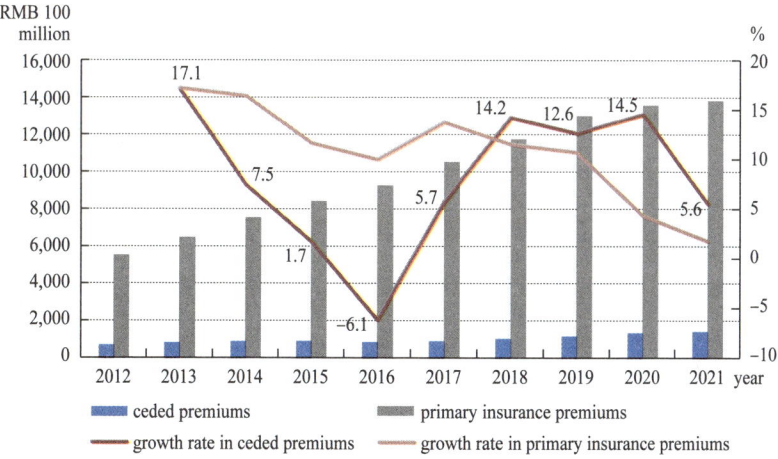

Figure16 Primary insurance premiums, ceded premiums and growth rates of P&C insurance (2012-2021)

(Sources: Yearbook of China's Insurance and CBIRC)

disclosed information from 15 reinsurance companies, if a catastrophe leading to a 50% increase in the cash outflow of reinsurance indemnity in the baseline scenario during the forecast period occurred at the end of the fourth quarter of 2021, the average liquidity coverage rate of the reinsurance companies would be 2265.50%; if a catastrophe occurred, which led to the fact that 20% of the fixed income assets maturing during the forecast period could not recover principal and interest, the average liquidity coverage of reinsurance companies would be 2423.45%.

International rating

In 2021, a total of 14 reinsurance companies obtained ratings from credit rating agencies. Most of the companies were rated by more than one credit rating agencies; 12 were rated A- and above by Standard & Poor's, 12 were rated A- and above by A.M.Best, 6 were rated A1 and above by Moody's, and 3 were rated AA- or above by Fitch.

II. P&C Reinsurance

(I) Market Size

Ceded premiums

In 2021, the total ceded premiums of China's P&C insurance companies stood at RMB 146.05 billion, up 5.6% year-on-year. During the same period, the total primary insurance premiums of P&C insurance companies amounted to RMB 1.38162 trillion, up 1.8% year-on-year, and the growth rate of ceded premiums was about 3.8 percentage points higher than that of

SARMRA review. The average score of reinsurers in the latest review session was 79.24, and the score of 6 reinsurers exceeded 80.

Liquidity

Insurance companies primarily reflect their liquidity risk with indicators such as net cash flow, comprehensive liquidity ratio, and liquidity coverage ratio.

In terms of net cash flow, according to the publicly disclosed information of 14 reinsurance companies, the reinsurers' total net cash flow in 2021 saw an outflow of RMB 2.73 billion in the first quarter, inflow of RMB 1.983 billion in the second quarter, inflow of RMB 2.792 billion in the third quarter, and outflow of RMB 4.796 billion in the fourth quarter. In each quarter, the total net cash flow of 8 reinsurers recorded a positive inflow, while that of 6 reinsurers saw a negative outflow.

In terms of comprehensive liquidity ratio, this indicator is the ratio of the total expected cash inflows from existing assets to the total expected cash outflows from existing liabilities, reflecting the cash flow distribution of all assets and liabilities of insurance companies in the future and the matching degree between cash inflows and cash outflows. According to the publicly disclosed information from 15 reinsurance companies, at the end of the fourth quarter of 2021, the average comprehensive liquidity ratio of the reinsurers was 246.37% within 3 months, 207.21% within 1 year, and 208.75% over 1 year.

In terms of liquidity coverage rate, this indicator is the ratio of the book value of high-quality liquidity assets at the end of a period to the net cash flow in the coming quarter, reflecting the liquidity of insurance companies in the coming quarter under stressed scenarios. According to the publicly regulatory ratio and the adequacy levels of P&C insurance companies and life insurance companies in the quarters.

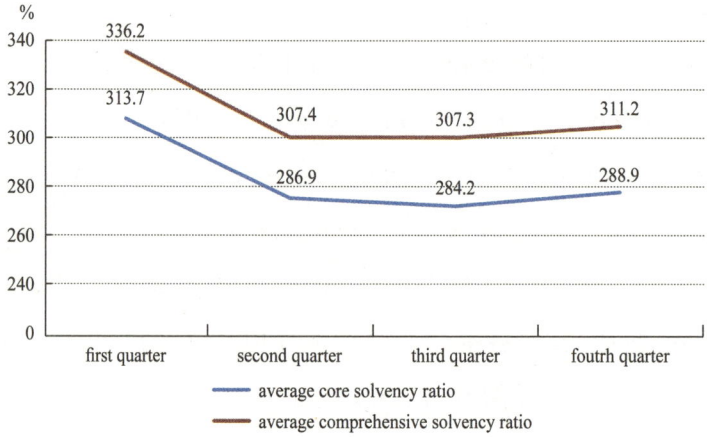

Figure 15 Solvency of reinsurance companies in 2021

(Sources: CBIRC)

Integrated Risk Rating (IRR)

IRR is the evaluation of the comprehensive risk of the solvency of insurance companies, which measures the overall solvency risk of insurance companies with 4 classes: A, B, C and D, and the required regulatory rating is B.

In 2022, a total of 14 reinsurers had received and disclosed their quarterly IRRs, all of which were rated Class B or higher, and 7 of them were rated Class A in four quarters.

Solvency Aligned Risk Management Requirements and Assessment (SARMRA)

SARMRA reflects the insurance companies' level of risk management with sound system and effective compliance. The CBIRC conducts the regulatory review and evaluation of SARMRA in insurance companies. When a company scores 80 or more, its solvency adequacy ratio can be raised.

As of the end of 2021, a total of 13 reinsurers had been evaluated with the risk management and control have become more diversified. In terms of risk index monitoring, the reinsurance industry mainly focuses on solvency and international rating indicators. In 2021, various reinsurance companies saw an excellent performance in terms of solvency and rating levels, providing effective support for the business expansion, risk management, market reputation and image.

Solvency[1]

Core solvency ratio and comprehensive solvency ratio

The core solvency ratio is the ratio of an insurance company's core capital to its minimum capital, which measures the adequacy of the company's high-quality capital, and the minimum required regulatory ratio is 50%. Whereas the comprehensive solvency ratio is the ratio of the actual capital to the minimum capital, which measures the overall adequacy of the company's capital, and the minimum required regulatory ratio is 100%.

From the first quarter to the fourth quarter of 2021, the average core solvency ratios of reinsurance companies were 313.7%, 286.9%, 284.2%, and 288.9%, respectively, exceeding the required 50% regulatory ratio and the adequacy levels of P&C insurance companies and life insurance companies in the quarters.

From the first quarter to the fourth quarter of 2021, the average comprehensive solvency ratios of reinsurance companies were 336.2%, 307.4%, 307.3%, and 311.2%, respectively, exceeding the required 100%

---

[1] The solvency data mentioned below are the statistical data under the regulations of C-ROSS II Phase I.

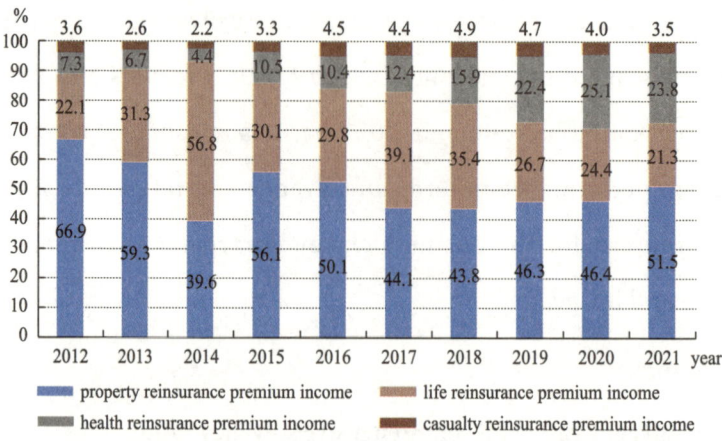

Figure 14　Share of reinsurance premium income by lines (2012-2021)

(Sources: Yearbook of China's Insurance and CBIRC)

(IV) Risk Management

Reinsurance functions to further transfer or share risks of the insurance industry, which is more prominent in addressing catastrophe risks, major risks, and special risks, helping insurance companies cross the restrictions of risk units and geographic locations to provide services and spread risks across a broader range of time and space around the world. Therefore, the reinsurance industry has higher requirements for risk management and a more systemic importance compared to the insurance industry. More importantly, more attention is paid to the management of cumulative liabilities for major risks such as catastrophes. Risk management has become one of the core competence in the reinsurance industry and has been highly valued by reinsurance companies.

In recent years, the overall development of the reinsurance industry's risk management system has been continuously improved, and tools for the

Table 8 Reinsurance premium income and growth rate by lines (2012-2021)

(RMB in 100 million)	Property	Growth rate	Life	Growth rate	Health	Growth rate	Casualty	Growth rate
2012	462.6		153.0		50.6		25.0	
2013	562.8	21.7%	297.3	94.3%	63.5	25.6%	24.8	−0.6%
2014	588.0	4.5%	799.6	168.9%	65.7	3.4%	32.7	31.7%
2015	598.1	1.7%	320.9	−59.9%	112.1	70.7%	35.1	7.4%
2016	480.7	−19.6%	285.9	−10.9%	100.1	−10.8%	43.5	23.9%
2017	484.9	0.9%	430.2	50.5%	136.1	36.0%	48.4	11.3%
2018	600.4	23.8%	484.4	12.6%	218.2	60.4%	67.1	38.5%
2019	729.9	21.6%	421.3	−13.0%	353.1	61.8%	73.6	9.7%
2020	840.1	15.1%	441.6	4.8%	454.5	28.7%	73.1	−0.7%
2021	1,075.6	28.0%	445.0	0.8%	496.5	9.2%	73.1	0.0%

Sources: Yearbook of China's Insurance and CBIRC.

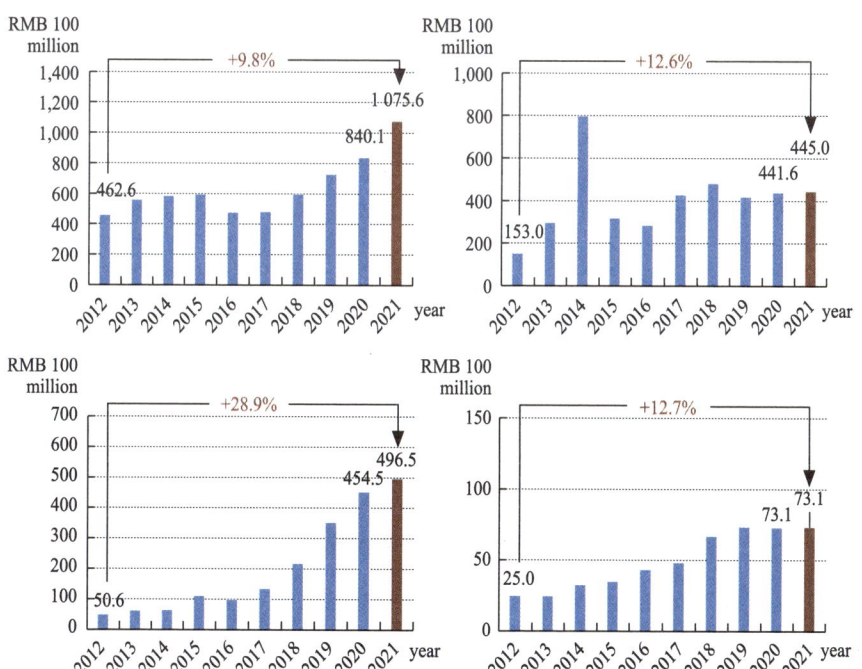

Figure 13 Property, Life, Health, Casualty reinsurance premium income and annual growth rate (2012-2021)

(Sources: Yearbook of China's Insurance and CBIRC)

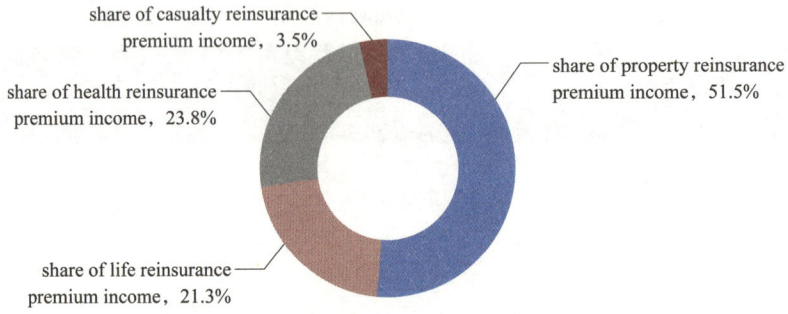

Figure 12 Share of reinsurance premium income by lines of reinsurance in 2021
(Source: CBIRC)

In summary, premium income of all lines in China's reinsurance market increased between 2012 and 2021. Property reinsurance premium income increased from RMB 46.26 billion in 2012 to RMB 107.56 billion in 2021, an average annual growth rate of about 9.8%; life reinsurance premium income increased from RMB 15.3 billion in 2012 to RMB 44.5 billion in 2021, an average annual growth rate of about 12.6%; health reinsurance premium income increased from RMB 5.06 billion in 2012 to RMB 49.65 billion in 2021, an average annual growth rate of about 28.9%; casualty reinsurance premium income increased from RMB 2.5 billion in 2012 to RMB 7.31 billion in 2021, an average annual growth rate of about 12.7%. Health reinsurance recorded the fastest growth. Its share of premiums has steadily increased over time, exceeding 20% for the first time in 2019, and its reinsurance premiums exceeded RMB 40 billion in 2020, which indicates great growth potential. However, growth in health reinsurance has slowed in recent years. As the share of health insurance business in P&C insurance companies increases, so does demand for health reinsurance, particularly the increase in demand for short-term health insurance, which is bound to generate higher reinsurance premium income.

Reinsurance premium income by lines of business

In 2021, property reinsurance premium income of China's reinsurance market was RMB 107.56 billion, up 28.0% year-on-year and accounting for about 51.5% of the total; life reinsurance premium income was RMB 44.5 billion, up 0.79% year-on-year and making up about 21.3% of the total; health reinsurance premium income was RMB 49.65 billion, up 9.2% year-on-year and accounting for about 23.8% of the total; casualty reinsurance premium income was RMB 7.31 billion, unchanged year-on-year and accounting for about 3.5% of the total. Overall, the reinsurance premium income of different types of reinsurance somewhat varied in terms of their respective growth rate: property reinsurance grew rapidly, followed by health reinsurance, while the size of life reinsurance and casualty reinsurance remained basically unchanged compared to the last year. At the same time, the growth rate of health reinsurance premium income was significantly slower than in previous years, consistent with the development of health insurance in the insurance market, which recorded a significant decrease in demand for health reinsurance in 2021. Compared with 2020, the share of property reinsurance premium income increased slightly, while that of life reinsurance, health reinsurance, and casualty reinsurance saw a moderate decline, indicating the impact of business structure adjustment in the insurance market on reinsurance.

Chapter II Development of China's Reinsurance Market in 2021

Table 7 Reinsurance premium income, growth rate, and share of treaty and facultative business (2012-2021)

(RMB in 100 million)	Treaty business	Growth rate	Share	Facultative business	Growth rate	Share
2012	681.9		98.7%	9.3		1.3%
2013	940.3	37.9%	99.1%	8.3	−10.7%	0.9%
2014	1,476.7	57.1%	99.4%	9.23	11.6%	0.6%
2015	1,055.2	−28.5%	99.0%	11.0	19.2%	1.0%
2016	917.9	−13.0%	95.8%	37.9	243.7%	4.0%
2017	1,080.2	17.7%	98.2%	19.4	−48.9%	1.8%
2018	1,339.4	24.0%	97.8%	30.7	58.5%	2.2%
2019	1,539.8	15.0%	97.7%	36.3	18.1%	2.3%
2020	1,774.3	15.2%	97.5%	45.8	26.2%	2.5%
2021	2,070.7	16.7%	97.7%	49.5	8.1%	2.3%

Sources: Yearbook of China's Insurance and CBIRC.

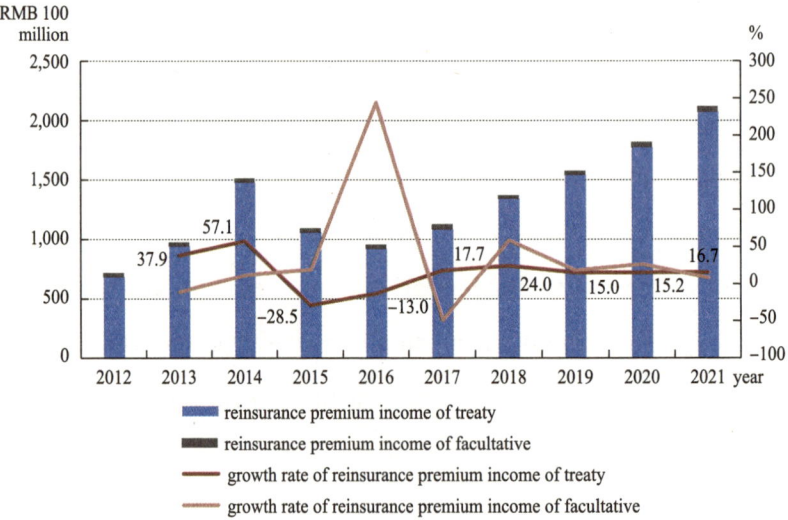

Figure 11 Reinsurance premium income and growth rate of treaty and facultative business (2012-2021)

(Sources: Yearbook of China's Insurance and CBIRC)

that of facultative business was RMB 4.95 billion, up 8.1% year-on-year and accounted for about 2.3% of the total reinsurance premium income. The treaty business saw steady growth, while the growth of facultative business slowed.

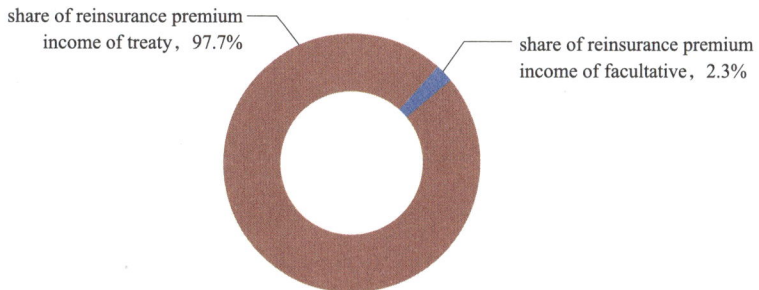

Figure 10   Share of reinsurance premium income of treaty and facultative business in 2021

(Source: CBIRC)

In summary, the reinsurance premium income of treaty business and facultative business increased between 2012 and 2021, with the former increasing from RMB 68.19 billion in 2012 to RMB 207.07 billion in 2021, an average annual growth rate of about 13.1%, and the latter increasing from RMB 0.93 billion in 2012 to RMB 4.95 billion in 2021, an average annual growth rate of about 20.4%. Overall, treaty business was the primary type of reinsurance business, holding a share of over 95% and showing relatively steady growth. The facultative business accounted for a small proportion and experienced relatively rapid growth, but has fluctuated significantly in terms of its growth rate over the years, which is closely related to the nature of the business.

Table 6 Distribution of branches of professional reinsurance companies in China

Company	Distribution of branches
China Reinsurance (Group) Corporation	Headquartered in Beijing
China Property and Casualty Reinsurance Company Limited	Headquartered in Beijing; Branches in Shanghai and Shenzhen
China Life Reinsurance Company Limited	Headquartered in Beijing; Branches in Shanghai and Shenzhen
Munich Reinsurance Group Beijing Branch	Branch in Beijing
Swiss Reinsurance Company Limited Beijing Branch	Branch in Beijing
General Reinsurance Corporation Shanghai Branch	Branch in Shanghai
SCOR SE Beijing Branch	Branch in Beijing
Hannover Re Shanghai Branch	Branch in Shanghai
XL Reinsurance (China) Company Limited	Headquartered in Shanghai
Reinsurance Group of America, Incorporated Shanghai Branch	Branch in Shanghai
Taiping Reinsurance (China) Company Limited	Headquartered in Beijing; Branch in Shanghai
Qianhai Reinsurance Company Limited	Headquartered in Shenzhen
People's Insurance Company of China Limited	Headquartered in Beijing
Korean Reinsurance Company Shanghai Branch	Branch in Shanghai
China Agriculture Reinsurance Corporation	Headquartered in Beijing

Sources: Yearbook of China's Insurance and annual reports of the reinsurance companies.

(III) Business Structure

Reinsurance premium income by type of business

In 2021, the reinsurance premium income of China's reinsurance market stood at RMB 209.02 billion. Meanwhile, the reinsurance premium income of treaty business stood at RMB 207.07 billion, up 16.7% year-on-year and accounted for about 97.7%[①] of the total reinsurance premium income, while

---

[①] The impact of related party transactions between companies was considered in terms of reinsurance premium income but not in terms of reinsurance premium income by business type.

Name of Company	Date of founding	Place of registration	Nature of registration	Nature of company
People's Insurance Company of China Limited	2017	Beijing	Single company	Chinese-invested
Korean Reinsurance Company Shanghai Branch	2020	Shanghai	Subsidiary	Foreign-invested
China Agriculture Reinsurance Corporation	2020	Beijing	Single company	Chinese-invested

Sources: Yearbook of China's Insurance and annual reports of the reinsurance companies.

In summary, the number of entities in China's reinsurance market has increased between 2012 and 2021, from 9 to 15, with 4 new Chinese-invested companies and 2 new foreign-invested companies. Every year between 2014 and 2017, a new reinsurance company was added, and in 2020, there were 2 more.

Company distribution

Unlike insurance companies that mainly rely on organizational expansion to drive business growth, reinsurance companies have a simpler structure and more concentrated personnel and resources. At present, China's professional reinsurance companies establish branches primarily concentrated in Beijing, Shanghai, Shenzhen, and other core cities with the developed economies in China.

As of the end of 2021, 9 of 15 reinsurance companies had set up branches in Beijing, 8 in Shanghai, 3 in Shenzhen. Meanwhile, 9 reinsurance companies established their headquarters or regional center in Beijing, making it the city with the most offices, followed by Shanghai.

Table 5 Overview of professional reinsurance companies in China[①]

Name of Company	Date of founding	Place of registration	Nature of registration	Nature of company
China Reinsurance (Group) Corporation	1996	Beijing	Group	Chinese-invested
China Property and Casualty Reinsurance Company Limited	2003	Beijing	Single company	Chinese-invested
China Life Reinsurance Company Limited	2003	Beijing	Single company	Chinese-invested
Munich Reinsurance Group Beijing Branch	2003	Beijing	Subsidiary	Foreign-invested
Swiss Reinsurance Company Limited Beijing Branch	2003	Beijing	Subsidiary	Foreign-invested
General Reinsurance Corporation Shanghai Branch	2004	Shanghai	Subsidiary	Foreign-invested
SCOR SE Beijing Branch	2008	Beijing	Subsidiary	Foreign-invested
Hannover Re Shanghai Branch	2008	Shanghai	Subsidiary	Foreign-invested
XL Reinsurance (China) Company Limited[②]	2011	Shanghai	Single company	Foreign-invested
Reinsurance Group of America, Incorporated Shanghai Branch	2014	Shanghai	Subsidiary	Foreign-invested
Taiping Reinsurance (China) Company Limited	2015	Beijing	Single company	Chinese-invested
Qianhai Reinsurance Company Limited	2016	Shenzhen	Single company	Chinese-invested

---

[①] The name of each reinsurance entity is abbreviated as follows: China Re Group or China Re, China Re P&C or China Re, China Re Life or China Re, Munich Re or Munich Re Beijing Branch, Swiss Re or Swiss Re Beijing Branch, General Re or General Re Shanghai Branch, SCOR SE or SCOR SE Beijing Branch, Hannover Re or Hannover Re Shanghai Branch, XL Re, RGA or RGA Shanghai Branch, Taiping Re (China), Qianhai Re, PICC Re, Korean Re or Korean Re Shanghai Branch, and China Agriculture Re.

[②] XL Insurance (China) Company Limited was established in 2011 and changed its name to XL Reinsurance (China) Company Limited in 2020.

Table 4 Total assets and share of reinsurance, insurance, and financial industry (2012-2021)

(RMB 100 million)	Reinsurance	Insurance	Reinsurance/ Insurance	Financial industry	Insurance/ Financial industry
2012	1,437.2	68,425.6	2.1%		
2013	1,765.4	77,576.7	2.3%		
2014	3,183.2	96,177.8	3.3%		
2015	4,722.0	119,295.7	4.0%		
2016	2,343.9	142,659.0	1.6%		
2017	2,699.3	146,816.7	1.8%		
2018	3,358.3	163,641.0	2.1%	2,940,000	5.6%
2019	4,261.3	187,495.6	2.3%	3,186,900	5.9%
2020	4,956.3	216,156.5	2.3%	3,531,900	6.1%
2021	6,057.5	248,874.0	2.4%	3,819,500	6.5%

Sources: Yearbook of China's Insurance, CBIRC, and People's Bank of China website.

(II) Market Pattern

Market entities

By the end of 2021, there had been a total of 15 professional reinsurance companies in China, including 7 China-invested reinsurance companies (including 1 group company, namely China Re) and 8 foreign-invested reinsurance companies. There are also over 100 P&C and life insurers competing in the reinsurance market to varying degrees, and over 500 foreign reinsurance entities that do not have a branch in China conduct reinsurance business offshore.

that of reinsurance premium income. The total assets also saw significant volatility between 2014 and 2016 due to the C-ROSS II. Since 2016, the asset volume of the reinsurance industry has steadily increased, consistent with changes in reinsurance premium income.

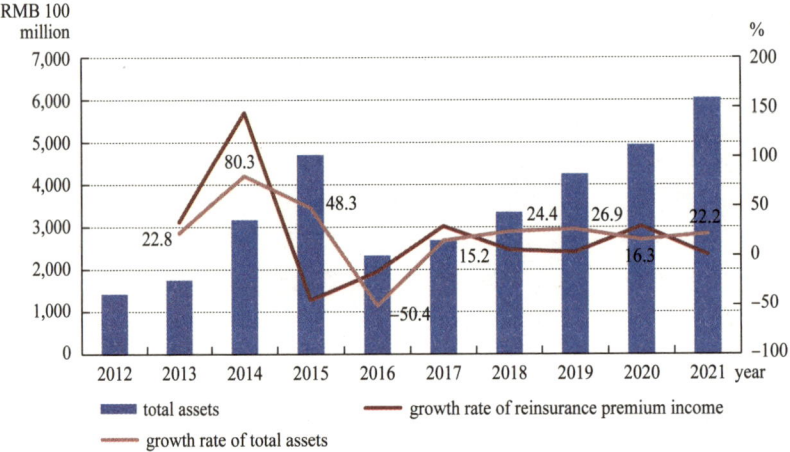

Figure 9　Total assets and growth rate of China's reinsurance industry (2012-2021)
(Sources: Yearbook of China's Insurance and CBIRC)

From 2012 to 2021, the total assets of the reinsurance industry accounted for a relatively stable share of the total assets of the insurance industry, which stood at about 2.4% at the end of 2021, indicating that the reinsurance industry grew with the development of the insurance market, sustained steady growth despite changes in the regulatory policies and in the market environment. Meanwhile, the share of total assets of the insurance industry in the total assets of the financial industry steadily increased from 5.6% in 2018 to 6.5% in 2021, indicating a stronger role and position of the insurance industry in the financial industry.

Table 3 Reinsurance claim payouts (2012-2021)

(RMB in 100 million)	Claim payouts	Growth rate	Share of total reinsurance premium income
2012	303.8		44.0%
2013	383.7	26.3%	40.5%
2014	433.2	12.9%	29.2%
2015	668.5	54.3%	62.7%
2016	1,119.3	67.4%	116.8%
2017	489.0	−56.3%	44.5%
2018	541.2	10.7%	39.5%
2019	677.6	25.2%	42.5%
2020	746.5	10.2%	41.3%
2021	852.6	14.2%	40.8%

Sources: Yearbook of China's Insurance and CBIRC.

In summary, the claim payouts of China's reinsurance industry increased between 2012 and 2021, from RMB 30.38 billion to RMB 85.26 billion, with an average annual growth rate of 12.2%. Overall, the reinsurance claim payouts saw a significant increase in the early stages of the implementation of the C-ROSS in 2016. The life reinsurance claim payouts saw a significant increase, and then declined significantly in 2017, indicating that there was significant volatility during the period of policy changes.

Asset volume

In 2021, the total assets of China's reinsurance industry stood at RMB 605.75 billion, up 22.2% year-to-date, which was 6.7 percentage points higher than the growth of reinsurance premium income.

In summary, the total assets of China's reinsurance industry increased between 2012 and 2021, from RMB 143.72 billion to RMB 605.75 billion, with an average annual growth rate of about 17.3%, which is higher than

Chapter II Development of China's Reinsurance Market in 2021

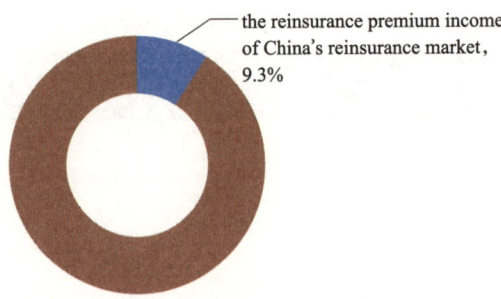

Figure 7 Share of China's reinsurance market in the global reinsurance market in 2021
(Sources: Yearbook of China's Insurance, CBIRC, and data from A.M.Best)

Claim payouts

In 2021, the claim payouts of China's reinsurance industry was RMB 85.26 billion, up 14.2% year-on-year and accounting for 40.8% of the total reinsurance premium income of the year. The 6 Chinese-invested companies had claim payouts of RMB 49.1 billion in total, up 13.5% year-on-year, while that of the 8 foreign-invested companies was RMB 36.16 billion in total, up 15.2% year-on-year.

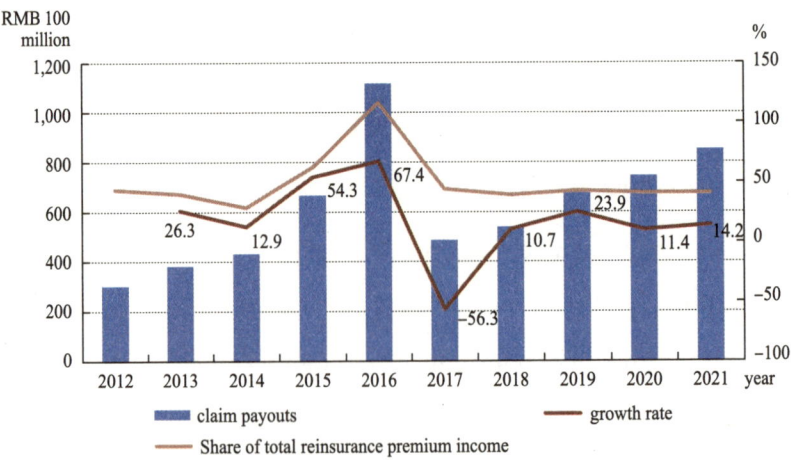

Figure 8 Reinsurance industry claim payouts (2012-2021)
(Sources: Yearbook of China's Insurance and CBIRC)

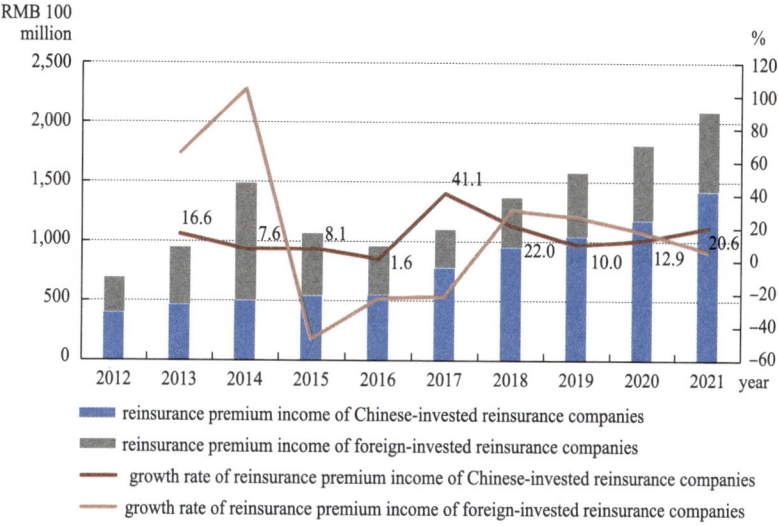

Figure 6 Reinsurance premium income and growth rate of Chinese-invested and foreign-invested reinsurance companies (2012-2021)

(Sources: Yearbook of China's Insurance and CBIRC)

In 2021, the reinsurance premium income of the world's top 50 reinsurance companies stood at about USD 353.75 billion[①] (approximately RMB 2.2554 trillion[②]). The reinsurance premium income of China's reinsurance market was RMB 209.02 billion, accounting for about 9.3% of the global reinsurance market.

---

① Data from A.M. Best.

② The exchange rate of RMB in the interbank foreign exchange market on December 31, 2021: USD 1= RMB 6.3757.

significant volatility, with a growth rate of over 100% in 2014, which then declined by almost 47% in 2015, indicating the different business strategies between Chinese-invested and foreign-invested companies.

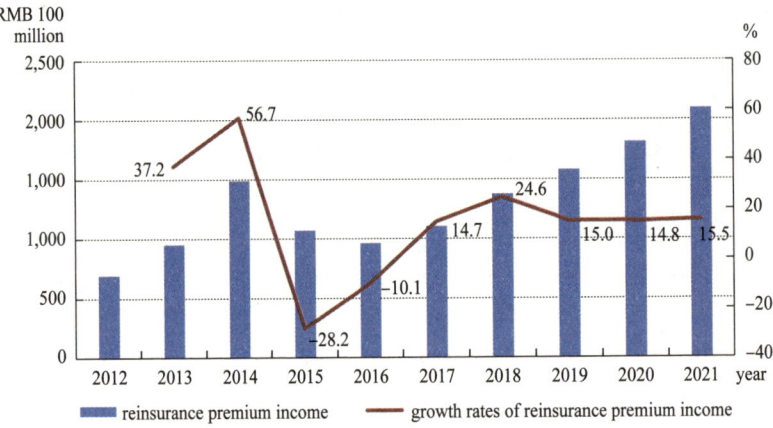

Figure 5 Reinsurance premium income and growth rates (2012-2021)

(Sources: Yearbook of China's Insurance and CBIRC)

Table 2 Reinsurance premium income and growth rate of Chinese- and foreign-invested reinsurance companies (2012-2021)

(RMB in 100 million)	Total reinsurance premium income	Chinese-invested companies	Growth rate	Share	Foreign-invested companies	Growth rate	Share
2012	691.2	400.3		57.9%	290.9		42.1%
2013	948.6	466.8	16.6%	49.2%	481.8	65.6%	50.8%
2014	1,486.0	502.5	7.6%	33.8%	983.5	104.1%	66.2%
2015	1,066.3	543.4	8.1%	51.0%	522.9	−46.8%	49.0%
2016	958.6	552.0	1.6%	57.6%	406.6	−22.2%	42.4%
2017	1,099.6	778.7	41.1%	70.8%	320.9	−21.1%	29.2%
2018	1,370.1	949.8	22.0%	69.3%	420.2	31.0%	30.7%
2019	1,576.1	1,044.9	10.0%	66.2%	533.0	26.8%	33.8%
2020	1,809.2	1,180.1	13.1%	65.2%	629.1	18.0%	34.8%
2021	2,090.2	1,422.9	20.6%	68.1%	667.3	6.1%	31.9%

Sources: Yearbook of China's Insurance and CBIRC.

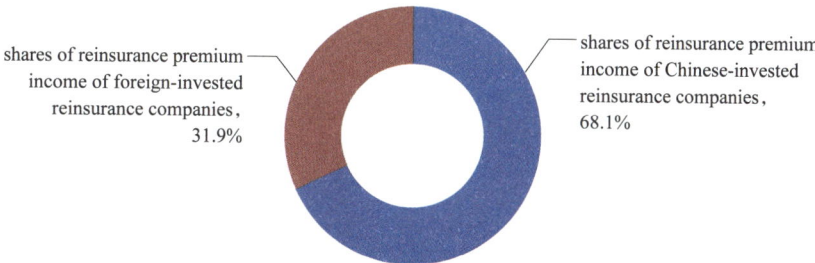

Figure 4 Shares of reinsurance premium income of Chinese-invested and foreign-invested reinsurance companies in 2021

(Sources: Yearbook of China's Insurance and CBIRC)

In summary, the reinsurance premium income of China's reinsurance market increased between 2012 and 2021, from RMB 69.12 billion to RMB 209.02 billion, with an average annual growth rate of about 13.1%. The reinsurance premium income of Chinese-invested companies increased from RMB 40.03 billion to RMB 142.29 billion, with an average annual growth rate of about 15.1%, while that of foreign-invested companies increased from RMB 29.09 billion to RMB 66.73 billion, with an average annual growth rate of about 9.7%. Overall, the average growth rate in ceded premiums basically keeps pace with that in primary insurance premiums. However, these growth rates of reinsurance income varied from year to year, and showed high volatility. Between 2014 and 2016, in particular, the reinsurance premium income of reinsurance companies saw significant fluctuation due to the interim period of the C-ROSS II regulatory policy. Since the official implementation of the C-ROSS II in 2016, reinsurance premium income has steadily increased year by year; reinsurance premium income of Chinese-invested reinsurance companies maintained positive growth between 2012 and 2021, while that of foreign-invested reinsurance companies saw

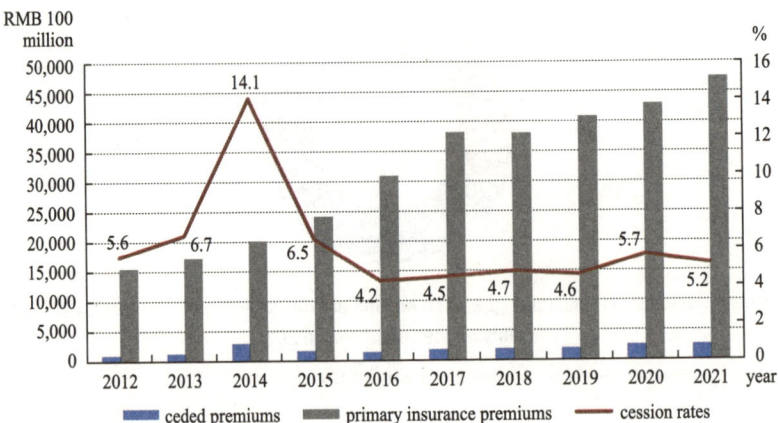

Figure 3 China's reinsurance cession rates (2012-2021)
(Sources: Yearbook of China's Insurance and CBIRC)

Reinsurance premium income

In 2021, the reinsurance premium income of China's reinsurance market amounted to RMB 209.02 billion, up 15.5% year-on-year. The total reinsurance premium income of the 6 Chinese-invested companies was RMB 142.29 billion, up 20.6% year-on-year and accounting for about 68.1% of the total, while that of the 8 foreign-invested companies was RMB 66.73 billion, up 6.1% year-on-year and accounting for about 31.9% of the total.

Overall, reinsurance premium income maintained a double-digit growth rate, which was greater than that of primary insurance premium, indicating a positive momentum in the industry as a whole; the market shares of Chinese-invested and foreign-invested companies remained relatively stable.

was officially released in February 2015, and entered an interim period prior to its official implementation in the first quarter of 2016. Unlike the size-oriented C-ROSS I, the risk-oriented C-ROSS II led to dramatic changes in the capital demand of businesses with different risk features in the insurance industry, which had a substantial impact on the reinsurance demand and strategy of insurance companies. From 2014 to 2016, the premiums ceded by insurance companies declined sharply from RMB 282.98 billion to RMB 131.45 billion, a drop of over 50%. Since 2016, the amount of premiums ceded by insurance companies has stabilized and begun to increase year by year.

In 2021, the cession rate of China's reinsurance market stood at about 5.2%, with that of P&C reinsurance around 10.6% and of life reinsurance around 3.0%. With more diverse risks and more prominent catastrophe risks, compared with the life insurance market, the P&C insurance market saw a greater demand for reinsurance, hence a significantly higher cession rate.

Between 2012 and 2021, the average cession rate of China's reinsurance market stood at about 6.2%. During the interim period of the C-ROSS regulatory policy from 2014 to 2016, the cession rate fluctuated greatly. In 2014, demand soared with a cession rate up to 14.1%, which subsequently declined. Excluding the influence of fluctuations between 2014 and 2016, the average cession rate was about 5.3%. Since 2016, the reinsurance cession rate has been on an upward trend, indicating that the demand for reinsurance in the insurance market is growing.

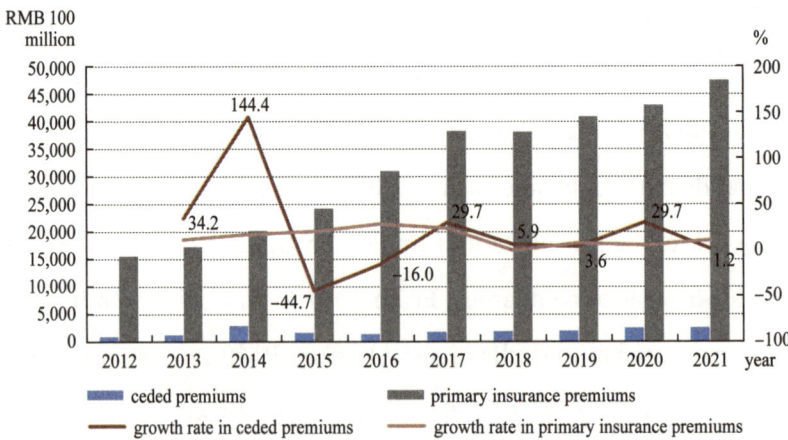

Figure 2 Primary insurance premiums, ceded premiums, and growth rates (2012-2021)

(Sources: Yearbook of China's Insurance and CBIRC)

Table 1 Ceded premiums, primary insurance premiums, and reinsurance cession rates (2012-2021)

(RMB in 100 million)	Ceded premiums	Growth rate	Primary insurance premiums	Growth rate	Cession rate
2012	862.9		15,487.9		5.6%
2013	1,157.8	34.2%	17,222.2	11.2%	6.7%
2014	2,829.8	144.4%	20,133.2	16.9%	14.1%
2015	1,564.8	-44.7%	24,167.6	20.0%	6.5%
2016	1,314.5	-16.0%	30,957.6	28.1%	4.2%
2017	1,705.0	29.7%	38,188.2	23.4%	4.5%
2018	1,806.2	5.9%	38,032.8	-0.4%	4.7%
2019	1,871.0	3.6%	40,857.7	7.4%	4.6%
2020	2,427.1	29.7%	42,952.4	5.1%	5.7%
2021	2,456.8	1.2%	47,452.1	10.5%	5.2%

Sources: Yearbook of China's Insurance and CBIRC.

In terms of the amount of ceded premiums, demand for reinsurance saw significant volatility from 2014 to 2016, mainly due to the impact of the C-ROSS II. In 2012, China initiated the development of C-ROSS II, which

and life insurance each accounted for about 60% and 40% of the total, which means that the ceded premiums of P&C insurance made the largest contribution.

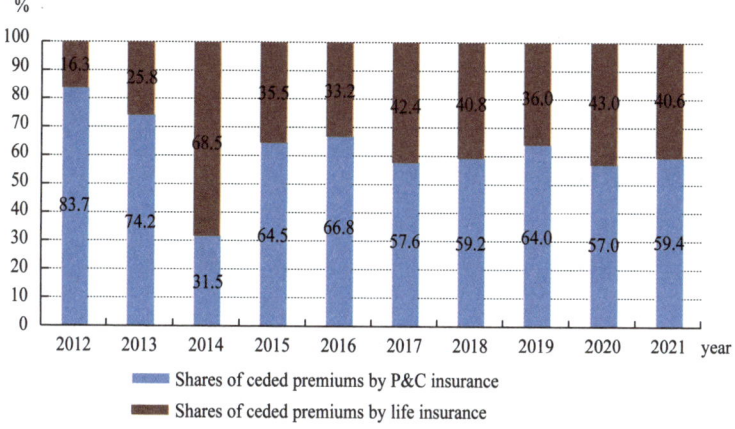

Figure 1 Shares of ceded premiums by P&C and life insurance (2012-2021)
(Sources: Yearbook of China's Insurance and CBIRC)

In summary, with the steady development of China's insurance market, the demand for reinsurance continued to rise from 2012 to 2021, and the amount of ceded premiums increased from RMB 86.29 billion to RMB 245.68 billion, an average annual growth of about 12.3%. During the same period, primary insurance premiums increased from RMB 1.54879 trillion to RMB 4.74521 trillion, an average annual growth of about 13.2%. Overall, the average growth rate in ceded premiums basically keeps pace with that in primary insurance premiums. However, these growth rates vary from year to year, and the volatility of the ceded premiums was significantly higher than that of the primary insurance premium, which proves to be also a notable feature of the reinsurance business model, reflecting reinsurance's role in sharing risks and smoothing volatility in the primary insurance business cycle.

Chapter II Development of China's Reinsurance Market in 2021

In 2021, the first year of China's 14th Five-year Plan, despite the COVID-19 and the tough situation at home and abroad, China's reinsurance market continued its stable operation, saw sustained growth in business size, steady improvement in operating profit, and increasing international influence, effective risk prevention and control, and secured a good start as an industry.

I. Reinsurance Market

(I) Market Size

Premiums ceded by primary insurers

In 2021, the gross premiums ceded by China's insurance market were RMB 245.68 billion, up 1.2% year-on-year. Premiums ceded by P&C insurance market were RMB 146.05 billion, up 5.6% year-on-year and accounting for 59.4% of the total, whereas that by life insurance market was RMB 99.63 billion, down 4.5% year-on-year and accounting for 40.6% of the total. During the same period, China's primary insurance premiums totaled RMB 4.74521 trillion, up 4.9% year-on-year.

Overall, ceded premiums showed a moderate increase, approximately 3.7 percentage points lower than that of primary insurance, mainly due to the significant impacts of policy changes and structural adjustments in the insurance market, particularly the comprehensive reform of motor insurance ("comprehensive reform" for short) and the second-generation solvency regulatory system phase II (C-ROSS II) on the demand for reinsurance. According to the overall structure of the reinsurance market from the annual ceded premiums in recent years, the ceded premiums of P&C insurance

Chapter II Development of China's Reinsurance Market in 2021

I. Reinsurance Market
II. P&C Reinsurance
III. Life Reinsurance

listed on the main board of the Stock Exchange of Hong Kong Limited, and completed the acquisition of the UK's century-old Chaucer Insurance Group. In 2020, it ranked among the *Fortune* Global 500 companies for the first time, becoming the largest reinsurance company in Asia and the sixth-largest in the world. It has set up subsidiaries in 11 countries or regions, including the UK, Hong Kong SAR of PRC, Ireland, Denmark, Norway, the United Arab Emirates, Singapore, Malaysia, Australia, and Bermuda, covering P&C reinsurance, life reinsurance, and asset management. China has steadily accelerated its efforts to build into an international hub for reinsurance, and is moving towards becoming an Asian regional reinsurance hub to increase its presence in Asia and around the world. Sixth, continuous improvement in the ability to innovate. China Re has gradually developed earthquake, typhoon, and flood catastrophe models with independent intellectual property rights and continued the efforts to build the life tables, critical illnesses tables, and other industrial facilities, which laid an important foundation for insurance risk pricing and product innovation. The company issued catastrophe bonds for the first time in Bermuda and Hong Kong SAR of PRC, providing a useful exploration for using the capital market to build a multi-channel catastrophe risk spread mechanism. Munich Re supported the first parametric insurance policy for carbon storage on grasslands in Inner Mongolia of PRC using satellite remote sensing technology, and Swiss Re was instrumental in securing China's first insurance scheme for the value of the wetland carbon sink ecosystem. In a word, reinsurance has played a significant role in driving product innovation, model innovation, and service innovation within the insurance industry.

the impacts of major disasters and accidents, safeguarding the sound and steady development of our social economy and the whole industry. The total reinsurance claim payouts in 2021 stood at RMB 85.26 billion, an increase of 2.8 times compared to 2012. For example, after paying claims for the 2013 SK Hynix Plant in Wuxi fire and the 2015 Tianjin Port explosion, insurance companies recovered RMB 5.3 billion and RMB 8.1 billion from reinsurers, respectively, accounting for 97% and 83% of the total claims. With sufficient underwriting capacity and risk management technology, reinsurance provided insurance support for agriculture, transportation, energy, nuclear power, and other large and special risks. For example, in 2021, the China Nuclear Insurance Pool provided comprehensive insurance coverage for 53 operating nuclear power units at all 17 nuclear power plants in China, covering nearly RMB 1 trillion in assets and 24,000 frontline employees, thereby effectively supporting the growth of China's nuclear power industry. Reinsurance plays an essential role in serving the national strategies, contributing positively to social governance, scientific and technological innovation, the national economy and people's livelihoods, the Belt and Road Initiative, rural revitalization, and green insurance. Fourth, opening up to foreign countries. In 2021, the reinsurance premium income of foreign professional reinsurance companies accounted for 31.9% of the reinsurance premium income of professional reinsurance companies in China, and over 500 foreign reinsurers conducted cross-border transactions in China's insurance market. Reinsurance is one of the most internationalized and open sectors of China's financial industry. Fifth, steady increase in international competitiveness. China Re Group, a leading company in the industry, was issued a series of measures to open itself to the outside, like steadily lifting the restrictions on the ratio of foreign shares and significantly reducing the quantitative threshold as to the requirements for foreign investment access. The first foreign insurance holding company, wholly foreign-owned life insurance company, wholly foreign-owned insurance asset management company, and foreign-invested pension insurance company were established in China. From 2012 to 2021, the market share of foreign-invested insurance companies increased from 3.5% to 7.8%. In regions like Beijing and Shanghai, the share had reached 20%.

IV. Major Achievements of China's Reinsurance Industry

With the rapid growth of China's economy and the development of China's insurance industry, China's reinsurance industry also grow rapidly and formed six major characteristics.

First, diverse specialized entities. As of the end of 2021, the number of professional reinsurance companies in China had increased from 1 in 2000 to 15, of which six companies were newly established after 2012. Second, steady expansion of market size. Premiums ceded by cedants increased from RMB 86.29 billion in 2012 to RMB 245.68 billion in 2021, up about 12.3% year-on-year. Meanwhile, reinsurance premium income increased from RMB 69.12 billion in 2012 to RMB 209.02 billion in 2021, up about 13.1% year-on-year, and held a global reinsurance market share of about 9.3%. Third, maintaining its function effectively. Reinsurance continued to give full play to the functions of loss compensation and risk spreading, reducing trillion, with an average annual growth of 14.51%. The industry saw steady improvement in international influence. From 2012 to 2021, the share of the premium income of China's insurance industry in the global insurance market increased from 5.34% to 10.1%. China has been the second-largest insurance market in the world for five years in a row since 2017. In 2021, 10 Chinese insurance companies ranked among the world's top 500 companies. Second, the insurance function has seen significant improvement. The insurance industry adhered to its original aspiration, adjusted and optimized the product mix to reinforce the nature of insurance protection. From 2017 to 2021, the total premium income of the insurance industry increased from RMB 3.66 trillion to RMB 4.49 trillion, up 22.7%; total insurance coverage provided for the real economy increased from RMB 4,154 trillion to RMB 12,146 trillion, up 192.4%; total claims paid increased from RMB 1.1181 trillion to RMB 1.5609 trillion, up 39.6%. Both total insurance coverage and claims paid saw much higher growth than that of total premium income. Third, the advantages of insurance funds became more prominent. From 2012 to the end of 2021, the balance of insurance funds in use increased from RMB 6.85 trillion to RMB 23.23 trillion, with an average annual growth of 14.53%. The industry gave full play to the strength of insurance funds being long-term and stable to support the development of the real economy. By the end of 2021, the total direct financing raised by insurance funds had invested in stocks, bonds, and equities to support the real economy stood at RMB 18.88 trillion, accounting for 81.27% of the balance of insurance funds in use. Fourth, more efforts were made to keep China's insurance market more open to the outside. In recent years, the insurance industry has

Breakthroughs were made in some core technologies. Strategic emerging industries were developed and strengthened. Significant achievements were made in manned spaceflight, lunar and Mars exploration, underwater and underground exploration, supercomputers, satellite navigation, quantum information, nuclear power technology, new energy technology, large aircraft manufacturing, biomedicine, among others. China joined the league of innovative countries.

III. Major Achievements of China's Insurance Industry

Since the 18th National Congress of the Communist Party of China, the insurance industry has implemented the decisions of the Central Committee and State Council, improved the insurance's functions, deepened the reform and opening up, supported the development of the real economy, and followed the bottom line thinking in dealing with risks. Over the past decade, the insurance industry has made tremendous achievements in pursuing high-quality development and supporting China's economic and social development. First, the insurance market has secured steady development. The market saw rapid growth. From 2012 to 2021, the premium income of the insurance industry increased from RMB 1.55 trillion to RMB 4.49 trillion, with an average annual growth of 12.55%; The insurance penetration increased from 2.98% to 3.93% while the insurance density increased from RMB 1,144 per person to RMB 3,179 per person. The total assets of the insurance industry increased from RMB 7.4 trillion to RMB 24.89

II. China's Major Achievements in Economic and Social Development

Since the 18th National Congress of the Communist Party of China, China has put forward and implemented new development philosophies, made tremendous efforts to boost high-quality development, fostered a new development pattern, conducted supply-side structural reforms, formulated a series of major regional strategies essential for China's overall development, and achieved a historic leap in economic strength. From 2012 to 2021, China's gross domestic product (GDP) increased from RMB 53.9 trillion to RMB 114.4 trillion, which accounted for 18.5% of the world economy, up 7.2 percentage points, and ranked second in the world; its per capita GDP increased from RMB 39,800 to RMB 81,000. China led the world in total grain production, effectively protecting the food and energy security of its over 1.4 billion people. Its urban population increased by 11.6 percentage points to 64.7% of the total population. It had the largest manufacturing industry and was the biggest holder of foreign exchange reserves. It built the largest high-speed railway and expressway networks and made remarkable achievements in building airports and ports, water conservancy, energy, information, and other infrastructures. China accelerated its efforts to develop independent and self-reliant technologies. Its total R&D investment increased from RMB 1 trillion to RMB 2.8 trillion, ranking second in the world, while the total number of R&D personnel ranked first. Basic research and original innovation saw continuous improvement.

insurance industry. Since the reform and opening up, China has embarked on a comprehensive reform to strengthen the reinsurance industry gradually. When China officially joined the World Trade Organization (WTO) in 2001, the reinsurance market was the first financial sector to embrace foreign competition. From 2002 to the end of 2005, restrictions on cross-border transactions of reinsurance and reinsurance broking were gradually abolished, and the compulsory reinsurance was completely replaced by the commercial reinsurance. Since then, China's reinsurance market has become the earliest and most open market in China's financial sector.

(IV) Reinsurance's Functions

As "insurance for insurers", reinsurance plays an irreplaceable role at the macro, meso, and micro levels. Viewing the social and economic system at the macro level, reinsurance is a market-oriented and commercial "safety net" that can reduce the impact of black swan and gray rhino events on the economic system and can play a social role in easing the state's financial burden and public administration costs. It is also an effective means of international economic cooperation. Viewing the industry at the meso level, reinsurance is the "safety valve" and "stabilizer" for the development of the insurance industry, which plays an essential role in ensuring insurance market security, supporting market regulation, and strengthening industry risk management. Viewing the industry at the micro level, reinsurance plays a vital role in sharing claim cost, enlarging underwriting capacity and providing catastrophe protection for insurance companies.

(II) Origin

Reinsurance arose from marine insurance in the 14th century, and reinsurance companies emerged in the mid-19th century. The modern reinsurance industry began in 1347 when an Italian merchant in Genoa issued the first marine insurance policy. In 1370, an Italian merchant underwrote the marine insurance policy for a voyage from Genoa to Sruth, Netherlands via Cadiz, Spain, transferring the Cadiz-to-Sruth risks to another insurer, which is recognized as the origin of reinsurance. The Cologne Re[1] was founded in 1846 in Germany as the world's first professional reinsurance company. Subsequently, Swiss Re and Munich Re were founded in 1863 and 1880, respectively. Since then, reinsurance has gained ground and become a means of risk control widely adopted by insurance companies around the world.

(III) History of China's Reinsurance Industry

The history of China's reinsurance industry is much shorter than that of the global reinsurance industry. It began before the War of Liberation and expanded alongside the development of the People's Republic of China. In 1949, the People's Insurance Company of China, the national insurance institution of New China, was established, with overseas branches for international insurance and reinsurance business. Before the reform and opening up, reinsurance sustained the survival and development of China's

---

[1] The Cologne Re was acquired by the General Reinsurance Group in 1994.

I. Overview of the Reinsurance Industry

(I) Major Concepts

Clause 1 of Article 28 of the Insurance Law of the People's Republic of China states that "Reinsurance is the practice of one insurer insuring part of its underwritten policies with another insurer." Reinsurance, also known as reinsurance ceded, is an insurance business whereby an insurer transfers some or all of its risks and obligations to other insurers by signing a contract, and thus it is, so to speak, "insurance for insurers". By signing a reinsurance contract and paying an agreed reinsurance premium, an insurer transfers part of its risks and obligations to one or more insurance or reinsurance companies to spread the risks and obligations and ensure stable business operations while an accepting company shall, in accordance with the terms of the reinsurance contract, be liable for a claim covered in the insurer's primary insurance policies.

Reinsurance is a specialized line of business. It is an insurance service and an insurance mechanism that functions as an indispensable part of the modern insurance industry. Reinsurance is a business derived from insurance, while insurance acts as the foundation and premise of reinsurance. There would be no reinsurance without insurance. Reinsurance supports and safeguards insurance; without the support of reinsurance, insurance cannot withstand significant adverse impacts. In other words, the two turn out to be inseparably interconnected, mutually supplementary and beneficial to each other.

Chapter I Overview of the Development of China's Reinsurance Industry

I. Overview of the Reinsurance Industry

II. China's Major Achievements in Economic and Social Development

III. Major Achievements of China's Insurance Industry

IV. Major Achievements of China's Reinsurance Industry

Chapter IV Overview of China's Reinsurance Regulation in 2021 — 73

I. Current Regulatory Framework of the Reinsurance Industry — 76

II. Special Policies Regulating the Reinsurance Industry — 83

III. Important Regulatory Policies for the Reinsurance Industry in 2021 — 88

Chapter V Prospects of China's Reinsurance Industry Development — 97

I. Prospects of Overall Market Development — 99

II. Prospects of P&C Reinsurance Development — 108

III. Prospects of Life Reinsurance Development — 112

IV. Prospects of Development of Foreign Reinsurance Companies in China — 116

V. Prospects of the Regulation Trend of the Reinsurance Industry — 119

Appendix Major Events in the Development of China's Reinsurance Industry (1949—2021) — 123

Contents

Chapter I Overview of the Development of China's Reinsurance Industry ... 1

I. Overview of the Reinsurance Industry ... 3
II. China's Major Achievements in Economic and Social Development ... 6
III. Major Achievements of China's Insurance Industry ... 7
IV. Major Achievements of China's Reinsurance Industry ... 9

Chapter II Development of China's Reinsurance Market in 2021 ... 13

I. Reinsurance Market ... 15
II. P&C Reinsurance ... 39
III. Life Reinsurance ... 44

Chapter III Development of Foreign Reinsurance Companies in 2021 ... 51

I. Outline of Foreign Reinsurance Companies' Development in China ... 53
II. Development of Foreign Reinsurance Companies in China ... 54
III. Overview of Foreign Reinsurance Companies' Operations in China ... 59
IV. Human Resources of Foreign Reinsurance Companies in China ... 66

Preface II.

Under the guidance of the Specialized Committee on Statistics and Research of the Insurance Association of China, China Reinsurance Group as the head member of the Specialized Committee published its first *Report on the Development of Reinsurance Industry in China (2022)*, to comprehensively review the development of China's reinsurance industry during the past 10 years and well demonstrate the important roles played by this industry. The report addresses issues such as China's reinsurance industry's assistance in the transformation and development of the insurance industry, promoting the development of the real economy, and ensuring national financial safety. China Re also documents the high-quality development achievements of the reinsurance industry in China, shows its practices in strengthening its responsibilities and undertaking as one of China's central government-owned enterprises, and celebrates the holding of the CPC's 20th National Congress with effective actions.

We expect the *Report on the Development of Reinsurance Industry in China* to deliver more fruitful theories for the development of China's reinsurance industry, as well as better services for the high-quality development of the insurance industry.

Yu Hua, President of Insurance Association of China

December 2022

healthy growth. Reinsurance has played a critical role in preventing and resolving systemic industry risks and reducing business volatility of ceding companies, especially in post-disaster compensation, risk management, and technical support. With advantages in underwriting capacity, modeling and pricing, and professional talents, reinsurance provides high-level and high-limit protections for major and special risks, sharing more than 50% of catastrophe losses of property and engineering risks as well as nearly 40% of catastrophe losses of agricultural risk. Reinsurance is also an essential booster for industry reform and innovation. For instance, by utilizing its platform and technical advantages, it gathers data of the insurance industry, develops new insurance products based on data analysis, thus acting as the main driving force for product-and-service innovation and upgrade in the insurance industry. To protect Chinese enterprises in expanding their business under the "Belt and Road" initiative, China's reinsurance industry has issued the first Chinese political risk policy. When faced with domestic demands for pandemic prevention and control as well as work and business resumption, China's reinsurance industry developed a variety of insurance products. Furthermore, when coping with challenges caused by climate change and assisting in the "carbon peaking and carbon neutrality" strategy, China's reinsurance industry led the way in exploring new green insurance products such as clean energy insurance, energy storage insurance, carbon insurance, weather insurance, and biodiversity protection insurance.

Preface II.

Since the CPC's 18th National Congress, particularly the 5th National Financial Work Conference, China's insurance industry has vigorously implemented the decisions and deployment of the Party Central Committee and the State Council, strengthening its protection functions, deepening its reform and opening up, serving the real economy, and safeguarding the society's bottom line of risks. This has helped the industry make tremendous achievements based on high-quality development, enabling leap-forward development. The insurance industry's total assets have increased from RMB 7.4 trillion at the end of 2012 to RMB 24.9 trillion at the end of 2021. Premium volume has increased from RMB 1.5 trillion at the end of 2012 to RMB 4.5 trillion at the end of 2021, with a compound annual growth rate of more than 12%, making China the world's second-largest insurance market. China's insurance penetration has increased from 2.98% to 3.93%, and its insurance density increased from RMB 1,144/person to RMB 3,179/person, getting much closer to developed countries.

The term "reinsurance" refers to "the insurance for insurance." In recent years, reinsurance industry has played an indispensable part in the high-quality development of insurance industry in China. Reinsurance has served as a safety valve and stabilizer for the industry's industry since the CPC's 18th National Congress and shows the panorama of the reinsurance market's evolution. We are confident that the publication of the Report will be of great interest and benefit to the general public, allowing them to gain a thorough understanding of and conduct in-depth research on the development of the reinsurance industry in China. It will also help to improve communication between the reinsurance and insurance industries both at home and abroad, and enhance the reinsurance industry's social influence.

He Chunlei, Chairman of China Re

December 2022

all fronts. It has formed the market pattern of full competition with more than 500 Chinese-invested and foreign-invested, on-shore and off-shore entities. By giving full play to the role of risk diversification, technical guidance, and financing mechanism, the reinsurance industry stabilizes and controls the insurance market in China. As the founder and a key force of China's reinsurance industry in China, China Reinsurance (Group) Corporation (hereinafter referred to as "China Re") has been unswervingly implementing the decisions and the deployment of the PCC and the State Council. China Re focuses on reinsurance as its core mission and principal business while having developed parts of its direct insurance business, expediting its digitalization, continuously improving industrial infrastructure, and stepping up efforts to innovate its products and services. This enables China Re to collaborate with partners to provide one-stop customized and comprehensive risk management solutions, spare no efforts to serve national strategies, spread economic risks, and help people lead better lives.

On the occasion of the CPC's 20th National Congress, under the comprehensive guidance of CBIRC and the Insurance Association of China, and with the strong support of the insurance industry and the reinsurance industry in China, the first annual development report prepared by China Reinsurance Institute, i.e., *Report on the Development of Reinsurance Industry in China (2022)* (hereinafter referred to as the "Report") was officially released. The Report systematically summarizes the achievements of China's reinsurance

Thanks to the strong guidance of the China Banking and Insurance Regulatory Commission (hereinafter referred to as "CBIRC"), as well as sustained economic growth and industry collaboration, China has become the world's second-largest insurance market and the most important emerging market. The insurance industry's ability to serve the real economy, and safeguard people's livelihood has been continuously improved. At the critical moment of the "Two Centenary Goals", China's insurance industry is stepping up its efforts to transform and upgrade itself. Keywords such as security, digitalization, greenness, pension, and affordability have changed the industry's outlook from passive risk bearing and pure economic compensation to active risk mitigation and comprehensive protection services. This will enable the industry to fully integrate itself into the larger ecosystem of social risk management and fully leverage the protective role of insurance. As a result, the industry is in a better position to vigorously serve national strategies, participate in social governance, and protect the public's life and property. By doing so, it integrates the tiny streams of the entire industry into the grand rivers of our nation and people's great undertakings, keeping pace with the national rejuvenation and resonate with the people's pursuit of a better life.

During the evolution of the international insurance industry, every developed insurance market has been backed by a strong and sound reinsurance system. As the "insurance for insurers," China's reinsurance industry has been a pioneer in opening up the financial industry on

Preface I.

Since the CPC's 18th National Congress, the Party Central Committee (PCC) has designed a grand blueprint for a new era with "Three News and One High," i.e. the introduction into a new development stage, the implementation of new development philosophies, the establishment of new development paradigms, and the achievement of high-quality development. As a result, the PCC has been able to inspire our Party and our nation to secure historic accomplishments and transformations.

Nowadays, the world is filled with uncertainties. With the accelerated evolution of profound global changes of a magnitude unseen in a century, turbulence caused by global geopolitical situations, global economic recession, recurrence of the global pandemic, and increased frequency of extreme weather as well as meteorological and geological disasters caused by climate change, the external environment for economic development in China has become more complicated, leading to increased risks. Acting as a primary tool to reduce such risks, insurance will play a more significant role in providing risk protections, serving the real economy, and ensuring people's better life.

Editorial Board

Chief Editor:
　　He Chunlei

Executive Deputy Editor:
　　Zhuang Qianzhi

Deputy Editors:
　　Zhu Hailin　Xiao Li　Zhu Xiaoyun
　　Lei Jianming

Members:
　　Zhang Renjiang　Tian Meipan　Dou Xujie
　　Cao Shunming　Zhu Rifeng

Report on the Development of Reinsurance Industry in China

(2022)

CHINA REINSURANCE (GROUP) CORPORATION

 CHINA FINANCIAL PUBLISHING HOUSE

EMPOWER YOUR INSURANCE BY EXPERTISE